Understanding Russia

The Challenges of Transformation

Marlene Laruelle
The George Washington University

Jean Radvanyi
*National Institute for Oriental Languages
and Cultures*

ROWMAN & LITTLEFIELD
Lanham • Boulder • New York • London

Executive Editor: Susan McEachern
Editorial Assistant: Katelyn Turner
Senior Marketing Manager: Kim Lyons

Credits and acknowledgments for material borrowed from other sources, and reproduced with permission, appear on the appropriate page within the text.

Published by Rowman & Littlefield
An imprint of The Rowman & Littlefield Publishing Group, Inc.
4501 Forbes Boulevard, Suite 200, Lanham, Maryland 20706
www.rowman.com

Unit A, Whitacre Mews, 26-34 Stannary Street, London SE11 4AB, United Kingdom

British Library Cataloguing in Publication Information Available

Library of Congress Cataloging-in-Publication Data
Names: Laruelle, Marlène, author. | Radvanyi, Jean, author.
Title: Understanding Russia : the challenges of transformation / Marlene Laruelle, Jean Radvanyi.
Description: Lanham, Maryland : Rowman & Littlefield, [2018] | Includes bibliographical references and index.
Identifiers: LCCN 2018014334 (print) | LCCN 2018030613 (ebook) | ISBN 9781538114872 (electronic) | ISBN 9781538114858 (cloth : alk. paper) | ISBN 9781538114865 (pbk. : alk. paper)
Subjects: LCSH: Russia (Federation)—Politics and government—1991– | Russia (Federation)—Economic conditions—1991– | Russia (Federation)—Foreign relations.
Classification: LCC DK510.76 (ebook) | LCC DK510.76 .L37 2018 (print) | DDC 947.086—dc23
LC record available at https://lccn.loc.gov/2018014334

Printed in the United States of America

Contents

Figures, Maps, and Tables

FIGURES

MAPS

TABLES

Introduction

Russia inspires fear. For decades, American presidents viewed the Soviet Union as an "evil empire," and the 2014 Ukrainian crisis, as well as the 2016 "Russiagate"— Russia's alleged meddling in U.S. presidential elections—has added a new chapter to this narrative inherited from the Cold War. Russia's behavior is regarded with distrust and its "nuisance power" arouses frustration in the West. In 2014, at the peak of the Ukrainian crisis, Hillary Clinton compared Vladimir Putin to Adolf Hitler,[1] and since Donald Trump's election in November 2016, Democrats are persuaded that Russia is responsible for their failure to win the presidential race. Moscow is seen as the "hidden hand" behind the rise of illiberalism in Europe and the political polarization of the U.S. domestic scene. That Russia finds itself enmeshed in issues deeply linked to America's own past, such as the August 2017 Charlottesville racist riots and multiple polemics about taking down statues of Confederate heroes, encapsulates the current overheated and emotional attitude of U.S. elites and public opinion toward Moscow. The country's image in the United States has never been so negative since Cold War decades. Western pundits seem happy to rekindle fear of Russia, which provides a useful and easy-to-use toolkit for creating political consensus, since it turns attention away from domestic failures and contradictions.

At the same time—and this is a key point of this book—Russia is fearful, too. More than twenty-five years after the end of the Soviet Union, and thirty years after the beginning of the transformations brought by perestroika, multiple ghosts haunt both the Russian elites and the society, from concerns about demographic and economic decline to worries about the country's vulnerability to external intervention. Opened up practically overnight under President Boris Yeltsin, the country has had to deal with a rapid and traumatic globalization. Faced with a West that emerged victorious from the Cold War, a shockingly dynamic China, and former Soviet republics claiming their right to emancipate themselves from

Moscow's stranglehold, Russia is constantly questioning its identity, its development path, and its role on the international scene. Vacillating between reformist aspirations and a fear of liberal society, the country hesitates between two strategies: Take refuge in a new isolation and revive the old notion of being a "besieged fortress," or replay the messianic myth of a Third Rome, having for mission to establish a new world order in the face of a decadent West.

The negative image of Russia in the West has deep roots. This was apparent even before the Marquis de Custine and his famous letters, for it was Stendhal who wrote from Smolensk: "In this sea of barbarism, not a sound responds to my soul! Everything is coarse, dirty, putrid, physically and morally."[2] Russian society is at once profoundly European in its history and culture *and* different from Europe. Its existential dilemmas permeate the country's greatest creations, from the novels of Dostoevsky and the plays of Chekhov to the symphonies of Shostakovich. Throughout the twentieth century and to this day, Russia's ideological and political choices have been regarded with both fascination and repulsion. When the Soviet system disintegrated, many hoped that Russia would finally align itself more closely with the West and magically "return" to the European fold. This naïve expectation was doomed to be defeated. Many analysts who subscribe to this simplistic "transition" ideology continue to analyze Moscow's supposedly erratic and inexplicable policies from the standpoint that Yeltsin's Russia was the norm of a pro-Western and liberal Russia. Seen from Russia, however, the Yeltsin years are anything but the norm. Indeed, they serve as an anti-model, illustrating a path Russia does not wish to go down again.

The collapse of the Soviet Union was seen as a victory for the Western liberal order—one remembers Francis Fukuyama's "end of history" theory—without the West being able to understand how much Soviet history and the Marxist doctrine that inspired it were part of its own history, too. The West thus became orphan both of its main geopolitical primordial enemy—now replaced by Islamic terrorism—but also of its leftist ideologies. The 1917 Revolution was an event of global significance that shaped not only Russian history but also the West's twentieth century. To borrow a metaphor from Oscar Wilde's *Dorian Gray*, Soviet and post-Soviet Russia has in many ways served as the West's mirror, amplifying many aspects of the West's own development, excesses, mistakes, and failures over the course of the century by testing, on its own soil, socialism, totalitarianism, democracy, and neoliberalism.

In this book, we do not see Russia as an "Other" that is fundamentally and radically different from "us," but on the contrary as part of a continuum with the West. It seems to us more necessary than ever to apply to Russia those analytical frameworks that the social sciences have gradually developed for other parts of the world, rather than to look upon Russia as an "exception." Indeed, what is happening in Russia today is deeply inscribed into broader global trends that can also be observed in the West. Distrust of the post–Second World War global order and established institutions, doubts about the direction taken by the world economy and the processes of globalization, the rise of conservative values and suspicion of some elements of the democratic system are not unique to Russia, but can also be found in Western societies. The unexpected attraction and emulation between Vladimir Putin and Donald Trump highlights this commonality. Russia's difficulties in accepting the loss of its empire could be also compared to France's post-colonial wounds, from the trauma of the Algerian war to opaque mechanisms of influence in the "France-Afrique"—comparable to Russia's use of its soft power and Soviet legacy in the post-Soviet space.

Russia is not the "hidden hand" so much as an echo chamber that amplifies American and European societies' own doubts and transformations. The difficulty of the exercise of assessing today's Russia is that it is largely based on value judgments and has a normative character, as when German chancellor Angela Merkel described Putin as living in "another world,"[3] or when observers insist on the supposed "unpredictability" of the regime. Who is in charge of determining the rationality and predictability of political decisions? Indeed, the Western view of Russia depends largely on how each observer looks at his or her own society. The most vocal critics of Russia are often convinced of the correctness of the Western system and its status as an indisputable international standard, while those with some reservations about the Western model adopt a form of relativism that may be more favorable to some of Russia's arguments.

In addition, analysis of Russia's stance is often focused on internal determinants— mostly Putin's personality and KGB background—as if tracing a natural and predestined path, without regard to influential external events that have arguably caused changes to the Russian position. But Russia's path is not written in the DNA of the Putin regime; it resulted from three decades of interaction between Russia and the world, in particular the West, and from mutual interpretations and misinterpretations. This calls into question the supposed ideological continuity of the Putin regime and its internal logic. The many ongoing debates over its "nature" can be grouped into three main schools.

The first considers Putin's regime to be, above all, a kleptocracy, with corrupt members of Putin's inner circle seeking personal enrichment. Karen Dawisha's *Putin's Kleptocracy: Who Owns Russia?* offers the most detailed analysis of this aspect of the regime. Yet massive and well-organized schemes, bribe taking, money laundering, and the offshoring of national wealth are not enough to explain every logic at work in the political realm and shaping state-society interactions. Another school sees Putin's regime as a totalitarian, neo-Stalinist institution, motivated by nationalism, revanchism, and imperial aggression, among other principles. In this view, deeply entrenched ideological convictions explain Russia's actions on both the international and domestic stages. Charles Clover's *Black Wind, White Snow: The Rise of Russia's New Nationalism* and Marcel van Herpen's *Putin's Wars: The Rise of Russia's New Imperialism* provide good insights into this outlook. We disagree with their vision in that they accentuate certain very limited features and interpret them as a "grand design."

A third school, to which we belong, advances a more nuanced view that encompasses two levels of analysis. First, it states that the regime's relationship with Russian society is far too complex to be classified simply as patronal or authoritarian: It is based on an implicit social contract with the population that is continuously renegotiated and limits the regime's options. To maintain its societal relevance, the government spends millions of dollars every year to track the smallest whim of public opinion and billions to try to shape that opinion in the government's favor. The regime is on a permanent quest to draw inspiration from and co-opt grassroots trends, and there are many bottom-up dynamics that foreign observers typically do not see. Second, the internal configuration of the regime is closer to a plural conglomerate of opinions and ad hoc improvisations than it is to a uniform, cohesive group with rigid ideological boundaries.

It is therefore critical to take full measure of the upheavals and inertia that have characterized the recent evolution of a country struck by thirty years of convulsions and avoid being excessively focused on getting inside "Putin's mind." Russia is much more than its president. The poorly controlled mutations of perestroika were followed by the failed August 1991 coup, the collapse of the Soviet Union a few months later, a profound political crisis and a second putsch in October 1993, and three serious economic crises, in 1998, 2008, and 2014. Russians—both the ruling elites and a large part of the population—maintain a paranoid relationship with the massive opening that has taken place over these three decades. This mixture of fascination and fear, interest in and incomprehension of the world around them has resulted in contradictory realities. Russian elites send their children to the West to study, live, and obtain quality medical care, yet they often criticize Western lifestyles and behavior. While attracted by some autarkic mechanisms, the Russian economy remains dependent on the export of natural resources, making the country heavily reliant on international actors and customers, as well as on foreign trade partners, who provide most of the technological equipment it needs.

The list of Russia's ambivalences could be long. It would therefore be a mistake to see the country and its leadership as seeking to revive the Soviet past and still viewing Russia solely through the Soviet prism. First, several central points of Putin's policies—defense of a handful of neighboring states that are under Russian influence or neutralized, Moscow's leading role in a crusade for traditional values in the face of a "decadent" West, and increasing global outreach, in particular in the Middle East—cannot be evaluated without highlighting historical continuities that go back long before the Soviet regime. Second, and more importantly, if Russia faces an undeniable authoritarian streak in the economic, social, and cultural realms, there is also an acceleration of neoliberal practices far removed from the Soviet model. Today's Russia is thoroughly globalized. Many of its paradoxes and ambivalences are the result of precisely this openness to the world, and of Russia's adaptation to what it interprets as its integration into a globalized system.

Since his third term in office began in March 2012, Vladimir Putin has stepped up efforts to centralize power, which he regards as a determining factor in the restoration of Russia's statehood. With his fourth and probably last six years term, beginning in 2018, Putin will have to negotiate a new turning point in Russia's post-Soviet history, setting his country's trajectory for the decade to come and figuring out how a regime that was already in gestation in the second half of the 1990s can prepare itself for a post-Putin era. It remains to be seen whether the effects of these measures can put the country on a constructive path and deconstruct some of the current contradictions.

1

Territorial Fatigue

New State, New Borders

Russian Geography

Moscow and the city of Peter,[1] and the city of Constantine—
Here are the sacred capitals of the Russian royalty . . .
But where is its limit? Where are its borders—
To the north, east, south, and west?
In times to come, fate will be revealed . . .

Seven internal seas and seven great rivers . . .
From the Nile to the Neva, from Elbe to China,
From the Volga to the Euphrates, from the Ganges to the Danube . . .
Such is the Russian empire . . . And it will not pass through the centuries,
The Spirit foretold it, Daniel prophesized it.

—Fyodor Tyutchev, 1848

In an immense Russia of some 17,098,246 square kilometers (6,601,670 square miles),[2] the symptoms of the country's territorial malady tend to be underestimated. To paraphrase the filmmaker Dziga Vertov, this veritable continent can be thought of as a "seventh part of the world," and should be sufficient for its inhabitants. However, the annexation of Crimea, following a hastily organized referendum on March 16, 2014, and Vladimir Putin's affirmation two days later, at a ceremony to formalize the reunification, that this action was taken in defense of the "Russian world," confirmed that Russia's leaders have still not totally accepted the borders that were agreed when the Soviet Union disintegrated in late December 1991. For the second time in less than ten years, after recognizing the independence of the secessionist regions of Abkhazia and South Ossetia in 2008, a Russian president reneged on the commitment Boris Yeltsin made to respect the territorial integrity and inviolability of state borders following the breakup of the Soviet Union.

Yet these difficulties in accepting post-Soviet borders are intimately correlated to other inward-looking concerns about Russia's territorial integrity and the connectivity of its regions. Although Russian public opinion almost unanimously applauded the Federation's annexation of Crimea, the country was already having great difficulty managing its own territory. Whole regions of Russia are depopulated, especially in Siberia and the Far East, to the point that a bevy of specialists has become obsessed with the problem of maintaining national territorial integrity. Another aspect of this decline is that large parts of rural Russia have succumbed to desertification. The space Russians actually occupy is shrinking for the first time in about five centuries, further underscoring the symptoms of this territorial malady. Russia's many spatial challenges should therefore be among the first to be discussed.

A POST-IMPERIAL SYNDROME

For some of its elites, Russia can only be imperial. Nataliya Narochnitskaya, founder of the Paris-based Institute for Democracy and Cooperation and herald of political Orthodoxy, summarizes this point of view: "Russia is inconceivable outside of imperial thinking. It can only be an empire. We must have a grand policy, a great national idea—otherwise we cannot be aware of our national interests. We will not understand why it is necessary to have navigable rivers and harbors that do not freeze."[3]

But what is an empire without the domination of the territories at the margins of the national core? How can this periphery be defined in a continental space without obvious natural boundaries? "From the Volga to the Euphrates, from the Ganges to the Danube . . ." These forgotten words of Fyodor Tyutchev (1803–1873) sound familiar today, as two states with renewed geostrategic postures, Russia and China, question the limits of the middle continent that is Eurasia. To the west, Moscow no longer accepts the loss of its sphere of influence on its European flank, which occurred at its moment of greatest weakness, at the end of the 1980s and in the early 1990s; to the east, Beijing intends to impose its maritime vision against the wishes of its neighbors: Vietnam, Japan, the Philippines, and South Korea.

The feeling of being contested on its periphery makes Russia anxious. In turn, its actions provoke anxiety in others, primarily neighboring former Soviet republics with significant Russian or Russian-speaking populations, such as the Baltic states, Ukraine, and Kazakhstan. The defense of these populations served as the pretext for Russia's annexation of the Crimean Peninsula. Yet some national elites—in Estonia and Latvia, for example—did not wait for the annexation to paint Russian ethnic minorities as a "fifth column" that could be mobilized. A newly powerful Russia, resurgent after decades of weakness, also concerns Western leaders, who, even while intervening around the world, do not accept the idea that power can be applied in the early twenty-first century using the principles that prevailed in the nineteenth century—such as the Monroe Doctrine, under which U.S. leaders claimed the right to intervene in their regional space, the American continents.

In the aftermath of the December 1991 accords that ended the Soviet Union and created the Commonwealth of Independent States (CIS), a new formula appeared in Russian media and political discourse—the "near abroad" (*blizhnee zarubezh'e*). Andrei Kozyrev, foreign minister under Boris Yeltsin, and Andranik Migranian, one of his advisers, spread (if not invented) the term. From Moscow's point of view, it refers to the former Soviet republics that became independent. Adopted by most Russian authors as well as many Western commentators, the "near abroad" was quickly interpreted as an indicator of neo-imperialist thinking. By classifying the newly independent states separately from other foreign countries, or the "far abroad" (*dal'nee zarubezh'e*),[4] Russian leaders clearly indicated the existence of a different category of states over which Moscow would reserve a particular role for itself. Boris Yeltsin put forward this idea at the highest level.[5] "Russia," he wrote in 1992,

> located at the juncture of Europe and Asia, is obligated to finally fulfill its unique historical mission, i.e. to become a link connecting East and West. The resolution of this task presumes two essential conditions: assuring stability within the former Soviet Union and building constructive relations with the other states to strengthen international security.

The minister of foreign affairs and numerous of his advisers further specified Russia's new strategy. One of the most illuminating texts is a note prepared after one of the meetings of that ministry as early as 1992:

> As the internationally recognized heir of the Soviet Union, the Russian Federation must be based, in its foreign policy, on a doctrine that declares the geopolitical space of the former Soviet Union as its vital sphere of interest (like the "Monroe Doctrine" of the United States in Latin America); it must obtain international recognition of its role as the guarantor of political and military stability in the entire former Soviet territory.[6]

Between 1992 and 1995, during the many summits that brought together the presidents of all twelve CIS states (the three Baltic states did not join the new organization), Russian leaders offered a wide range of treaties to realize their design of this new community. It became clear that Yeltsin, though treading resolutely down the path of pro-Western liberal reforms, had no intention of giving up his country's role in the post-Soviet space.

Moscow, for instance, proposed the creation of a collective force for peacekeeping and a joint mechanism controlling all CIS airspace, as well as the organization of an integrated defense community, a sort of eastern North Atlantic Treaty Organization (NATO). More troublingly, Russian leaders suggested that the twelve CIS states should be regarded as a unique space, with external borders to be guarded and defended by a common force under a single command, and that this same space should also become a wider free trade area. It was obvious to all the partners that these proposals involved keeping Russian border guards in all the signatory states, and that the command of these forces and organizations would in large part be given to Russian officers, who had the most training in these functions. Moreover, in several countries

(Armenia, Belarus, Kazakhstan, Kyrgyzstan, and Ukraine), Russia did everything possible to maintain control of its military and naval bases. Even beyond Russia's legitimate strategic interest, it was well understood that these bases carried strong symbolic weight (particularly the Crimean port of Sevastopol and the Baikonur Cosmodrome in Kazakhstan) and embodied Russia's broader influence over its neighbors.[7]

In outlining what would become the foundation of their foreign policy in the "near abroad," Russian leaders tried to use the legacies of the collapse of the Soviet Union to their advantage. Nine of the fifteen new states are landlocked; in other words, they have no direct access to open seas. In addition to the five Central Asian states, this is true of Armenia and Azerbaijan (since the Caspian Sea is not connected to any ocean), Belarus, and even Moldova.[8] As part of imperial and Soviet policy, most major communications routes, roads, railways, and tunnels were directed toward Russia and its capital cities. This organization of networks inherited from the Soviet past has given Moscow leverage in orienting the trade policies of its newly independent neighbors. However, this is a double-edged sword in the case of oil and gas: while several countries (notably Kazakhstan and Turkmenistan) depend on Russia as a transit route for their exports, Russia is dependent on third countries (the Baltic states and Ukraine) for its deliveries to the European Union (EU)—at least until it completes the infrastructure necessary to bypass them and reach European markets directly.

Such attempts by the Russian leadership to rearrange the former Soviet space in its favor have faced strong resistance. Many of the newly independent states have sought all possible means of disengaging from what they see as imperial legacies: Uzbekistan, Turkmenistan, Azerbaijan, Georgia, Moldova, and Ukraine were all quick to oppose the presence of Russian guards on their borders. They have found significant support from their new Western partners. Systematically and repeatedly, U.S. diplomats in CIS capitals have reasserted that the organization is useless, a pure instrument of Russian policy, and that its treaties must be denounced. The approach that successive Russian presidents have taken to the territorial conflicts that have arisen at Russia's margins only substantiates these fears. Although these conflicts draw on factors that are internal and have often existed since the creation of the Soviet Union, it is obvious that after 1991, when these issues were exacerbated and became local wars, Moscow systematically intervened to exploit them and gain leverage over its neighbors. Support for breakaway regions was designed to eliminate the risk of these states' accession to NATO or the EU, since those organizations' statutes require that any territorial dispute be settled before accession. Since 2008, this strategy has complicated the essential question of the country's own borders.

WILL RUSSIA'S BORDERS EVER BE STABILIZED?

According to the 1991 agreement that created the CIS, the new Russian Federation inherited some 60,000 kilometers (37,282 miles) of borders from the RSFSR (Russian Soviet Federative Socialist Republic), of which approximately 40,000 kilometers

(24,855 miles) are maritime. This legacy has proven problematic, as questions concerning the demarcation of borders with other former Soviet republics, in addition to a number of outstanding disputes with other neighbors, were never settled during the Soviet period. Although Putin managed—as a result of Yeltsin's efforts—to resolve many of these disputes, others appear to reflect the ambiguities of the exercise of Russia's power.

The most notable progress was made in the final demarcation of the Russian-Chinese border along the Amur River. In May 1991, when Moscow finally recognized the international rule that makes the thalweg line (the main channel) the decisive factor, Russia surrendered a number of islands to China, ending a feud that had seen the two Communist powers confront one another in 1969. In returning part of the Bolshoi Ussuriiskii Island opposite Khabarovsk to China in 2004 (over the opposition of regional elites), Putin concluded the negotiations that Mikhail Gorbachev had begun.[9] Officially, there are no more territorial issues between the two large neighbors, although the Chinese still note on many maps that parts of the Russian Far East—and of Central Asia—were under their rule in different eras.

Similarly, in 2010, there was a surprise settlement with Norway of a difficult border delimitation issue in the Barents Sea, in an area deemed to be rich in fish and hydrocarbons.[10] The compromise reached demonstrates that Moscow is willing to make concessions when it sees fit. In this case, the two countries are a step ahead of the future division of the Arctic, which is a strategic and disputed point. Even if the common border does not reach to the North Pole—as the Russians claim it does—the maps added in the appendix of the agreement show that the latitude of the agreed border goes a long way in this direction. The same pragmatic attitude can be found in Russia's approach to maritime boundaries in the Caspian Sea. With two bilateral treaties, Moscow set its maritime borders with Azerbaijan (an area thought to lack hydrocarbons) and Kazakhstan (with agreements to share neighboring deposits). But it left open the question of sharing the sea with Turkmenistan and Iran, which in principle blocks underwater pipe construction between the two sides of the sea.[11]

This series of agreements could in the future be supplemented by a decisive move on the Kuril Islands, a sensitive issue that has prevented the signing of a peace treaty with Japan since 1945. When Putin offered in 2014 to recommence talks on the treaty, he knew that for the Japanese, the return of at least part of these islands would be a prerequisite. Some Russian leaders have taken a dim view of this possibility, just as they continue to criticize the U.S.-Soviet agreement on the delimitation of the Bering Strait, signed by Eduard Shevardnadze in 1990, as giving too much to the Americans. The Russian parliament has never ratified this treaty, but it functions as an ad hoc border and both sides have agreed on joint management of fisheries.

The demarcation of borders with the new independent states also held many surprises. The borders between the former Soviet republics were only administrative, and many towns and villages sat on lines that had simply never meant anything. With independence, several major Russian rail lines suddenly found themselves on foreign territory—parts of the famous Trans-Siberian railway, for instance, crossed into Kazakhstan—which implied the need for special transit arrangements. Although border demarcation has not been a particular problem with Kazakhstan or Belarus, this is not the case everywhere. Estonia and Latvia tried to reclaim some districts forcibly attached to Russia by Stalin in 1945, invoking treaties signed in 1920 with Bolshevik Russia that placed the areas under their tutelage. The prospect of joining the EU and NATO deterred them from reviving these conflicts, but the Russian Duma delayed the ratification of new border agreements, thus exerting pressure on the ultimate decisions.[12] In Azerbaijan, pragmatic interests likewise prevailed, and the clarification of the boundary along the Samur River saw Russia surrender several Dagestani villages south of the river. Yet the issue of water use remains unresolved, as Moscow has reserved the right to increase its quota.

Conversely, the demarcation of borders with Georgia and Ukraine led to a series of armed conflicts in which Russia was directly involved. In Abkhazia and South Ossetia, it has continued to support the claims of local secessionist movements, thereby weakening successive Georgian governments. Tbilisi's discriminatory policies toward national minorities contributed to increasing tensions, but the deadly escalation would not have reached the magnitude it did without the support of Moscow.[13] The Russian military also decisively intervened in the organization of the March 2014 referendum in Crimea that allowed Moscow to regain this region, as well as supporting secessionists in the Donbas region. These activities have led to unilateral boundary changes: recognizing the independence of Abkhazia and South Ossetia in 2008 (although Russia did not integrate these areas into its territory) and annexing Crimea in 2014.[14]

Russian officials' justifications have varied, from the right to popular self-determination to the defense of Russians and Russian-speakers abroad as part of the country's strategic interests. At a press conference on December 18, 2014, Putin added a special factor in Crimea: the sanctity of this region as the place where the Russian people were baptized into Orthodoxy.[15] This explanation was not enough to reassure all of its neighbors. There are Russian communities in Estonia, Latvia, and northern Kazakhstan, and in the 1990s, Russia-aligned movements sprang up to claim more autonomy. Putin has certainly reiterated that his country does not intend to expand its territory, but the veracity of such remarks became questionable after the annexation of Crimea. This action, like the procrastination around ratifying several border demarcation treaties, leaves the impression of a state that has not yet finished defining its own territory. Such a position is not without risk for Russia's neighbors, as well as, potentially, for itself. Were there to be a sustained weakening of Russia, could the possibility be excluded that some republics in the North Caucasus would claim independence, or that other neighbors, such as China or Finland, would make their own sovereign demands on Russian territories?

THE PARADOXES OF A SHRINKING SPACE

While Russia has been expanding its territory at the expense of Ukraine, whole sections of its own space lie abandoned, stirring up major anxieties in public opinion.

For decades, a number of regions have been losing population. This phenomenon stems from several factors. The first is the general demographic crisis, which saw the country's population decline between 1993 and 2010, as will be discussed in chapter 2. This decline is uneven across regions, and particularly affects the more northern and eastern parts of the country, where natural and economic conditions are toughest. These areas were colonized by methods that combined forced resettlement and deportation (Tsarist camps and then the GULAG), as well as economic incentives. A second decisive factor was the end of the Soviet planned system, which, with the exception of a few sectors such as hydrocarbons, weakened the benefits (bonuses, wage supplements, etc.) that for decades had allowed the government to attract pioneering young people to those frontiers. The near demise of benefits at the same time as prices (transport, heating, food) spiked drove a massive exodus to other parts of the country.

In the Russian Far East, the phenomenon of desertion is pervasive (See map 1.1.). This vast area, which covers 36 percent of the territory of the country, has lost 22 percent of its population since 1990. Chukotka has lost nearly 70 percent, the Magadan oblast (region) 60 percent, and Kamchatka over 40 percent. Young and old, especially ethnic Russians, have left these places en masse to return to the European part of the country. In some cities, whole neighborhoods have been drained of signs of life. This phenomenon can even be found in Primorskii krai (territory), which remains the most favored region in the Far East; the Pacific port city of Vladivostok, the provincial capital, has lost 7 percent of its population. This situation is even more paradoxical given that the Asia-Pacific region is one of the most dynamic in the world. This trend, which slowed but continued in 2016/17, is all the more worrisome to the authorities because the Far Eastern Federal District, with an average population density of only 1.1 inhabitants per square kilometer, is next door to

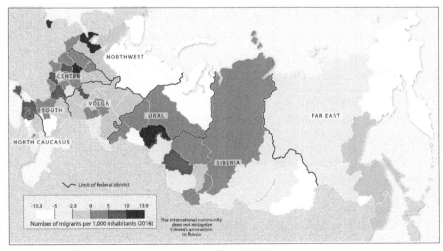

Map 1.1.   Migration between Russian regions (2013)

northern China, where population densities are a hundred times higher. This situation has revived ancestral fears of the "yellow peril," a Chinese invasion.[16]

Another, less visible phenomenon reinforces these territorial apprehensions: the bleeding of rural northern Russia, the so-called non–black soil areas—a name that contrasts these areas to the southern regions, known as Black Earth (*chernozem*) for their rich soil. This is not a new phenomenon: It appeared as early as the 1960s, as a result of Nikita Khrushchev's disastrous agricultural policy. Young people, then a large part of the working-age population, left under-equipped rural areas in the hope of finding a job and a more attractive way of life in the cities or in the so-called Virgin Lands. Since 1991, this depopulation trend has continued at a slower pace but in a way that is affecting more regions in the Urals and Siberia. It has two major consequences. The first is the narrowing of inhabited space, a veritable "shrinking skin" that sees whole villages disappear (wooden houses in the north, if they are not inhabited, rot in place within a few years) or their population reduced to a few elderly women. The 2010 census found that 36,000 of 133,700 Russian villages had fewer than ten permanent inhabitants; in non–black soil areas, 70 percent of villages had fewer than 100 residents, most of whom exceeded working age.[17] The second consequence is the abandonment of arable land. In many districts, the abandonment of unused gardens and meadows has allowed the forest to reclaim these areas after centuries of clearing. The total sown area fell by 36 percent between 1990 and 2012, from 118 million hectares to 76 million, before beginning a slow recovery that reached 79 million hectares in 2015.[18]

The phenomenon of shrinking populated space is not limited to the northernmost areas and the Far East; it also affects the European part of the country, including along the Moscow–St. Petersburg axis. Some regions are facing a depopulation crisis due to the decline of one-industry towns (*monogorod* in Russian) that owed their growth to a single factory or industrial group. The Pskov and Novgorod oblasts, for instance, have lost 22 and 18 percent of their populations, respectively, since 1989. Various initiatives have been proposed to curb these trends by directing immigrants to these areas. However, most migrants aspire to settle in the big cities, where they can find jobs and live in a multicultural environment more easily than in historic rural Russia.

Of course, these forms of territorial abandonment do not all have the same significance. In the European part of the country, they reflect economic and demographic adaptation crises, which also exist elsewhere: *Paris and the French Desert* was the title of a 1947 book by geographer Jean-François Gravier, who denounced the extreme monopoly of that city over French resources, and the North American continent abounds in "shrinking cities." Yet in the Far East, depopulation trends are likely to undermine the very integrity of the Russian state and have pushed the government to take urgent measures, such as a controversial program that offers one hectare of land to any new migrant. In both cases, the spatial fragility of the Russian Federation should not be underestimated.

ISSUES AND TABOOS OF RUSSIA'S INTERNAL "COLONIALISM"

In a book devoted to the post-Soviet space, Vladimir Kagansky wrote:

> An important element of a region is its coherence, the connections of its territory. The Russian Federation is much less "connected" than each of its parts. Numerous nodal regions intersect on its territory, but none match the Federation in its entirety. The preservation of Russia as a state entity requires large ongoing efforts. The opening of the country has made clear the attraction of a large part of its territory to the outside.[19]

Kagansky points out several major elements that are fragility factors in the new Russian state. The first is the weakness of communication networks that cover the whole country. They are often fragmented and outdated. Russia's famous rail network does not cover entire regions of the country and still lacks high-speed trains outside the Moscow–St. Petersburg corridor. Roads are being improved, with a real effort being made to upgrade major federal roads, but the interstate network is still in its infancy, limited to a few sections radiating out of Moscow and surrounding a few large cities. On main roads, there are still many deficiencies (no city bypasses, unpaved sections, dilapidated bridges, and the like); the thawing of permafrost (deep-frozen soil) in Siberia could further complicate matters. Thus, Russia's proverbial road deficit remains a genuine handicap. As for the air network, it is as vital as it is deficient. Hundreds of local airports closed in the 1990s and only recently has restoration of the major regional airports been launched. Whole areas are cut off from the rest of the country for part of the year or are poorly connected to it, limiting the mobility of people and goods.

One of the main legacies of Putin's terms in office will be his systematic address of the main infrastructure gaps that the country inherited from the Soviet era. In November 2009, he became president of the board of trustees of the Russian Geography Society, headed by none other than Sergei Shoigu (at that time minister of emergency situations; since 2012, he has been defense minister). Putin thereby seeks to personally participate in the symbolic mobilization of the Russian population around the natural potential and richness of the national territory. His role in protecting endangered species, from Siberian tigers to Baikal seals, is well known. But his highly publicized trip at the wheel of a Lada on roads in the Far East belongs to a different set of strategic concerns. Over the course of his successive terms, a twofold strategy has been at work. On the domestic front, the aim is to modernize all transport infrastructure. Significant emphasis has been placed on the large railway and road networks, as with the building of the first genuine highways and the first high-speed trains (the Sapsan, which travels from Moscow to St. Petersburg in five hours, has been operational since 2009). Less eye-catching but just as essential is the detailed work done on the black spots evoked above: to bypass the main cities, build or repair bridges on the country's main rivers, and upgrade the main airports to international standards. At the same time, a particular effort is being made to reorganize the country's main export routes, as seen in the exceptional development of Russian ports in the Baltic, on the Black Sea, and on the Pacific Ocean; the emphasis placed on the use of the Northern Sea Route in the Arctic; and the way in which Moscow is trying to slot into the Chinese "New Silk Road" project between Asia and Europe. Evidently, this focus on reinforcing the physical cohesion of Russian territory will continue to be one of the major policy planks of Vladimir Putin's presidency.[20]

The second major fragility factor is the enormous disparity between regions.[21] As seen in tables 1.1 and 1.2, more than 55 percent of the value of the country's total regional output is concentrated in the ten richest regions, while the ten poorest produce less than 1 percent. The range in GDP per capita goes from 1.6 million rubles for the richest to about a hundred thousand for the poorest (see tables 1.3 and 1.4). Moscow city and Moscow region, the two most attractive "subjects" of the Federation, alone account for one-quarter of Russia's GDP. Most economic indicators, such as the volume of retail trade and average wages, corroborate these differences. Outside of Moscow and St. Petersburg, the privileged areas produce hydrocarbons or metals, host heavy industry, or serve as hubs for the food industry or the transit of hydrocarbons. Only one territory, Krasnodar, is "mixed," with intensive agriculture, a transit function (Novorossiysk), and the Caspian Riviera (Sochi).

Conversely, out of the current total of 85 federal subjects, the 20 less-favored regions include 12 of the 22 national republics, almost all in the North Caucasus and Siberia, as well as typically Russian regions such as Pskov, Kostroma, and Ivanovo, which were hit hard by the industrial crisis and the decline of agriculture. The magnitude of these discrepancies is due to many factors, of course, with natural characteristics (remoteness, climate, and resources) playing a role. But the key lies in economic choices (such as the concentration on raw material sectors) and especially in policy decisions. Since the early twentieth century, Russia has had only two brief periods of relative decentralization—a very brief one under Khrushchev and a longer

Table 1.1.   Share of regions in Russia's federal output: Top ten most contributing regions (subjects), 2015

Region	Share (%)
1. Moscow city	21.0
2. Tyumen Oblast (including Khanty-Mansiysk Okrug and Yamalo-Nenets okrug)	9.1
3. Moscow Oblast	5.0
4. St. Petersburg city	4.7
5. Krasnodar Krai	3.0
6. Tatarstan Republic	2.9
7. Sverdlovsk Oblast	2.8
8. Krasnoyarsk Oblast	2.5
9. Bashkortostan Republic	2.1
10. Samara Oblast	1.9
Total of the 10 regions	55.0

Source: Goskomstat, *Regiony Rossii* 2017, tab. 10.1

Table 1.2. Share of regions in Russia's federal output: Top ten least contributing regions (subjects), 2015

Region	Share (%)
1. Altai Republic	< 0.10
2. Jewish Autonomous Oblast	< 0.10
3. Tuva Republic	< 0.10
4. Kalmykia Republic	< 0.10
5. Ingushetia Republic	< 0.10
6. Chukotka Autonomous Okrug	< 0.10
7. Karachay-Cherkessia Republic	0.1
8. Adygeya Republic	0.1
9. Magadan Oblast	0.2
10. Kabardino-Balkaria Republic	0.2

Note: This table does not include Sevastopol city, which is the least contributing region.

Source: Goskomstat, *Regiony Rossii* 2017, tab. 10.1

Table 1.3. Russian top ten richest regions (GDP per capita), 2015

Region	Rubles
1. Sakhalin Oblast	1,699,932.7
2. Tyumen Oblast (including Khanty-Mansiysk Okrug and Yamalo-Nenets Automonus Okrug)	1,625,998.2
3. Chukotka Automonous Okrug	1,269,343.9
4. Moscow city	1,103,453.3
5. Magadan Oblast	846,400.3
6. Sakha (Yakutia) Republic	782,629.4
7. Komi Republic (including Nenetsk Autonomous Okrug)	607,941.9
8. St. Petersburg city	580,562.9
9. Krasnoyarsk Krai	565,272.3
10. Kamchatka Krai	542,797.4

Source: Goskomstat, *Regiony Rossii* 2017, tab. 10.2

Table 1.4. Russian top ten poorest regions (subjects) (GDP per capita), 2015

Regions	Rubles
1. Ingushetia Republic	116,007.9
2. Chechen Republic	116,119.8
3. Karachay-Cherkessia Republic	143,789.5
4. Kabardino-Balkaria Republic	145,555.1
5. Tuva Republic	150,258.3
6. Ivanov Oblast	165,496.3
7. North Ossetia-Alania Republic	181,039.9
8. Adygea Republic	183,386.5
9. Dagestan Republic	186,370.4
10. Altai Krai	194,825.4

Note: This table does not include Sevastopol, which has the lowest GDP per capita at 92,899.6, and Crimea Republic at 130,569.9

Source: Goskomstat, *Regiony Rossii* 2017, tab. 10.2

one between perestroika and the end of the Yeltsin presidency. The hypertrophy of Moscow, where an abnormally high share of investment, skilled management, and high-level students and researchers is concentrated, was initially due to political hyper-centralization. This in turn had the effect of weakening regional cities and solidifying their subordinate role, which affected regional development overall.

Without going into detail, many surprising features can be observed that set the Russian case apart from most models worldwide. Border regions are often depressed, which is to say that the "border effect" does not play its usual dynamic role, but rather imposes a series of administrative constraints that impede development.[22] The same goes for many port cities that were long "closed" (i.e., required access permissions) and remain unattractive today. Finally, too many medium-sized cities are underdeveloped compared to the Russian average and therefore cannot act, as they should, as points of support for their surrounding areas.

The magnitude of these differences is all the more worrying because they broadly correlate with ethnicity. Many national republics are among the country's most disadvantaged regions, and this weighs on interethnic relations and migration. The economic and social developmental deficit of the North Caucasian republics is certainly one of the major drivers of the conflicts and tensions that have appeared there since the late 1980s.

The ethnic factor does strengthen broader criticisms concerning the resurgence of a very centralized policy, which is at the heart of debates on the relationship between the center (the federal government) and the periphery. There has been a series of controversies and claims on the topics of regional autonomy and the center's inability to manage the country. Two sensitive issues are at the heart of this debate. The first is how the regions can benefit from their specific advantages—location, natural resources, and potential specializations—rather than seeing them captured by federal lobbies that tend to monopolize these assets. The second issue is the way the federal government tends to reduce autonomy in regional decision-making in an array of important areas, from the distribution of tax revenues to the definition of school cultural programs, even as it credits the regions with having greater expertise in these areas.

While this does not translate to the political level, Russian oblast leaders have joined with republic leaders to denounce the hypertrophy of the center and the lack of economic, fiscal, and cultural autonomy in the peripheries, be they Russian (like Siberia or Kaliningrad) or non-Russian (like the Volga and Caucasus). This debate recalls the writings of the "regionalists" of the late nineteenth century, such as the Siberian Nikolai Yadrintsev (1842–1894), who denounced Tsarist policy on the borders of the empire.[23] In 2010/11, an important weekly, *Kommersant Vlast'*, published a series of surveys on the autonomist tendencies emerging in several regions. Indeed, it is possible to observe the revival of a long-held taboo, the idea of colonial exploitation of the periphery by the "Moscow hydra." Although it is not expressed in the form of political secessionism, as was the case in Chechnya in the 1990s, these debates point the finger at one of the serious weaknesses of the new Russian state: its over-centralization.

AN OVERLY CENTRALIZED REGIONAL POLICY

The Russian authorities are struggling to define a coherent regional strategy. This is apparent in the instability of the central government entity in charge of this issue. The latest, the Ministry of Regional Development, was dissolved in 2014 and had not yet been replaced as of early 2018.[24] It would be wrong to say that the federal authorities are not interested in these issues. On the contrary, there has been a proliferation of consultation meetings and regional plans for economic and social regional development, a management approach typical of the Soviet era. Obviously, the center still thinks of these issues as it did during Soviet times—in a purely administrative and hierarchical way. Symptomatically, to accelerate and control the development of the three most sensitive areas of the country—the North Caucasus, the Far East, and the Arctic—it created three new area-specific administrations.[25] Moreover, the federal government intervenes in individual cases by taking ad hoc decisions to address disparities, extinguish sources of tension through exceptional allocations, or attract foreign investors by creating "special development zones" where ineffective federal standards do not apply.

Although rarely implemented at full scale, the projects included in the development programs for the North Caucasus and the Far East are extremely ambitious, and impressive budgets have been announced for them—a sign of federal concern about regional disparities and development issues. The projects include both major infrastructure modernization (of ports, airports, and road and rail bottlenecks) and spectacular undertakings such as the planned development of international ski resorts in the North Caucasus or priority development areas in the Pacific Rim. Observers are cautious, stung by the profusion of such outlandish plans that have never actually been brought to fruition. One can, of course, single out the successful realization of the 2014 Sochi Olympics, but it took the direct intervention of the president and outsized investment to complete this exceptional site. Yet Russia is not the only country investing in expensive megaprojects today . . .

Another example of regional issues is the case of border regions where the attractiveness of the neighboring country has become a sensitive issue. This is the case for the Murmansk region and the republic of Karelia, which eye their Scandinavian neighbors, and for the Kaliningrad region, whose population long benefited from a special visa-free regime allowing them to shop in neighboring districts of Poland (this special regime was abolished by Polish authorities in 2016). It also includes the inhabitants of the Russian Far East, who are attracted to the Chinese border towns and almost exclusively drive Korean and Japanese used cars. The development of cross-border trade and employment is common in many countries, but in Russia these situations are often regarded as a kind of foreign invasion or even a possible challenge to territorial cohesion. While not prohibited, they serve as an example for those who argue in favor of limiting the autonomy of these borderlands—such that, far from being an advantage, being located on a border can actually become a handicap. In the case of the Kaliningrad "exclave" wedged between two EU states, Poland

and Lithuania, there is a difficult debate between the majority of the residents, who would like to see their region serve as a model for better integration of Russia into the European neighborhood, and a Moscow administration that seeks above all to better integrate the oblast into the Federation. The Ukrainian crisis and resulting sanctions and embargoes have only served to stiffen these positions. Meanwhile, several companies that had settled in the area to enjoy one of Russia's few effective free economic zones, such as carmaker General Motors, have announced their withdrawal.

All of these territorial issues remain highly sensitive for Russian society and its elite. This is partly due to the history of this state, whose borders have fluctuated for centuries. It is also linked to the country's size and the diversity of its territories. The answer to the uneasy question of how to manage Russia's immense size has yet to find a balanced solution. The current plan to go back to hyper-centralization is far from efficient. As early as 2001, Tatar president Mintimer Shaimiev commented on Putin's first reforms:

> Today it is not necessary to scare by saying that if we give autonomy to regions, Russia will collapse. If we succeeded in preserving the country's integrity at the most difficult moments of political reforms, there is no more room for such concerns today. Russia can only be strong through strong region. Such a large country cannot be governed in all its aspects from only one center.[26]

In 2017, Moscow refused to renew the power-sharing treaty (validated in 1994 and renewed a first time in 2007) with Tatarstan, putting an end to the republic's increased autonomy.[27] Beyond the difficulty of defining a genuine regional policy, it is critical to comprehend how the spatial issue is one of the major elements of the identity crisis Russia is facing.

2

A Troubled Identity

Diversity, Decline, and Migration

The breakup of the Soviet Union and the emergence of Russia as a new state named "Russia–Russian Federation" (*Rossiia–Rossiiskaia Federatsiia*) were a shock to the Russian population. Historically, such a state had never existed within these borders. In tandem with the rapid redefinition of political, economic, and institutional systems born of the Soviet collapse, concerns about the country's identity came to the forefront. Not only is Russia a territorial and cultural archipelago, characterized by large regional differences in living standards and socioeconomic dynamics, it is also an ethnic mosaic that reproduces the national diversity of the former Soviet Union on a smaller scale. While debates over national identity are by no means specific to Russia, the multiplicity of challenges facing the country and its citizens has no equal on the European scene.

The unstable relationship between state and nation inherited from the imperial tradition, the demographic crisis, migration flows, citizenship policies, and rising xenophobic tensions laid bare a country in transformation. The first question that needed to be resolved was the very designation of the nation. There were two options from which to choose: a new Russian nation-state (*russkoe gosudarstvo*), as proposed by the Russian nationalists very active since the 1980s, or a Russian Federation (*Rossiiskaia Federatsiia*) with a more inclusive nationhood.[1] It was this second option that reformers such as Yegor Gaidar supported in order to mitigate the risk of marginalizing non-Russian ethnic minorities and fueling secessionism, and which Boris Yeltsin chose when he signed the Minsk agreements on December 8, 1991. Yet this decision by no means put an end to the search for national identity, which remains one of the core issues facing the country.

19

A "RUSSIAN" VERSUS A "ROSSIAN" PROJECT

Each state has its own coding of difference—by race, ethnicity, religion, or class—which can be explained by the country's history and political culture, and which largely shapes debates on national identity and citizenship.[2] Russia is heir to a pre-revolutionary imperial scheme that for centuries assigned differentiated statuses to conquered peoples based on how they became a part of the empire, their numbers, and the Russian administration's ability to co-opt their indigenous elites. It is also heir to the Soviet system, which, beginning in the 1920s, made ethno-linguistic identity a key marker of individuals and communities, sometimes with benevolent results (the training and promotion of republics' national elites), but often with tragic ones (the deportation of "punished peoples," unofficial quotas limiting Jews' access to intellectual professions, etc.).[3] Today, Russia is not managing solely the legacies of previous regimes. Since the collapse of the Soviet Union, the identity debates that rage in Europe and the United States have also inspired discussions on the domestic scene. Samuel Huntington's "clash of civilizations" theory, the success or failure of the American melting pot and European multiculturalism, the uprisings in the French suburbs in 2005, and the terrorist attacks against *Charlie Hebdo* in 2015—all have been widely discussed in Russia, fueling controversy among intellectuals and influencing decision-makers' framing of the national identity question.[4]

In the early 1990s, the reformers around Yeltsin chose to promote a civic identity for the new Russian Federation, with the aim of following the path of Western liberal democracies. More pragmatically, they also sought to mitigate the risk of the country dividing along ethnic fault lines. This post-Soviet fear reverberated with Chechen demands for independence and autonomist pressures from Tatarstan,[5] pushing the Kremlin to quickly develop the project of a civic identity modeled on the Russian term *rossiiskii*, or "Rossian," which refers to everything related to the Russian state, as opposed to *russkii*, which applies specifically to Russian language, culture, or ethnicity. This Rossian identity was meant to unite all citizens of the Federation around a European-style civic patriotism and was symbolized by the dropping (in 1997) of the mention of ethnicity (*natsional'nost*) from the Russian passport.[6]

In the Rossian doctrine as promoted by its founders, such as Valery Tishkov, director of the Institute of Anthropology and Ethnology, ethnicity belongs to the private sphere. Yet this Rossian civic identity does not eliminate the multiplicity of local ethnic identities, which are still recognized with disparate rights inherited from the Soviet system. This is why Russia has thus far remained a federal state consisting of eighty-five subjects (if we include Crimea and Sevastopol), of which twenty-seven originate directly from the ethnic specificities of their populations. Through their national administrative territories (republics and autonomous districts), fifty ethnic groups have public policies that preserve their vernacular language and ethnic culture in the local education system, as well as give "titular" individuals (representatives of eponymous peoples) priority access to high positions in local government.[7] The 2010 census distinguished 194 "nationalities," a heterogeneous category that includes indigenous ethnic groups as well as diasporas and expatriate communities and quickly proves problematic.

Non-ethnic Russian citizens of the Federation represent about 20 percent of the population, and have varied symbolic statuses.[8] Ukrainians (about three million) and Belarusians (over eight hundred thousand) form significant minorities, but are considered "brother Slavs" who are so well integrated that public opinion does not view them as ethnic minorities. The Finno-Ugric populations (Karelians, Mordvins, Chuvash, Udmurts, Maris, and Komis), as well as peoples of Siberia and the Far North (Yakuts, Buryats, Altai, Nenets, Evenki, and Dolgan), are mostly Russian speakers and Orthodox Christians (even if many preserve shamanistic beliefs and some are Buddhists); their unique identity is seen first and foremost in folk expressions. The feeling of otherness is more consistently expressed toward nominally Muslim peoples (belonging to a traditionally Muslim culture does not automatically assume religious belief or practice). Among them, the Tatars are the most numerous (about 6 million), followed by the Bashkirs (1.6 million), Chechens (1.3 million), Kabards and Ingush (500,000 each), and various smaller groups from Dagestan. Political tensions in the North Caucasus and Volga, coupled with a growing sense of Islamic otherness, made these minorities the only ones deemed potentially problematic for Russia's national identity.

The Russian civic identity promoted during the Yeltsin era was both a success and a failure. It was a success inasmuch as the citizens of the Russian Federation widely recognized themselves as a part of the Russian state and did not display different levels of patriotism based on their ethnicity. It was a failure because the term *rossiiskii* did not take root and found itself increasingly challenged, first by Chechen leaders seeking independence and nationalist elites in the republics, for whom Russia's state identity remained too "Russian" and insufficiently "Rossian"—that is, it was lacking in federalism and multiethnicity. It also sparked harsh criticism from Russian nationalists, who denounced the civic identity as a "de-Russification" of Russia and submission of ethnic Russians to minorities' diktat, an old theme already present in some 1960s dissident circles.[9]

In the 2000s, the debate between Russian and Rossian underwent a series of semantic evolutions. First came the formalization of a new political language that expanded the space for patriotism, based primarily on the rehabilitation of the Soviet past, as the objective and the engine of social consensus under Putin (see chapter 4). This state-sponsored patriotism has resulted in the revaluation not only of the Soviet past, but also of the Russian imperial one. The state committed significant funds to commemorating the great symbolic battles of Russian history (Alexander Nevsky against the Swedes, Dmitry Donskoy against the Mongols, Mikhail Kutuzov against Napoleon, Alexey Yermolov commanding the imperial army in the Caucasus, etc.). It also gave new rights to Cossacks, the descendants of the peasant soldiers who formed the backbone of the Russian force that colonized the Caucasus and Siberia between the seventeenth and nineteenth centuries and who are now integrated into the army and police that patrol the south of the country.

Second, there has been a gradual formalization of the Orthodox Church as the right hand of the state. The Moscow Patriarchate is increasingly visible at official ceremonies, in the military, in the penitentiary system, in educational institutions, and on every societal, family-related issue, a fact that weakens the Rossian civic consensus, the explicit corollary of which is the secular nature of the state and equal rights for the so-called "traditional" religions (Orthodoxy, Islam, Buddhism, and Judaism). Third, some influential intellectuals and politicians, tapping into Russian nationalist sensitivity, have continued to raise the specter of the de-Russification of Russia. Many legislative projects, sometimes adopted but never implemented, have identified ethnic Russians as the only carriers of statehood and formalized Russian culture as primus inter pares.

The elites of the national republics and most minorities have reacted strongly to what they interpret as the breakdown of the Russian civic contract. Many advocate a proactive policy of preserving ethnic languages. Some want the reintroduction of ethnicity in passports, in order to protect minorities from assimilation or, in the case of Russian nationalists, to avoid a possible "dissolution" of Russianness. Others argue for strengthening federalism to give more autonomy to the national republics. President Putin has mentioned several times the need to eliminate all administrative differences between subjects of the Federation, and in 2004–2008 the incorporation of several small Siberian autonomous districts into neighboring oblasts or krais looked like the first step toward simplifying the administrative map at the expense of ethnic minorities. Yet this process ceased. For their part, Islamic institutions claim rights equal to those of the Orthodox Church in terms of their access to military and educational institutions.

Despite the centralizing will of Moscow, local situations are very—and increasingly—diverse. Official secularism no longer applies in Chechnya, where Sharia (Islamic law) has been partially introduced, forcing women to veil themselves and allowing polygamy. In Tatarstan and Bashkortostan, Islam is increasingly taught in public schools. In several other republics, textbooks offer a schizophrenic reading of history, presenting the federal perspective—"peaceful integration" of the territory into the Russian Empire—in the class on Russian history but celebrating local resistance to "Russian colonialism" in the class on local history.

State identity has been further complicated by the strategies Moscow has developed to maintain its influence in the "near abroad."[10] Russia initially facilitated the rapid acquisition of its citizenship for any former Soviet citizen who wanted it, but then took up a more selective policy—until the Ukrainian crisis, after which the policy became more inclusive again. In the 1990s, and more significantly in the next decade, Moscow developed the concept of "compatriot" (*sootechestvennik*) to refer to Russian minorities living in Soviet successor states, as well as to former Soviet citizens and descendants of the waves of outward migration that Russia has experienced since the nineteenth century more broadly.[11] Although the term "compatriot" does not guarantee any legal status, it allows Moscow to concretely practice asymmetric policies. For example, Russia distributed passports to Abkhazians and South Ossetians (as well as to the inhabitants of Transnistria and Donbas), then used this fact to justify its intervention in Georgia in August 2008 as undertaken in defense of its citizens.

With the annexation of Crimea and the emergence of a new conflict in eastern Ukraine, the boundaries of "Russianness" and the "Russian world" have blurred a little more. The internationally recognized borders of Ukraine have been forcibly changed to accommodate the symbolic boundaries of Russianness. In defense of its actions, Moscow has variously invoked its strategic security against NATO advances, its right to defend Russians abroad or those who identify with Russia, and even the baptism of Russia in Kherson in 988. This mixture of genres disrupts the identity repertoires created in the 1990s and 2000s. This expansion of Russianness—real and symbolic—is weakened by the breakdown of internal consensus between the "majority" and the country's minorities, and the progressive erasure of the difference between *russkii* and *rossiiskii*—the latter has gradually declined, while the former is increasingly used, even in reference to civic identity. These identity hesitations are exacerbated by fears of demographic decline and the changing ethnic balance within the Federation itself.

THE RUSSIAN EXCEPTION AND FEAR OF DISAPPEARANCE

On several occasions, Vladimir Putin has mentioned the grim demographic situation in Russia as a threat to the very survival of the nation and the sovereignty of the state. Russia is indeed the only developed country to experience a population decline with such severe potential consequences. Japan has maintained very low fertility rates and a near absence of immigration, but given long life expectancies, it was able, until recently, to avoid a statistical decline. However, the Japanese population could decline by almost half (from 128 million to 80 million) in the coming half-century. Life expectancies are also declining in the United States for public health reasons, but migration and relatively high fertility rates guarantee the country's demographic growth.

Russia is a unique case on the world demographic landscape. Throughout the twentieth century, the country's political upheavals influenced its demographics. Years of civil war, collectivization, Stalin's purges, and the massive losses of the Second World War cost tens of millions of human lives, compounded as the shrunken generations of the 1920s through the 1950s themselves had fewer children. During the Brezhnev years, falling fertility rates and excess mortality among working-age cohorts were partly obscured by the vitality of the Soviet Union's southern peoples. The reversal that occurred after the disintegration of the Soviet Union was thus particularly noticeable: the Russian population declined from 148.5 million in 1992 to 141.9 million in 2009. The correlation between this decline and the economic and political crisis in the country struck a chord with public opinion. The population issue became a main point of political struggle during the Yeltsin era, with conservatives linking demographic decline to liberal reforms.

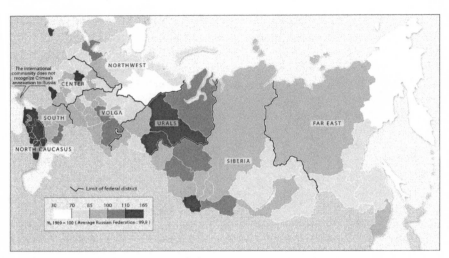

Map 2.1. Growth of Russia's population, 1989–2016 (1989=100)

However, population figures stabilized at the turn of the 2010s, with a minor increase in the population and, in 2013, a positive natural increase for the first time since 1992. In 2017, the authorities welcomed this success, loudly announcing a population of 146.8 million, including 2.3 million new citizens following the annexation of Crimea. Fertility rose from its lowest level in 1999, 1.17 children per woman, to 1.54 in 2009 and 1.78 in 2015. This has been supported by improvement in middle-class living standards, social optimism in young households, and the establishment of a pro-natalist policy, which includes financial support for families (a "baby bonus" allocated beginning with the second child), programs promoting large families, and slightly more restricted access to abortion.[12] Abortion was long used as a form of contraception, and it was not until 2006 that Russia finally had more births than abortions. Despite this modest demographic recovery, the outlook remains somber. Indeed, this rebound is primarily due to the naturalization of some immigrants and the arrival of more numerous age cohorts. But the rise in births cannot fundamentally change this situation. The number of women of childbearing age will decline by 20 percent around 2025 due to the age-cohort effect. The country simply no longer has enough young people: Only 4.5 million children were born between 1991 and 1995, and the increase to 6.5 million between 1996 and 2005 is still below replacement levels.[13]

In addition, the birth policy does not address the main challenge at the heart of the Russian population issue: excess male mortality.[14] Life expectancy for men at birth declined from 63 years in 1990 to 58 in 1996 (which was lower than the rate under Khrushchev), before slowly rising to 66.5 in 2016. The gender differential disproportionately increases with age: There are 105 men for every 100 women under 15, but only 92 men per 100 women between 15 and 65 years, and 44 men per 100 women over 65 years.[15] This excess male mortality is directly and indirectly explained by alcoholism (diseases related to alcohol consumption and poisoning with adulterated liquor), a very high number of accidents at work and on the road, suicides, and domestic violence. In terms of mortality for external causes (not related to a disease), Russia is tied with Burundi and Democratic Republic of Congo.[16] Added to this is Russia's unenviable status as a world leader in heroin use (the country shares first place with Iran). With about seventy tons consumed a year, or nearly a quarter of global consumption, about eight million Russia citizens are drug users.[17] This consumption also influences the growth of the AIDS epidemic, with Russia's infection rate among the highest in the world behind some sub-Saharan countries.[18] However, the authorities continue to ban alternative treatments such as methadone and syringe programs for risk groups.

The authorities have celebrated the rise in the birth rate with great pomp, interpreting it as Russia's awaited demographic rebirth and rightly highlighting an improvement in the welfare of households of childbearing age. They are quieter on male mortality, as the public policies that would be needed to improve the situation are more difficult to implement than natalist policies. Programs designed to combat it are few, but recent years have seen a slight decline in vodka consumption, greater control over its production, and the launch of some road safety policies. At the same time, however, recent health system reforms have reduced the number of hospitals and doctors, sparking fears of a further deterioration of health conditions.

The government also avoids lingering too long on the rise of regional differences, at least in the public arena. In fact, demography is doing well in some areas of the country (see map 2.1). Of the twenty regions with positive rates of population increase, nineteen are national republics or autonomous districts with relatively high percentages of non–ethnic Russian citizens. Chechnya is in the lead, with a natural increase of more than 2 percent (figures that should be taken with caution, given the propaganda of the Kadyrov regime on that question), followed by Ingushetia and Dagestan. After the North Caucasus come regions with Buddhist traditions, such as Tuva, and those with significant indigenous populations, such as Khanty-Mansiisk in Siberia. The thirty peoples considered nominally Muslim saw a sharp demographic increase (+25 percent) between the 1989 and 2010 censuses, to about fifteen million people (10.3 percent of the population).[19]

Despite their different methods of calculation, projections from the Russian statistics service as well as from the UN agree on the decline in the size of the Russian population. By 2030, population may fall to between 122 million and 135 million people,[20] which would have significant consequences in terms of labor, pension funding, and "securing" the areas near more populous neighbors such as China. Working-age population is certain to decline from 104 million in 2016 to around 92 million in 2030. Like European countries, Russia is therefore faced with a migration dilemma: The only way for the country to increase its population is to accept and naturalize the many migrants who come to its borders.

A COUNTRY PROFOUNDLY TRANSFORMED BY MIGRATION

Debates about national demographic collapse are directly associated with migration controversies. The breakup of the Soviet Union had a radical influence on population flows. In total, between 1991 and 2011, four to six million people left Russia for Europe (primarily Germany), the United States, Israel, and Canada.[21] These flows were massive in the early 1990s and then slowed. However, they resumed at a brisk pace after 2012 with the clouding of the country's "modernization" outlook, and have peaked at above three hundred thousand per year since 2014.[22] Emigrants are often younger and more educated than average citizens, contributing to the "brain drain" that has afflicted the country since the Soviet collapse. A land of emigration since the nineteenth century, Russia is now a country of immigration as well. It ranks second or third (depending how the Gulf countries' migrant inflows are calculated) in the world in terms of migration flows after the United States, with eleven million immigrants, or about 8 percent of the population (compared to 15 percent in the United States), in 2014, though this figure has decreased with the economic slowdown.

Since the 1979 Soviet census, there has been a reversal of migration flows, with people tending to "return" to Russia from the southern Soviet republics. The first to leave were Russians who had settled in the Caucasus and Central Asia in the context of the major industrial and agricultural projects of the Stalin and Khrushchev eras, and other Russian speakers (e.g., Slavs and Balts) who did not belong to the titular nationality. Germans and Jews have emigrated directly to Europe or Israel. Upon the collapse of the Soviet Union, flows in the direction of Russia accelerated with the mass migration of those fleeing the conflict zones in the South Caucasus and the civil war in Tajikistan. Poorly equipped Russian authorities had to learn to manage refugee camps in border areas and adopt international standards on the status of refugees and asylum seekers.[23] Compounding these flows was the influx of Russians and Russian speakers who were fearful of staying in the newly independent states. They were not fleeing anti-Russian pogroms but rather difficult economic conditions and "identity" anxieties related to the fear of having no future in the new nation-states. Of the twenty-five million people identified as ethnic Russians who lived in Soviet republics other than Russia at the 1989 census, several million "returned" to Russia (which was often a symbolic homeland, since most of these individuals had been born in the republics). There are no definitive figures, but around half of this group left the republics for Russia or more distant destinations (see table 2.1).[24]

However, since the early 2000s and the revival of the Russian economy, the nature of migration has changed. Labor migrants in search of wages to send home have largely replaced the former "identity migrants." Among these economic migrants, Uzbekistan tops the list, with about 3 million citizens in Russia, followed by Ukraine (1.5 million, much more since the 2014 crisis), Tajikistan (about 1 million), Azerbaijan (800,000), and Kyrgyzstan, Armenia, and Moldova (each of which has about half a million citizens in Russia). Evidently, Russia attracts mostly former Soviet citizens,

Table 2.1.   Russians in the former Soviet states

	Estonia	Latvia	Lithuania	Belarus	Moldova	Ukraine	Armenia	Azerbaijan	Georgia	Kazakhstan	Kyrgyzstan	Uzbekistan	Tajikistan	Turkmenistan
Population 2014 (millions)	1.3	2	3	9.5	4	44	3	9	4.5	16	5.5	28	7.5	5
Russians* (%)	25.5	27	6	9	6	18	0.4	2	1.5	24	12.5	2.5	1	2
Russians in 1989 (%)	30.3	34	9.4	13.2	13	22.1	1.6	5.6	6.3	37.8	21.5	8.3	7.6	9.5

*Figures from the last census conducted in each country

Sources: Statistical committees of the USSR and the different states

although there are also immigrant communities from Afghanistan, China, and Vietnam, with the latter two communities mainly located in the Far East.

As in Europe, these migrants fill specific economic niches scorned by Russian citizens: construction, road services, minor commercial activities, hotel and restaurant work, taxi driving, and, increasingly, human services (as home health aides or caring for children and the elderly). Some nationalities specialize in certain sectors: young Ukrainian and Moldovan women dominate the market for home health aides; Kyrgyz invest in restaurants; Tajiks are mostly in construction; and Azerbaijanis and Uzbeks have pursued petty commercial activities, such as the fresh fruit and vegetables stands in the markets of major Russian cities, since the Soviet period.[25]

These labor migrants have become an integral part of the economy. Ads call for "Tajiks"—now a generic term designating a low-skilled worker—to work at construction sites, taxi and bus drivers speak "accented" Russian, "people of color" (several derogatory terms exist in Russian) clean the sidewalks, and women in colorful clothing run the market stalls. These migrants have fundamentally changed the urban landscape, with the emergence of ethnic neighborhoods (not on a par with the segregation of American cities, but new for Russia), often in the suburbs of large cities, and the development of ethnic restaurants and mosques, including in Russian regions without traditional Muslim populations.[26] Most migrants work in difficult conditions without official contracts or health insurance, putting them at the mercy of their bosses. Workers at construction sites and wholesale markets tend to live in barracks or units without access to personal hygiene facilities, and workplace accidents are common. Each year, Tajikistan collects around six hundred bodies of compatriots who died in Russia due to accidents or untreated illnesses.[27]

In 2013, the Federal Migration Service recorded about two million foreign citizens working legally in Russia—the rest were unregistered and undocumented. Whatever the exact number of migrants, the Russian authorities are struggling to establish a functional migration policy. The country remains liberal on the matter, as CIS citizens can enter Russia without a visa. They then have one month to declare themselves to the relevant services (the infamous OVIR) and register their place of residence and employment contract before they become "illegal."[28] At their own expense, migrants drive another part of the Russian economy: the corruption of the law enforcement agencies and migration services. Those who can afford to do so purchase Russian passports; the less fortunate secure fake registrations, work permits, and health insurance certificates. The departments in charge of migrants are so intimately involved with administrative malfeasance that it becomes almost impossible to know whether migrants have proper papers, hence the emergence of the term "real-fake" documents, which the official services create but do not actually record.[29]

Since 2007, the Russian authorities have tried several times to improve the regulation of migration.[30] Controlling flows at the borders is illusory; no customs service can operate effectively along the entire 7,000-kilometer (4,350-mile) border with Kazakhstan, and in any case, Russia wants to remain an open space for citizens of Eurasian Economic Union member states (see chapter 6). Instead, it is through integration into the national economy that the authorities try to regulate migrants. They initially introduced a quota system requiring companies to notify the municipal and regional administration of their labor needs for the forthcoming year. However, this system was both too rigid (a company could not know the number of employees it would need in a year) and maladaptive (companies preferred to hire underpaid, undocumented migrants rather than play the costly and time-consuming game of legalization). In addition, the penalty measures for businesses that employ illegal labor were largely inefficient, given the endemic corruption of the law enforcement agencies.[31] Since 2015, Russia has replaced the quota system with a duty (*patent*) system that is easier, because each migrant can become his or her own employer. The authorities also introduced a Russian-language test for legalization, but this requirement was for sale on the growing market for false documents before it ever took effect.[32]

Meanwhile, the economic crisis has reduced the number of migrants leaving their countries of origin to work in Russia. Yet even in a context of economic downturn and long-term contraction, the country will continue to need cheap and undemanding labor. In addition, a growing number of migrants settle permanently in Russia and obtain dual citizenship. Between the 2002 and 2010 censuses, the number of Russian citizens of Tajik origin rose by more than 150 percent, and by 70 percent for those from Uzbekistan, Kyrgyzstan, and Armenia.[33] These migrants see Russia as their second home and bring their families, which implies the increasing entry of migrant women to the labor market and the need to adapt the Russian school system for the arrival of non-Russian-speaking children. On this, Russia is in tune with broader, pan-European societal evolutions.

A SOCIETY HAUNTED BY XENOPHOBIA

As in Europe, the influx of migrants attracts the attention of public opinion and media, and has given rise to an unprecedented increase in xenophobia. Since the mid-2000s, about two-thirds of Russians have displayed various xenophobic beliefs, although this number has decreased since the Ukrainian crisis.[34]

In the early 1990s, polls showed strong ethnic sentiment among minorities, whereas the majority of Russians seemed relatively indifferent to ethnic classifications and instead clung to Soviet symbols and the slogan of "friendship of the peoples." With the first Chechen war, xenophobic discourse directed against Chechens—and North Caucasians in general—gained in popularity, with the idea that North Caucasians were "unable" to assimilate to Russian cultural values. Symptomatically, in the late 1990s, several Russian leaders believed it would be better to grant Chechens independence and erect a wall between the region and the rest of the country.[35] Vladimir Putin then exploited a series of terrorist attacks—against Moscow apartment buildings in 1999, the Dubrovka theater in 2002, and the school in Beslan in 2004—and appropriated the American post-9/11 rhetoric of the "war on terror" to mobilize public support. In the 2000s, this xenophobia was transformed with the arrival of labor migrants. Sociological surveys conducted by pollsters such as the Levada Center showed the gradual transformation of "danger": People from the North Caucasus and other groups that had traditionally faced discrimination (Roma, Jews, and expatriates or students from sub-Saharan Africa and Asia) were gradually overtaken by Tajiks and Uzbeks, who had become more easily identifiable targets for violence.[36] This trend was even given a new term in Russian: "*migrantofobiia.*"

Nowadays, about two-thirds of the Russian population, and an even higher proportion of the population of Moscow, thinks their country welcomes too many migrants, that they are responsible for rising crime, and that they pose serious health risks. They want a policy of deporting illegal immigrants and call for the establishment of a visa regime with the southern former Soviet republics. Migrants are generally accused of not wanting—or of being unable—to integrate, and of not respecting Russian values and lifestyles.[37] Many ambiguities accompany this xenophobia.[38] It concerns not only foreigners but also North Caucasians, who, although they are full citizens of the Russian Federation, are considered culturally foreign. While republics such as Dagestan are experiencing massive departures for other parts of the country, given high youth unemployment,[39] polls show that mainstream public opinion wants them to be "parked" in their republics and not settled elsewhere in the country. Other Muslim populations of Russia, such as the Tatars, display xenophobia at rates similar to ethnic Russians but reject the growing trend of conflating migrants and Islam. The main institutions representing Islam in Russia, in particular the Moscow-based Council of Muftis, now consider it their religious duty to meet the needs of migrants and therefore increasingly play a mediating role between the government and diaspora Muslim communities. The conflation of migrants and Muslims and the rise of Islamophobia have also taken root in Russia, yet to a lesser extent than in Europe.[40]

This xenophobia is not only expressed in discourse and attitudes, but has led to unprecedented violence. In the 1990s, only the Roma and sub-Saharan and Asian expatriates were victims of aggression; some Jewish cemeteries were desecrated. In the following decade, the extent of the phenomenon and its victims grew, with skinhead groups—up to fifty thousand of them at the peak of their success—taking the lead in this street violence.[41] Between 2004 and 2007, the number of attacks exploded from 270 (of which 47 were fatal) to 632 (67 of them fatal), without the authorities implementing repressive or preventive responses. The riots in Kondopoga in Karelia in the fall of 2006, which followed a brawl between ethnic Chechens and Russians, ignited Russian nationalist movements and increased clashes between skinhead groups and security forces in Moscow city and region, pushing the authorities toward a more repressive policy. The laxity that had previously characterized police attitudes toward skinhead groups was called into question.

The incidence of street violence initiated by skinheads declined in the years that followed—even if it remains under-recorded, especially in the provinces.[42] But another type of violence emerged: mass clashes between Russian nationalist and North

Caucasian groups following large xenophobic demonstrations. In 2010, some five thousand young Russian nationalists and football fans occupied Manege Square near the Kremlin, shouting racist slogans never heard in the country on such a vast scale. In 2011, street militias organized to violently expel Azeris and Roma (who were suspected of being mafia members) from the village of Sagra, near Yekaterinburg. In 2013, Biryulyovo, a Moscow suburb, ignited after a bloody settling of scores between a victim who was identified as Russian and killers identified as North Caucasians. Youth groups fighting in the streets took the opportunity to loot neighboring stores, especially those belonging to ethnic minorities.[43]

The authorities were not neutral spectators of the rise of xenophobia. The mayors of some cities have quietly backed the skinhead groups as "street cleaners" and celebrated their willingness to restore law and order. The Moscow municipality—under its former mayor, Yuri Luzhkov, as well as under its new one, Sergei Sobyanin—has openly played to xenophobic slogans and conducted media campaigns for the arrest of illegal immigrants in the city's markets. The presidential party's youth movements, Young Guard and Nashi (Ours), have set up "trainings" to explain to migrants how to "behave" in Russia and respect its "national traditions." Several official figures, meanwhile, have expressed concern about migrants deteriorating the quality of spoken Russian and the fact that ethnic Russians are accused of racist violence but never recognized as victims of minorities. Assertions that migrants are responsible for the reactions they generate—a topic largely cultivated by the media—and that the country is threatened by a creeping Islamization have become more mainstream.

This partly explains the success of the so-called national-democratic opposition to Vladimir Putin, embodied by the blogger and lawyer Alexei Navalny, who has combined his sharp criticism of the regime's corruption with an admixture of xenophobia.[44] Both nationalist and liberal opposition has denounced the Kremlin's refusal to tackle the corruption of the security and justice organs. Putin's support for Chechnya's President Ramzan Kadyrov is often cited as an example, since Chechen groups that use brutal methods to dispose of their economic competitors are the most successful example of "ethnic mafias." In recent years, identity debates in Russia have taken on a more political tone and now seem closely related to the nature of the regime. These identity crises are a good indicator of the consensus between society and the state. In the great moment of unanimity that followed the annexation of Crimea, propelling Putin to record popularity ratings, xenophobia has suddenly fallen, a sign of its close articulation with broader issues of threat perception and identification of Russia's "foes."

3

Society

Fragmented but Reinvented

Russian society has profoundly changed over the past three decades. The data published by the State Committee for Statistics (Goskomstat, now Rosstat) and hundreds of sociological surveys conducted by the main polling centers, such as FOM, VTsIOM, Romir, and the independent Levada Center, sketch the contours of a society disrupted by mutations of a scale and speed so great that, in many cases, one can speak of genuine social trauma. Three features characterize Russia's post-Soviet society: its high level of adaptability, its need for stability, and calls for predictability.

The first finding of these sociological studies is indeed the remarkable adaptability of Russian society to changes. In 2014, about 25 percent of respondents said they live as they did before, 10 percent that they were able to take advantage of new possibilities, and 30 percent that they are "tougher." However, this adaptation also obscures a real divide in the population. Twenty-five percent indicated they had had "to get used to deprivation" and nearly 10 percent felt they could not adapt at all (this figure was 16 percent in 2001).[1] The second finding is the overwhelming need for stability. To the question of feeling confident about the future, those responding no (50 to 60 percent) always outnumbered the yeses (40 to 45 percent), with the exception of a short period between 2010 and 2012 and in the first months of 2014.[2] Even if the Levada Center noted a remarkable rise in what it calls the "stability reserve" (the ratio of those for whom it is possible to live in or bear conditions, to those who say that it is no longer bearable), all these years were marked by anxieties or fears in much of the population. In 2013—that is, even before Ukraine-related tensions with the West—respondents said they feared, in descending order, the death of their relatives (52 percent), war or pogroms (38 percent), old age and disease (34 percent), poverty (30 percent), hunger (20 percent), and the arbitrariness of authority (19 percent). In 2014, 77 percent of respondents admitted their fear of another world war (this figure was 65 percent in 1994), 71 percent of natural disasters, and 49 of the hardening of the political regime.[3]

The third finding is the need for "predictability": The number of those who say they are reassured about their futures in the next one or two years increased from 15 percent in the early 1990s to 40 percent in 2014, but only 13 percent felt the same way about the next five or six years and 37 percent said they did not know where they would be in a few months (this figure was over 60 percent in 1990/91).[4] Obviously, the war with Ukraine and the economic crisis in 2014 worsened both personal outlooks and those regarding the country—55 percent feared for the future of Russia.

ONE RUSSIA, SEVERAL RUSSIAS

If one looks beyond the traumas of the early post-Soviet years, the exceptional cohesion of public opinion around its president obscures one of the fundamental characteristics of the Russian society: its fragmentation into several parallel realities. During the 1980s and 1990s, the whole society underwent radical changes: the impact of perestroika, the end of the Soviet system, a sharp reduction in territory, and major political and economic reforms, accompanied by hyperinflation and the evaporation of accumulated savings, the emergence of unemployment and devaluation of skills, and the loss of ideological certainties. It is very difficult to comprehensively assess the effects of shocks that were both physical (the loss of jobs for some, and loss of purchasing power for most) and psychological.

While caution should be maintained in drawing direct links between a deep economic and social crisis and its demographic rendition, it appears certain that this crisis has had a major effect. Two indicators are often cited to get closer to some of these effects. The general fertility rate (average number of children per woman of childbearing age), which was consistently greater than 2 in the 1980s, dipped below this threshold in 1990, reached a low of 1.1–1.2 in 1999–2000, and then slowly rose to 1.78 in 2015. At the same time, the suicide rate per 100,000 people, at 23–24 in the mid-1980s, spiked to a peak of 46 in 1992, remained above 35 until the early 2000s, and fell to 15.4 only in 2015.[5] Many saw these abrupt discontinuities as two symptoms of the psychological trauma induced by rapid changes.

However, classic economic and demographic indicators shed little light on significant variation between regions, social classes, or families. The range of individual reactions to this tumultuous period is infinite. Some Russians, especially the elderly and those in rural areas, truly fell into destitution. One can recall cohorts of women and retirees reduced to selling goods, clothing, or everyday objects on sidewalks or at Sunday markets in order to support themselves. At the same time, many former party officials and administrators, teachers, medical professionals, technicians, and researchers left their posts, often letting their skills fall into disuse as they sought gainful employment, particularly in the services sector. Trade, banking, insurance, and private agencies of all kinds formed in the early 1990s (notaries, lawyers, consulting, advertising, and travel) attracted thousands of defectors from formerly state-sponsored sectors.

One of the fascinating aspects of these changes is the speed with which some individuals, beginning in 1988/89, resolutely embraced new endeavors such as trade, banking, and starting companies—even in the total absence of certainty about the management, legislative, and regulatory guidelines that would govern these activities. The first laws on cooperatives and the timid beginnings of privatization were enacted under Gorbachev. Former Communist Party cadres and members of the Communist youth organization (Komsomol), who were relatively well informed, well connected, and trained as accountants or engineers, launched new ventures during this particularly troubled period. Some would become oligarchs, others simply traders or owners of small and medium-sized enterprises. Many would disappear as a result of score-settling or forced mergers, which were common throughout the 1990s. But the massive scale of these vocational shifts is an unmistakable sign of the adaptability of a part of Russian society and of the maturation of aspirations for change under the late Soviet system.

More than a quarter of a century after the start of these ruptures, it is possible to try to sketch out the new Russian society and its key features. The primary difference from Soviet society is the impressive increase in inequality, which has brought Russia closer to most Western countries on this metric. Of course, the equality claimed by Soviet ideology was only a facade that concealed a variety of situations. The Brezhnev era was based on the stabilization and reproduction of elites; members of the *nomenklatura* and their families had privileged networks (special shops, hospitals, and holiday resorts) and thus a very different way of life than common citizens. Most Soviets had to adapt to modest choices as well as shortages, but the regime offered a level of security that explains why nostalgic attitudes persist: free compulsory education, a basic guaranteed health system, the virtual absence of unemployment, and a highly monitored but largely accessible cultural infrastructure.

Thereafter, social differences quickly emerged. Russia's Gini coefficient (a measurement of income inequality, according to which 0 represents complete equality and 1 represents complete inequality, with all income accruing to a single individual) leapt from an estimated .289 in 1992 to .395 in 2000, and continued to grow (though much more slowly) throughout most of the Putin era, reaching .421 in 2010. This put Russia around the level of the United States and substantially higher than Western Europe.[6] The vast majority of Russians considers that inequality in their country has increased since the end of Yeltsin's rule, with 68 percent saying so in 2014 and only 11 percent arguing that it had fallen.[7] Russia's Gini coefficient seems to have since leveled off and actually started a slow decline, falling to .377 in 2015.

One can observe the presence of a sizable class of the extremely poor, those with incomes below the subsistence level, in each region of the country. This group has declined significantly, from 36.5 million Russians (24.8 percent of the total population) in 1995 to 16 million in 2014 (11 percent). This reduction is due in large part to the proactive social policy initiated by the authorities, which has resulted in a substantial increase in pension payments and a more than doubling of purchasing power. Adding to this effective remedial policy is the maternity allowance, which has helped reduce the number of the extremely poor. However, the fact remains that the poorest 20 percent receive only 5.2 percent of total income, while the richest 20 percent collect more than 47 percent.[8] The 2014 crisis led to a new rise in poverty, with almost twenty million people—or 13 percent of the population—below the poverty line, the highest level since 2006.[9]

According to surveys, the poor live mostly either in rural areas (49.5 percent) or in small towns of under fifty thousand people (24.8 percent). In 2014 the average monthly wages of the most common sectors in these areas (at purchasing power parity,[10] US$679 in textiles, $758 in leatherworking, $833 in agriculture, and $875 in woodworking) were the lowest of all sectors in the Russian economy, much lower than the national average wage (US$1,527) and vastly below those of privileged sectors (such as mining—$2,088; fossil fuel extraction—$3,138; and finance—$3,222).[11] It is not surprising that many members of these impoverished social classes reported individual agricultural plots as one of their sources of income. Such extreme precariousness has become a constant for this part of the Russian population, with the same consequences as in the West: deteriorating housing conditions, lack of access to certain types of care (e.g., dental) or services (culture and travel), spending a significant share of income on food, and an inability to help children establish themselves. Retirees constitute an important share of the poor, with monthly income often around $200 to $300.

At the same time, attention has been focused on the emergence of the small group of ultra-rich, the oligarchs, whose activities and lifestyles continuously arouse media curiosity. If one restricts the definition of this group to the criterion of accumulated wealth, their numbers have exploded since Putin's arrival in power. According to the Russian version of *Forbes* magazine, there were 7 Russian billionaires in 2002, 30 in 2005, and 111 in early 2014, before the onset of the Ukraine crisis and sanctions, which have not spared them—the number declined to 76 in 2016. Moving the threshold to US$500 million brings the figure to 189 people.[12] Their lifestyles have made headlines, with purchases of yachts, football clubs, and sumptuous residences on the French Riviera, in Switzerland, or in London.

But more important than this jet-setting lifestyle is the oligarchs' role in the economy and society. The sources of their wealth are known. Under various conditions, they have benefited from the privatization (Russians crafted the term *prikhvatizatsiya*, a combination of the words privatization and seizure) of the most profitable sectors of the economy: rent-generating sectors (gas, oil, minerals, metallurgy, and chemistry); the military-industrial complex (which still benefits from state controls); and some service industries (banking, telecommunications, and media). They took advantage of offshore investments and globalized financial speculation early, and their wealth became closely associated with corruption scandals and the permeation of the public and private sectors. Almost all have benefited one way or another from their proximity to political power, either during the Yeltsin era or later under Putin. It is hardly surprising that in Levada Center polls, 73 percent of respondents thought it is impossible to become a millionaire in Russia by honest means.[13] In addition, the media sensationalized the fact that many of the early oligarchs were of Jewish origin, feeding implicit anti-Semitism.

Naturally, the vast majority of the population falls between these extremes of abject poverty and extravagant wealth. Observers' attention has long focused on the emergence of a true middle class, the boundaries of which are disputed. The Russian middle class is commonly understood as being made up of families earning approximately (before the 2015 devaluation) US$1,000–1,500 per month per person (more in Moscow), but the definition of the category has as much to do with lifestyle as with income. The average representative of this class is an executive or manager in a private firm who not only earns a relatively high salary but also has a retirement system and supplemental insurance that gives him or her access to good private clinics. He or she is an inhabitant of a large city, owns a home in the city center or in one of the protected suburbs as well as a *dacha* (holiday home), is able to invest in his or her children's education (including one or two years abroad for the better-off), and can buy quality consumer goods. The family owns a car and spends some time abroad: summer and winter trips to Turkey or Egypt, and Europe or Southeast Asia for the wealthier. The number of Russians traveling to the "far abroad" (that is, outside of the former Soviet Union) increased from ten million in 2000 to thirty-eight million in 2014, of whom half were tourists.[14] Yet, only a quarter of the population has a passport for overseas travel, and 59 percent of them are Muscovites.

According to the calculation methods used by the sociological institutes, the middle class represents 25 to 40 percent of Russia's population. Enamored with stability, it plays a growing role in public opinion, a point to which we will return. Despite the undeniable emergence of this new middle class, the country lacks the professions—skilled personnel and executives—that are traditionally associated with it. Russia is the only country in the world with such a high number of young people engaged in upper secondary or tertiary education and such a low number of new scientific or technical patents.[15] This lack of a qualified labor force has weighed on the Russian economy since the mid-2000s. Major business leaders, such as Alexey Mordashov, the head of the steel holding Severstal, and representatives of business associations, have emphasized the dire need to educate new engineers and specialists and to revitalize the hard and applied sciences.[16] In 2009, a survey conducted among business leaders revealed that more than half of them could not recruit enough staff. The country's largest mining holding, Norilsk Nickel, was forced to conduct recruitment campaigns in the neighboring states of Ukraine and Kazakhstan in order to overcome the lack of qualified engineers.[17]

This shortage is even more acute in the area of new technologies and applied sciences. Former president Dmitry Medvedev launched Skolkovo, a major technology innovation center located just outside of Moscow, as a symbol of his signature "modernization" through which Russia was supposed to make its mark on the global market for new technologies. Yet the country has not been able to produce a new generation of specialists in this highly competitive field. Brain drain has hit Russia hard. Since the collapse of the Soviet Union, nearly thirty thousand researchers have left the country, and the Soviet scientific heritage has been reduced to the bare minimum.[18] Advances remain in some theoretical subjects (mathematics and physics), but there are worrying gaps in most applied areas, with the exception of some IT sectors. In 2010, the authorities launched a major project to finance scientific institutions in the hope of attracting foreign talent and bringing back some expatriates, but without much success.[19] Since Putin returned to power in 2012, the marginalization of the country following the Ukrainian conflict, the economic crisis, and strained relations with the West have directly affected foreign investment and scientific partnerships. Symbolizing the resumed brain drain were the departures of the rector of the Higher School of Economics, Sergei Guriev, and the founder of the main Russian social media, equivalent to Facebook, Vkontakte (vk.com), Pavel Durov.

Of course, this new social stratification of the Russian population has a significant impact on the range of values and political attitudes that the different strata share. But before analyzing them, it is necessary to linger on another differentiating factor—the complex differences between types of geographical environments that strengthen these features.

REAFFIRMED OPPOSITIONS BETWEEN URBAN AND RURAL

In analyzing the social and professional changes in progress, many Russian scholars concentrate on spatial oppositions within Russian society. Nataliya Zubarevich, director of a major regional program,[20] divides the country into four regions according to their degree of "social modernization." Building on this classification, one can clarify the tangible operating conditions of this new Russian society.

Moscow city certainly holds a special place in this evolution. It is the undisputed capital in all regards, a showcase for both the country and the regime, and a model of the economic transformations from which it directly benefits, with Moscow city and its wider region earning more than a quarter of the country's GDP. St. Petersburg is seeking to bring itself in line with its old rival; although it can claim cultural and tourist assets, the northern metropolis remains provincial in many ways. It is Moscow that defines all political trends, as well as cultural ones, from architecture to the art market and fashion. Profoundly transformed by the privatization of real estate and the application of a liberal model of development, the city is now socially and functionally segregated. Gentrification has gradually won out in the city center, Moscow's administrative and commercial core. The wealthier segments of the population are concentrated in protected virtual islands, luxury buildings in some central areas such as Ostozhenka or, more often, in the gated communities and new residential neighborhoods that have mushroomed in the western part of the city. They are well preserved from an ecological point of view, especially around the lakes of Serebriannyi Bor or toward Rublevka, where most of the official residences of the country's political elite are located. Other central areas, where prices have soared, focus on the new middle classes, who benefit from a dense network of services; chains such as IKEA, the Azbuka Vkusa (Alphabet of Taste) network of luxury stores, and the popular Auchan hypermarkets; restaurants and trendy cafes; theaters and cinemas; and agencies of various sorts.

The rapid privatization of housing benefited the tenants installed at the end of the Soviet era, initially providing some social diversity. But the rapid rise in prices has made access difficult for newcomers, the young, and the lower-middle classes from the periphery. Life on the wide margins of the urban area, whether inside or outside the administrative boundaries of the city, is infinitely more difficult, with significant commutes made longer by permanent traffic jams. The communal apartments (former "bourgeois" apartments shared by several families) that were once a part of Soviet daily life have disappeared from the city center but proliferated in the periphery in new ways. Migrants from Central Asia are crammed ten or twenty people per apartment, often of the same sex and grouped by region of origin. Social tensions related to ethnicity, which were virtually unknown but are now beginning to be felt, take, for instance, the form of unease about the crowds of young Muslims who fill the streets and squares adjacent to the Grand Mosque in Moscow's city center on every major Islamic holiday.

A second spatial category consists of the dynamic regions that not only enjoy promising economic sectors—oil or other mineral production, large modernized companies, and rich agriculture (in the south)—but also benefit from the driving role of their metropolis. This category encompasses the fifteen "millionaire cities" (those with more than one million inhabitants), as well as some less populated administrative capitals (see map 3.1). Although the difference from Moscow is still marked, rapid and major changes can be observed all around: the transformation of city centers into trendy neighborhoods that are partly pedestrian, reserved for shops, restaurants, cultural facilities, and services; the construction on the outskirts of American-style malls; and the development of tertiary economy segments for qualified cadres. An important element of this success is that many people from the provinces are unwilling to live in the capital, which they consider unfriendly, polluted, and exhausting. They want to maintain a balanced life that involves limited commuting times, real proximity to nature, and more direct forms of participation in neighborhood life and interaction with local authorities. This provincial dynamism is essential to understanding an understudied aspect of "deep" Russia. Some lively cities are image conscious and concerned about their branding. The most vibrant examples rely on fairs, festivals, or academic centers that create annual forums and become important dates on the national calendar. As always, much depends on the personality of the governor and having a team that knows how to seize opportunity and resist the temptation of patronage networks that divert a share of resources from actual needs.

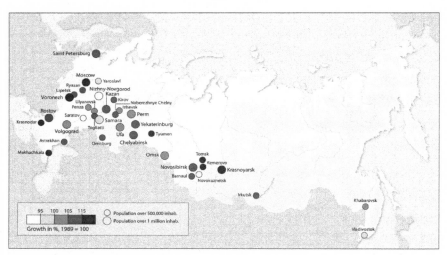

Map 3.1. Russia's main cities

The third category is the mass of intermediate regions, in which a few vibrant cities manage to thrive by taking advantage of a resource or local company that has resisted the crisis, or simply by having a more enterprising mayor or "city manager." The majority of rural areas and small towns (classified in Russian statistics as those with fewer than fifty thousand inhabitants), however, fall into the fourth category: depressed regions. This category includes the villages of northern Russia and Siberian towns, which continue to suffer from dying industries and a weak road network that prevents any modernization. As already mentioned, the elderly tend to populate these small villages or hamlets. At best, the nearest urban centers become "*dacha villages*" that are popular among urban dwellers; this may save a few old wooden houses, but does not change the overall balance. For decades, there has been a little more dynamism in peripheral areas closer to towns, while the most distant margins have withered both economically and demographically.

The cities of these depressed areas often make for a worrying picture. Signs of modernization are everywhere: a hotel or mansion, a couple of restaurants, a few shops that are much better stocked than at the end of the Soviet era, and widely available Internet access. But this does not dispel the impression of abandonment: streets punctured with ruts, broken sidewalks, and historical buildings left in ruins. In some public housing neighborhoods in depressed workers' cities, it is not uncommon to lack running water or district heating, such that residents are reduced to fetching water from pumps in the street and heating apartments with wood.

Next to this, and sometimes in the same region, it is possible to find villages or small towns that have escaped this curse thanks to a savvy mayor or a dynamic collective movement that took over the affairs of the city and was able to draw on—or grow—economic resources in the form of tourism or agro-industrial activity. The facades of the houses are renovated, streets are paved, and some museums and new shops have opened. In the south, Krasnodar, Stavropol, and Rostov-on-Don have escaped the depressive tendency through agricultural means. Much more compact and densely populated, these large rural towns maintain collective functions, family assets, and mutual assistance mechanisms that are more common among Caucasians and Cossacks. Houses have been enlarged and enhanced with new additions, large courtyards are planted with fruit trees, and cars and trucks are omnipresent—all testaments to these households' commitment to successful inter-regional trade.

These differences in development and modernization, coupled with the sense of abandonment that the inhabitants of many villages and small towns feel, feed high levels of disillusionment and depression. Against such a background, it is easier to understand the nostalgia expressed for the Soviet era, when the material aspects of life seemed more assured. These feelings often reflect a rejection of Moscow and Muscovites, a mixture of jealousy and envy that was already present in Soviet times but has been revived by differences in income and lifestyles. The flashes of frustration born from such disparities can quickly turn against convenient scapegoats—the Roma, Caucasians, and migrants, who are accused of benefiting from this situation. There have been incidents where private citizens, convinced of the laxity of complicit local authorities, have taken it upon themselves to "punish" neighbors considered undesirable. These actions, which are covered in the media only when they lead to bloodshed, bear witness to the growing gap in lifestyles and cultural values in a society that has become increasingly complex over the past three decades.

THE GROWING GAP IN CULTURAL VALUES

The socioeconomic fragmentation of Russian society directly impacts the diversity of cultural values expressed by different social groups. It is difficult to identify dominant trends, as the variety of reactions to openness to the world and globalization has led to complex processes in a country that was long closed to outside influences.

The first massive reaction was the extraordinarily rapid spread of a number of foreign models, largely dominated by American examples, once seen only through the distorted prism of the Soviet media. One can easily date this craze to the January 1990 opening of the first McDonald's, on Pushkin Square in central Moscow, which created incredible queues. As of late 2014, the company had 471 stores in the country. There are many other examples of the "Westernization" of Russian consumer society, from the IKEA and Auchan networks already mentioned to the presence in virtually all cities of such companies as Pizza Hut, Le Pain Quotidien, Starbucks, Coca-Cola, and Apple. It is important to note that this openness is not only to the West. The country has also experienced strong Asian influences, including Chinese and Japanese food, the Japanese cars that make up the bulk of the automotive fleet east of the Urals, the fashion for martial arts, and a craze for Caucasian and Central Asian cuisine (exemplified by the Alaverdi and Chaikhona No. 1 restaurant chains). Far from being limited to trade or food, this trend is also reflected in architecture:

The new Sochi ski resort resembles the major resorts of the Rocky Mountains, and the amusement park adjacent to the Olympic Stadium is a Russian copy of Disney World. Television (Brazilian and Turkish series) and women's magazines (the Russian versions of *Elle, Cosmopolitan*, and *Vogue*) are part of the same globalizing trend.

This diffusion certainly contributes to increased foreign travel by Russian citizens. But these influences are also to be found at much deeper levels. By the late 1990s, there was virtually no city, large or small, that did not have a Protestant church started by an Adventist, Baptist, or Pentecostal proselytizing group. This took advantage of people's critical need for new points of reference in the wake of the disappearance of the Soviet ideological system, but also relied on funding from American, German, or Korean parent organizations.[21] Their aggressive activities in the spiritual realm, as well as with school programs (they circulated textbooks translated into Russian) and charities, soon disturbed the Orthodox Church, which tried to prohibit their expansion by promoting the adoption of restrictive laws. The authorities came to view the new churches as a Western attempt to subvert Russian society.

Russia's religious landscape is widely diversified, despite the thundering declarations of the Orthodox Church, which claims to represent the Russian nation as a whole.[22] In surveys asking Russians about their religious identification in the sense of cultural identification, between 70 and 80 percent claim Orthodoxy. However, if one asks about their specific religious identifications, a different picture emerges. Only 40 percent of citizens choose Orthodoxy, almost 25 percent identify as "spiritual but not religious," 13 percent claim to be atheistic or agnostic, and 4 percent call themselves unaffiliated Christians. To these numbers can be added 300,000 Protestants, 140,000 Catholics, a similar number of Hindus and Krishna worshippers (expatriates from South Asia as well as converts), and over a million neo-pagans.[23] Of course, there are also the other major traditional religions of Russia: Islam (dominant in the Caucasus and Volga, it now has active communities even in the far north and important ethnic Russian converted communities), Buddhism (in Buryatia, Kalmykia, and Tuva), and what remains of Judaism.[24]

The result of thirty years of opening is contradictory. One often has the feeling of a sort of disorganized copy-and-paste of the most popular and commercial Western models, a mix of European hipness and Disney aesthetics, somewhere between New York, Berlin, and Dubai but with a Russian coloration. Yet a closer look reveals other trends. The globalization of food, for example, quickly sparked resistance that can be seen in the appearance of new, typically Russian fast-food networks, such as Mu-Mu or Yolki-Palki. During the Olympic Games in Sochi, the impressive Olympic Park restaurant served more Russian specialties—soups, *pirogi* (pies), *pelmeni* (Siberian dumplings), and *blini* (pancakes)—than global dishes (pizzas, hamburgers, hot dogs, and rolls). A strong patriotic movement resurfaced, demanding a return to "real" Russian values. This current, riding the wave of nostalgia induced by the destabilizing effects of the reforms, has continued to assert itself in all areas. In architecture, it is seen in the revival of wooden buildings, the proliferation of churches and chapels on the urban landscape, and the overwhelming presence of icons and other religious symbols. It is also exemplified by the reappropriation of re-invented traditional crafts: linen and felt, leather and wood, ceramic and porcelain. On top of this, there are attempts to make space for products "Made in Russia" in the hope of reviving economic patriotism.

Media play a critical role in both shaping and reflecting this diversity. Television remains the primary source of information for the population, and two-thirds of Russian citizens consider it "relatively reliable" in its analysis of national and world events. However, its dominance is increasingly challenged by the rise of the Internet, which really took off in the second half of the 2000s. Half of Russians go online at least daily, almost all to check their email and participate in social networks such as Odnoklassniki ("in the same class at school") and Vkontakte. Online recreation ranks second. Searches for alternative information online remain modest, rising from 6 percent to 17 percent between 2011 and 2013—a significant increase, but still far from dethroning the omnipresence of television (as everywhere, print media are in decline).[25] In the fifteen to thirty age group, however, the Internet has become the primary source of information.

The proliferation of sites providing pornographic content and incitement to racial hatred and religious extremism served as a pretext for the authorities to introduce "filters" and block some blogs. The public has mixed feelings about government control of the media. Polls have found that 58 percent of the population agrees to some extent with the notion that countries ought to have television channels that criticize the government and are free from censorship.[26] On the other hand, an overwhelming majority of Russians think the government ought to restrict or ban immoral books and films.[27] The population generally supports the authorities' increased control over the media: In 2013, 44 percent of respondents wanted the state to maintain the same level of control over the media, 24 percent wanted more control, and only 16 percent wanted less.[28] These results are explained by the widespread sense (of course cultivated by the authorities) that a media liberated from state control is a place of perdition and that the younger generations must be protected.

Yet despite the authorities' desire to control society, a growing number of communities are coalescing around specific practices, cults, and ideas outside of the mainstream favored by the regime and the official media. From time to time, on the occasion of some scandal or diversion, the press refers to the existence of these various groups and sects, from fire worshippers of Ramakrishna to environmentalist communities. The two extremes of this wide spectrum are the Old Believers, on one side, and the "bobos" (bourgeois bohemians), on the other.

Russia's territorial vastness makes it possible for certain religious communities to preserve their lifestyles and operate almost hermetically, like the Amish in the United States. This is the case for Old Believer communities. Born of an internal schism in the Russian Orthodox world in the seventeenth century, they managed to survive Tsarist and Soviet persecution due to their isolation. It is estimated that there are as many as two million Old Believers today, including the descendants of relatively large groups that emigrated to North America. In Russia, these communities total around four hundred thousand people and are concentrated mainly in eastern Siberia and the far north. The Old Believers, divided into several sub-branches, are now out of hiding; the main groups have returned to the bosom of the Orthodox Church and recognize the authority of the Patriarch,[29] but have preserved the specificity of their rituals and even inspired some Russian nationalists to convert. There are also some communities belonging to another schismatic movement, the Dukhobors. Several hundred Dukhobor families were repatriated from Georgia to Russia, mainly to the Tambov region, in a publicized but relatively marginal move.[30] Orthodox traditionalists, they are easily recognized by their appearance—long dresses for women, beards and old-fashioned shirts for men—and their large families.

In addition, there are some New Age communities that call for a return to nature and the rehabilitation of pre-Christian rites derived from neo-Druidism, Wicca, and so forth. Some of these movements advocate a doctrinal neo-paganism with books of faith, priests, and rituals; they often incorporate nationalist elements. Others are more eclectic and remain faithful to the New Age principle that a holistic spiritual quest can only be individual. Some New Age communities practice rituals dedicated to pre-Christian Slavic gods at ceremonies in the forest or near water sources during the winter and summer solstices. Their members are "baptized" and change their names when they enter the brotherhood. Some groups have become specialized in the revival of traditional Russian wooden crafts.[31] The archaeological site of Arkaim, near Chelyabinsk, has become the Russian Stonehenge. Dating from the seventeenth century BC, the site is particularly well preserved, but its historical value has been completely overtaken by the New Age cult that has been established there. Presented as "the city of the swastika," the ancient capital of a so-called Aryan civilization, the site receives tens of thousands of curious visitors in search of esoteric mysticism and holistic medicines every year. The tourist draw is so strong that even the regional administration has got into the game, emphasizing the exceptional nature of the place as "connected" to higher powers.[32]

At the other end of the ideological spectrum, the upper-middle classes of large cities—primarily in Moscow and St. Petersburg—have seen the slow emergence of "bobos," a phenomenon common across Europe. These families are financially comfortable, have strong cultural capital, possess advanced degrees, and are accustomed to consuming cultural goods (books, films, music, and art). They are well integrated into the global world, regularly traveling abroad and sending their children there to study. They promote eclectic Western or liberal values—environmentalism, feminism, antiracism, the rejection of established hierarchies, and cultural diversity—though without necessarily seeing these as entailing politicization against the regime.

The phenomenon of neo-ruralization—young families of modest middle-class means moving to rural areas to improve their quality of life while engaging in urban occupations—is not as developed as it is in Europe, since rural areas in Russia are under-equipped in terms of infrastructure. However, the 2000s saw an increase in people owning second homes around large cities, especially Moscow, which has led to the gentrification of parts of the countryside. In some villages, the traditional wooden houses inhabited by the elderly stand alongside the new "cottages" of urban-ites who come for weekends and holidays.

In the three decades of transformation that have followed the onset of perestroika in 1985, Russian society has been fractured to its core. To a large extent, it has adopted Western societies' consumerism, values, and ways of living. This is, in part, the acceleration of a natural trend that was delayed by the ideological and material barriers once imposed by the Soviet system. But this process uncovers much deeper contradictions. When the Levada Center asked how current Russians differ from So-viets, 26 percent said that they understand the world better, 29 percent that they are freer, and 30 percent that they are poorer—but 35 percent also indicated that they are more intolerant of others and 58 percent that they have become more cold and calculating.[33] When asked in March 2014 about what historical path Russia should take, 21 percent responded with the path of European civilization, 22 percent would prefer to return to the path forged by the Soviet Union, and 46 percent believe that Russia must choose its own, special way.[34]

This is the paradox of the current situation. While the population largely identi-fies with Europeans' lifestyles and dreams of a European-style welfare state, surveys note the rise of anti-Americanism and wider anti-Westernism, as well as genuine debate over which values to defend. It is these rifts that are instrumentalized by the Kremlin and of which Putin takes advantage when he declares:

> For me it is important to defend our population from certain quasi-values, which are alien to our citizens. . . . As for our traditional values, I believe that we should pay more attention to them for a very simple reason. A certain ideology dominated in the Soviet Union, and regardless of our feelings about it, it was based on some clear, in fact quasi-religious, values. The Moral Code of the Builder of Communism . . . has the same commandments [as the Bible]; they are just written in simple language [and] shortened drastically. This code has passed on; it does not exist anymore. A new generation of Russian citizens, young people, do not even know what it is. But the only thing that can replace it is those traditional values. . . . Society falls apart without these values. Clearly, we must come back to them, understand their importance, and move forward on the basis of these values.[35]

4

The Political System

A Quest for Consensus

Thirty years after perestroika, the Russian political regime still relies on the deep traumas that shaped the society. These have been numerous: the sudden disappearance of the Soviet system, the bloody confrontation between Boris Yeltsin and the Supreme Soviet (the parliament) in October 1993, the two Chechen wars, numerous terrorist incidents, several economic shocks that weakened the stability of the middle classes, and a revival of tensions with the West to an unprecedented level . . . and simply the unknown: *Everything Was Forever, Until It Was No More* is the title of a book by anthropologist Alexei Yurchak on the last Soviet generation and the impossibility of imagining the collapse of the Soviet Union.[1] On the other hand, the Russian political system itself has cultivated a situation of fear and chronic instability, exerting constant pressure on representatives of the critical opposition (including the unexplained murders of its most prominent figures, such as Anna Politkovskaya and Boris Nemtsov) and oligarchs who refused to play by the regime's rules (the legal saga of Mikhail Khodorkovsky and the death in prison of Sergei Magnitsky).

This complex interplay between the exploitation of popular fears born in this new time of troubles and the exercise of state violence is a major feature of the Putin system. These fears explain much of the Russian regime's capacity to cultivate consensus and avoid serious questions about its methods of exercising power, but they cannot hide the various forms of resistance that have emerged. Growing discontent cannot be controlled only with historical feats such as the annexation of the Crimea or by increasing repressive measures and establishing an ever more rigid and standard-setting discourse. From being a blessing, the regime's stability has indeed become a curse: The stability that remains at the foundation of Putin's popularity is more and more difficult to sustain in its current form. The 2018 election campaign, widely expected to inaugurate Putin's final term, has brought several readjustments, confirming the general but still implicit agreement that changes are to come—but that the regime can still count on a few years of consensus, even among younger generations.

THE "EUROPEAN HOME" AND THE DELEGITIMATION OF LIBERALISM (1989–1993)

From the last years of perestroika until 1993, the Russian elite engaged in a discourse that advocated for the establishment of a "normal country," anxious to make up for what was seen as lost time, and to terminate as soon as possible the path of development that the Soviet Union had taken. Seeing Europe as the model to follow, Gorbachev himself sang the praises of the Soviet Union joining the "European home." The conservative putsch of August 19, 1991, which ousted the general secretary from office for three days, did not enjoy the support of the population; rather, it served to discredit the proponents of the status quo and strengthened the position of the reformers. The supporters of liberal "shock therapy" gathered around Boris Yeltsin, who was elected chairman of the Supreme Soviet of Russia in March 1990 and then president of Russia on June 12, 1991. In the midst of this pro-Western consensus, only two dissenting voices asserted themselves: those of the Communist Party of the Russian Federation (CPRF), which was formed from the ashes of the old Communist Party of the Soviet Union, and the Moscow Patriarchate. Both sought continued consideration of the specific character of Russian civilization, thought to be unassimilable into the Western model and needing to be preserved from it.

After the Soviet Union was dissolved in December 1991, however, the violent impact of social and economic change was such that the wide support enjoyed by what was seen as the march toward a double Westernization (the introduction of a market economy and the establishment of a parliamentary system) weakened quickly. Soaring prices, the loss of savings accumulated during the Soviet period, the collapse of living standards, massive closures of factories and businesses, the liquidation of social benefits (especially for pensioners), and late payment of salaries to civil servants all broke the pro-Western consensus in 1992/93. A brutally impoverished society, the wild privatization of large industrial enterprises, and the birth of a privileged class enjoying social success based on their control of the shadow economy all deeply offended a population accustomed to Soviet uniformity of ways of life.

Unlike in Central Europe, the Communist *nomenklatura* was the main agent of the transition to a market economy. While former dissidents were completely absent from the post-Soviet political scene, former party members easily benefited from privatization, fueling the view that the Soviet collapse had been programmed and plotted by elites who had betrayed the egalitarian ideal of the Soviet regime.[2] As a result of these unprecedented changes, "democracy" was equated with the ravages of capitalism and gradually became a negative, even insulting term in a system that refused to recognize the oligarchs' pillaging of wealth: The Russian word *dermokratiya*, revealingly coined around this time, mixes the words for democracy and shit. The discourse on the absence of a new ideology for the country was also seen as hypocrisy. The presence of Western donors was interpreted as a proof of Western economic diktat, and liberalism was perceived as a new ideology imposed by force. References to the "European example" faded, and political rights were considered secondary to dealing with the material issues of individual survival and social justice.

The first political shock to hit the fledgling Russian democracy came in the fall of 1993, after Boris Yeltsin barely won a referendum on continued reforms (though he garnered 58 percent of the vote, turnout was only 53 percent). The president presented a draft constitution to the Supreme Soviet, then dominated by Communists and nationalists, which rejected it. Yeltsin decided to dissolve the parliament, which responded by voting for his dismissal. A state of emergency was proclaimed on September 24, and military troops loyal to the president stormed the parliament building on October 4, officially leaving more than 150 dead.[3] This bloody event has played an important role in the collective memory of post-Soviet Russia, as it seemed that the democratic project ended in bloodshed and the country nearly descended into civil war. The event also marked the beginning of the presidentialization of the regime: To avoid what was perceived as a step backwards, democratic and liberal parties—supported by Western countries—backed Yeltsin in his muscular demonstration of power and demonization of the Communist opposition. They propagated the idea that in its march toward the West, Russia needed to maintain an authoritarian regime—legitimate because liberal—that would be able to disregard defiant conservative opinion.

The crisis in the fall of 1993 also revealed the fragility of the new Russian Federation. Local leaders took to heart the famous phrase that Yeltsin had uttered to regional leaders in August 1990, when he was first elected president of Russia and still struggling with Soviet president Gorbachev: "Take as much autonomy as you can swallow." The situation in many regions was grave due to the brutal economic crisis and rampant embezzlement by those in power, who took advantage of the situation to capture what remained of profitable businesses. In the republics, the new nationalist parties were trying to capitalize on their influence by mobilizing minorities sensitive to growing inequalities.[4] To protect considerably weakened regional markets, some did not hesitate to propose radical measures such as creating local currencies, imposing customs barriers, and setting credit limits for their regions. Added to the battle between democratic reformers and Russian conservatives was the so-called "revolt of regions." In September 1993, a motley union of regional leaders hostile to President Yeltsin was set to initiate proceedings to remove him from office.[5] The specter of the implosion of the Soviet Union was everywhere.

Concerns about the identity of the new Russian state were accentuated by the situation in two key regions. In 1993, the republics of Tatarstan and Chechnya defied the president and refused to sign a new federal treaty intended to redefine the balance of power between the center and the regions. In fact, Tatar authorities, under the leadership of Mintimer Shaimiev, had voted for their own constitution in a March 1992 referendum. The document proposed federalism from below, wherein the subjects of the Federation would delegate sovereign powers (military, security, monetary policy, etc.) to the federal center while retaining control of any regional economic, political, and cultural issues. But the situation was even more dangerous in Chechnya. Since the collapse of the Soviet Union, this small North Caucasian republic had been demanding its independence. Taking advantage of the withdrawal of the federal center, it was existing almost independently of Moscow, with a criminalized economy (bombings and kidnappings) marked by significant intra-Chechen rivalries.

GETTING BACK ON THE PATH OF POLITICAL CONSENSUS (1994–2000)

From the beginning of 1994, Yeltsin tried to erase the deep divisions that had led to the previous autumn's violence and sought to limit the polarization between "liberals," on the one hand, and "Communist-nationalists," on the other. Prime Minister Viktor Chernomyrdin, representing the interests of the military-industrial complex and the oil and gas industry, granted amnesty to the August 1991 coup plotters and the October 1993 insurgents, allowing conservative figures like Alexander Rutskoy and Ruslan Khasbulatov to return to the political scene. In May 1995, the celebration of the fiftieth anniversary of the end of the Great Patriotic War—the name given in Russia to the Second World War (1941–1945)—was an opportunity to strengthen national unity by reigniting the flame of patriotism.[6] Yeltsin's reelection campaign was marked by an implicit agreement with the oligarchs and their media companies that they would back his candidacy in exchange for financial advantages—all with the unspoken support of the Western powers, which feared the possible return to power of the Communists. Upon his election to a second term in 1996, Yeltsin accelerated the quest for consensus. On June 12, 1996, the date on which the Declaration of Sovereignty of Russia had been adopted in 1990, he declared, "The most important thing for Russia is looking for a national idea, a national ideology."[7] The government newspaper, *Rossiiskaia gazeta*, launched a contest on the new Russian idea and collected hundreds of slogans sent by readers.[8]

Over the course of 1994, a transformational year, the two main regional conflicts would have totally different outcomes that would profoundly affect Russian society for years to come. In February, a political compromise was reached between Moscow and Kazan with the signing of a treaty on the division of powers. The Tatar leadership agreed to enter the more centralized institutional framework defined by the 1993 constitution in exchange for some concessions: participation in the management of the republic's large enterprises, control of domestic politics and cultural life, and the right to engage in some diplomatic activities to defend their economic interests abroad.[9] But Chechnya would not have the same fate as Tatarstan. In December 1994, for reasons mainly related to the internal balance of power in the

Kremlin,[10] Yeltsin sided with the "hawks" in his government and launched an attack in Chechnya. The largest military operation organized by Moscow since its intervention in Afghanistan in 1979, the war would be a military and humanitarian failure that would bog down Russian troops. In 1996, during the presidential election campaign, a peace agreement signed in Khasavyurt allowed Chechnya, renamed the Islamic Republic of Ichkeria, to obtain de facto autonomy and the promise of independence talks in the future, which was seen as a deep humiliation for Russia. Chechnya became the nexus of Russian fears, and threats to national unity one of the leitmotifs of power.

The 1998 economic crisis also came to cast doubts on the market economy and wiped out the first middle-class stabilization efforts, with Russian citizens losing all of their savings for the second time in less than ten years. The feeling that young Russian capitalism was a sham spread rapidly in the population, while the wealth and political omnipotence of the oligarch bankers close to Boris Yeltsin aroused criticism. In 1999, the domestic situation hardened again with respect to Chechnya. In August, local warlords announced that they wanted to establish an Islamic state in Dagestan. A few days later, several attacks on suburban Moscow apartment buildings (which the Kremlin blamed on separatists, although the real planners remain unknown) led to the deaths of over three hundred people and served as a pretext for the new prime minister, Vladimir Putin, to embark on a second Chechen war.

In this context, the so-called democratic and liberal parties were largely discredited. Yabloko and the Union of Right Forces were denigrated because they were unapologetic about the social price of liberal reforms. In the eyes of the public, these parties embodied the brutality of the changes of the Yeltsin years, the negative impact of privatization in the 1990s, and the oligarchs' monopolization of national wealth.

Russia traveled a long road in that first decade after independence. At the time of the Soviet collapse and into the early Yeltsin years, all surveys showed that Russians had very negative views of themselves. According to VTsIOM, between the beginning and end of 1991, agreement with the phrases "we are worse than anyone else" or "we bring only negative things to the world" rose from 7 percent to 57 percent.[11] This feeling was soon combined with the idea that only a return to a powerful state could overcome this shame. Surveys conducted in 1995/96 confirmed that the majority of Russians were ashamed of the current state of their country and viewed the reign of Peter the Great (1672–1725) as the greatest time in national history. Nearly half of respondents saw the notion of great power (*derzhava*) as a unifying element that transcended partisan divisions.[12] The stage was set for Vladimir Putin—a virtual unknown before Yeltsin appointed him prime minister a few months before his resignation on December 31, 1999.

All the elements that would give birth to Putinism indeed took shape in the second half of the 1990s. New personalities gained visibility on the political stage: General Alexander Lebed (d. 2002), former prime minister and minister of foreign affairs Yevgeny Primakov (d. 2015), and Moscow mayor Yuri Luzhkov. For them, the dangers of two extremes—liberalism and Communism—had to be avoided, and the country needed to find a middle way that put the interests of the Russian state above all else. By stating that there was no shame in thinking of Russia as a strong state in terms of domestic politics and a great power in foreign policy, these advocates of a "third way" strengthened patriotic discourse and marginalized the pro-Western stance of the last remaining liberals. In the legislative elections of 1999, the idea of a specific Russian path of development became consensual even within parties considered liberal, as all were critically analyzing the country's situation and recognizing the need for more authoritarian policies that could meet the Chechen security challenge.[13] The new presidential party, Unity, deftly hijacked the need for consensus and security, co-opting the election niche established by Primakov and Luzhkov's rival Fatherland (*Otechestvo*) party to make Vladimir Putin the embodiment of national consensus.

PUTIN I: THE POWER VERTICAL

Vladimir Putin very quickly achieved the dual feats of bringing about Russia's economic recovery and its social stability. Pursuing the logic of "patriotic centrism" pioneered by Primakov and Luzhkov, the new president started the official reconciliation with the Soviet past. In December 2000, a new law on the emblem, flag, and anthem of Russia brought about an ideological compromise that reconciled the three major periods of the nation's history: the Tsarist regime, the Soviet Union, and independent Russia. The former red flag of the Soviet army was reintroduced as the flag of the Armed Forces of the Russian Federation. The state launched its first patriotic education program for citizens, with the aims of giving a "new impetus to the spiritual rebirth of the people of Russia," "maintaining social stability, restoring the national economy, and strengthening the defense capability of the country."[14]

Putin's first term (2000–2004) was organized around the ideas of stabilization and recovery, with themes like order, authority, and state effectiveness, and two slogans: the "power vertical" and the "dictatorship of the law." The president complained about society and elites' lack of political and moral conscience, but refused to claim any ideology, instead citing his pragmatism and qualities as a "technologist" of power charged with righting the boat. Several traumas fed into the authorities' will to strengthen the state. The sinking of the nuclear submarine *Kursk* (and the inability to save its crew) in August 2000, a few months after the inauguration of the new president, was experienced as a humiliation that confirmed the decline of the most prestigious aspects of the country's military and industrial capacity. Public opinion condemned the opacity of the investigation procedure and the military leadership's general contempt for soldiers. Putin promised to take on the issue of military leadership and reinvest in the military-industrial complex.

With North Caucasian violence reaching Moscow through the hostage-taking at the Dubrovka Theater in October 2002, the Kremlin called for a return to "constitutional order" across the entire national territory. It legitimized Putin's tough talk about Chechen terrorists ("we'll whack them in the outhouse") and his promotion of security slogans, reinforced by the global atmosphere that followed the 9/11 attacks, including the U.S. discourse of a war on terror. However, the regime remained careful not to over-correlate acts of terrorism with Islam in general, so as not to offend Muslim minorities. The authorities thus created a double-edged discourse on religion: They emphasized the secular nature of Russia, but attributed a growing symbolic role to the Orthodox Church; they recognized the rights of the country's four "traditional" religions, including Islam, under the leadership of the Spiritual Boards, but disparaged and limited the others as "non-traditional."[15]

The Kremlin also sought to recentralize the country by ending the asymmetric federalism that had emerged in the 1990s. The first step was limiting the role of the Federation Council, the upper house of parliament, whose members consisted of regional leaders and had originally counted republic presidents and regional governors among their number. In May 2000, Putin established seven super-districts (*federal'nyi okrug*), which overlapped with the military regions and were led by plenipotentiary representatives of the president. These have been responsible for restoring a unified constitutional space and confirming the supremacy of federal laws over republics' constitutions and charters. The districts were revised to remove oversized spaces of autonomy that had been granted to Federation subjects. These super-districts moved the system for nominating heads of regional agencies (customs, tax, and police) from the regions, where under Yeltsin governors had often exchanged their support for political and economic benefits, to the federal center.[16]

The regime also reduced the space for political parties by redefining their registration rules while putting in place a structured and hierarchical partisan machine, United Russia (*Edinaia Rossiia*), in order to assert control of the parliamentary institutions and guard against any risks that might come from the legislature. Last but not least, the Kremlin led the offensive against oligarchs who sought to use the media they controlled to stop this takeover by the central government. In 2001, the government raided the main opposition media channels—ORT, NTV, and TV-6. Oligarchs expressing any hint of opposition that could harm the president saw their economic empires dismantled. Boris Berezovsky and Vladimir Gusinsky were forced into exile; Mikhail Khodorkovsky, the head of Yukos, then the largest Russian oil company, resisted the new rules of the game and was arrested in 2003.

The exceptional popularity of Vladimir Putin, who advanced in the opinion polls at record rates, allowed him to win reelection in March 2004 in the first round, with 71 percent of the vote. In this paradoxical campaign, the country's other political leaders (Gennady Zyuganov for the Communists, Vladimir Zhirinovsky for the nationalists, and Grigory Yavlinsky for the liberals) chose not to run, leaving unknown personalities to stand against the incumbent president.[17] The liberal party Yabloko did not even manage to win representation in the Duma; its successor, the Union of Right Forces, moved closer to the regime in a case of semi-co-option.

PUTIN II: THE CHALLENGE OF THE COLOR REVOLUTIONS

In Putin's second term (2004–2008), the regime went on the political offensive. The bloody hostage-taking at a school in Beslan (North Ossetia) in September 2004 helped the authorities stoke popular fears and increased demands for security. Putin announced his desire to further weaken the power of governors, whom he framed as sources of corruption and negligence. Governors would no longer be elected by popular vote but appointed by the regional assembly at the request of the president (a measure that was later partly abolished). This decision, which allowed Putin to dismiss resistant individuals, spurred regional elites to become members of United Russia in droves, such that the party of the president also became the party of governors. The twenty-nine Duma committees moved, without exception, into the hands of United Russia members; the Duma chairman, former interior minister Boris Gryzlov, was the president of both the party and a parliamentary group of the same name. The system of selective coercion and intimidation of opposition forces, already well established, was now accompanied by a growing manipulation of the associative spectrum, embodied by the creation of a third chamber, the so-called Social Chamber, to co-opt the patriotic elements of civil society.

The "power vertical" initiated during Putin's first mandate was reinforced with the progressive structuring of the president's inner circles and their step-by-step conquest of Russia's high-level official functions, especially in the economic sectors. A Russian analyst, Evgeny Minchenko, describes this network as Politburo 2.0, a reference to the highest body in the Soviet system.[18] However, in our view, this comparison is not relevant. Except during the Stalinist period, the Soviet Politburo was a collegial body, based on the rules of the Communist Party, and functioned on the basis of rather precise operation mechanics. As far as we can tell, the "consortium" around Putin has rested on different bases, namely loyalty to the president and a form of co-optation under his direction, thus ensuring both its coherence and its fragility. The "consortium" bridges positions of economic management and explicitly political posts, with the two functions performed simultaneously or successively. It offers a multifaceted career path that can pass through major state bodies (the presidential administration, government, various ministries and committees, and regional governments) and large enterprises, making it perhaps not fundamentally different from similar patterns in major Western countries.

This "Russia, Inc.," as several Russian scholars describe it, consists of a narrow group of fifty to sixty people whom Vladimir Putin had selected to direct all the key branches of the economy and the state: banking and finance, the fuel and energy complex, transportation and infrastructure, and the military-industrial complex, along with metallurgy and chemistry, media and communications, sports and tourism, and the alcohol market. "The president's men," as Yevgenia Albats and Anatoly Yermolin dubbed them in a *Novoe vremia* article from 2011,[19] can be classified into four categories according to the origin and duration of their personal relationships with Putin. The most numerous are the "men in uniform," those commonly referred to as *siloviki* (from *sila*, force), who come mainly from the KGB and its successor, the FSB, and to a lesser extent from the army and police. Among those in the president's innermost circle are men who worked with Putin in the KGB's foreign service in East Germany. Since 2000, the Russian press has repeatedly highlighted the increasing number of former KGB/FSB members who have been promoted to executive functions in the state or economy. According to *Novoe vremia*, in 2011 they occupied about 40 percent of the upper echelons of power of the main Russian firms. A second, slightly smaller category consists of the "men of St. Petersburg," whose leading ranks include Putin's colleagues from the time when he held various administrative positions in that city under the leadership of Mayor Anatoly Sobchak (1990–1996). From this period, too, comes the third group, a few members of the Ozero (Lake) cooperative, an association created with the future president to build a series of dachas.[20] They remain close to Putin and have occupied decisive positions in his regime, as ministers, financiers, and traders of petroleum products. A final, diversified category consists of other family members, and friends from these three circles.[21]

Putin's second term also saw the first turning points in terms of ideology. The color revolutions, especially the 2004 Orange Revolution in Kiev, took the Kremlin by surprise and revealed the impossibility of continuing to present the Russian state as "non-ideological." The presidential administration set about reconstructing the image of the regime under the leadership of Alexander Voloshin, the head of the all-powerful presidential administration, and Vladislav Surkov, its deputy director and Putin's "gray cardinal."[22] The administration developed the concept of "sovereign democracy" (*suverennaia demokratiia*) to describe Russia's right to forge its own development path without interference from the West. More successful was the Kremlin's response to the popular dynamics of the color revolutions in the form of pro-regime youth movements such as Nashi. The patriotic education program was strengthened in the hope of motivating young people to complete their military service (which many avoid) and, more generally, to "make the patriotic consciousness of Russian citizens one of the most important values, one of the foundations of spiritual and moral unity," such that patriotism would become the "spiritual backbone of the country."[23]

The government also decided to invest heavily in culture, which it considered an important means of cultivating consensus and consolidating implicit support for the regime. Although outright *political* nostalgia for the Soviet regime has been diminishing (the Communist Party collects fewer votes each year), *cultural* nostalgia for the Brezhnev era, the golden age of Soviet culture, has been massive and exists across class and age divisions.[24] Movies, songs, and literature from that time have been largely rehabilitated, as have some fashions and consumer products; Soviet vintage has been a commercial success. The presidential administration has used this wave of Soviet nostalgia to its advantage. It offers generous funding for major historical anniversaries (especially military ones), patriotic concerts, and the development of movies and television series, often of very good quality, to promote national sentiment by revisiting the Soviet (and, to a lesser extent, Tsarist) past.[25]

Although the rehabilitation of the Brezhnev years is widely consensual, the Stalin years continue to be interpreted in contrasting manners. In 2004, Boris Gryzlov, State Duma spokesman and the leader of United Russia, laid flowers on Stalin's grave and called on Russians not to forget his contributions in difficult times, implying that at this pivotal time in its history, the country needed an authoritarian leader more than ever.[26] The same year, Putin asked that in preparation for the sixtieth anniversary of the end of the war, the name Stalingrad replace Volgograd at the Tomb of the Unknown Soldier in Moscow, to "respect the heroism of the defenders of Stalingrad in order to preserve the history of the Russian state."[27] In March 2005, the municipality of Volgograd took this one step further, deciding to erect a monument to Stalin alongside Franklin D. Roosevelt and Winston Churchill as the victors of the Second World War.[28] Yet the Orthodox Church has maintained a reverse reading of Stalinism by canonizing the victims of state repressions, even while positioning itself as a staunch supporter of the regime. In 2007, Putin went to Butovo, a large memorial dedicated to the victims of the Stalinist purges, for the seventieth anniversary of the great trials,[29] with the goal of speaking to both sides—those in favor of forgetting Stalin's crimes and those calling for remembrance and mourning.

DMITRY MEDVEDEV: A LIBERAL INTERLUDE?

In 2008, Dmitry Medvedev, who had been Putin's prime minister, became Russia's new president, while Putin became his prime minister. Medvedev's arrival in power thwarted many Western predictions: Putin may not have respected the spirit of the constitution, but he complied with the letter of it by rejecting many proposals to change it so that he could serve a third consecutive presidential term. Although Medvedev had been a part of Putin's inner circle since the 1990s, his election was not a pure political fiction. By becoming prime minister, Putin risked losing control of his protégé and finding himself unable to return to power in the next election. He was careful, however, to transfer the essential functions previously exercised by the president (supervision of the Ministries of the Interior and Defense, FSB, etc.) to his new role as head of the government.

For four years, the Medvedev-Putin diarchy affected the general political system.[30] With Putin positioned as head of both the government and the presidential party, those two institutions suddenly gained increased media visibility and policy credibility. Members of the government more clearly emerged in the public eye as figures with their own personalities, and the presidential party, which had until then essentially functioned as an electoral machine, became more structured. Ideological trends emerged within it, from "liberals" to "conservative patriots," representing a wide range of interests and deploying openly contradictory discourses.[31] Previously hidden conflicts of interest also went on public display, for instance that between Igor Sechin, head of the oil company Rosneft, known for his conservative and *siloviki* views, and Yuri Trutnev, the minister of natural resources and ecology, who supported greater openness to foreign and private capital.

Medvedev created an autonomous space for the revival of liberal thought, symbolized by the Institute for Contemporary Development (INSOR), Igor Yurgens's think tank, which addressed sensitive issues such as the sustainability of the political regime, the need to reform inefficient post-Soviet regional institutions, and the possibility of NATO membership.[32] From a practical political standpoint, however, the liberals no longer existed. The presidential party gradually absorbed the Union of Right Forces, and only the small Solidarity movement—which included former chess player Garry Kasparov, former prime minister Mikhail Kasyanov, and former deputy prime minister Boris Nemtsov—and some members of the Yabloko party still embodied pro-Western liberal ideas.

Medvedev's presidential term was marked by the theme of "modernization"— mainly economic in nature (see chapter 5), but also social and political. Although Putin and Medvedev maintained their popular legitimacy, polls showed the progressive disengagement of the middle and upper classes, who believed less and less in the regime's ability to point out the path to modernization.[33] This was reflected in local and municipal elections in Moscow and St. Petersburg, where the ruling United Russia party struggled to earn a majority. It was no longer seen as an instrument of progress, but as a bureaucratic machine that represented the interests of a privileged caste.

Although greater ideological diversity was noticeable among the Russian elite, this was also the time when some elements of the future "conservative turn" began to take shape. The Moscow Patriarchate was gaining power: Having already established a presence in the penitentiary system and within the military, it now aimed to enter the education system and influence social legislation more generally. Several church figures managed to obtain various positions within the working groups of the Duma Committee on the Family, Women, and Children, then headed by Yelena Mizulina, who spearheaded the passage of more restrictive laws on protecting children from online content and championed pro-life slogans. The president's wife, Svetlana Medvedeva, positioned herself as a mediator between certain religious figures who served as "confessors" for the president and his inner circle—such as Father Tikhon, Father Vladimir Volgin, and Father Kiprian—and the strongmen of the regime, including Putin himself.

In 2010, Medvedev approved the introduction of a new subject into the school curriculum: "Fundamentals of Spiritual and Moral Culture of the Peoples of Russia," later renamed "Fundamentals of Religious Cultures and Secular Ethics." After trial runs in some parts of Russia, the course became mandatory across the country in 2012. Several versions were available, allowing parents to pick and choose course content. The results did not meet the expectations of the Moscow Patriarchate, which had hoped to see the beginning of formalized Orthodox education in public schools, and demonstrated the deep roots of secular values within the population and the educational realm. In 2012, more than 40 percent of parents chose the Ethical

Values option for their children, only 30 percent chose Orthodox Values, and more than 20 percent selected the more neutral Introduction to World Religions.[34] There were many criticisms of the implementation, as a lack of trained teachers sometimes resulted in Orthodox priests teaching catechism disguised as ethics courses, while in several Muslim republics, such as Chechnya, this course became an invitation to adopt Islamic rules.

The "liberal temptation" that was noticeable during the Medvedev presidency remained weak and did not manage to drive a radical transformation of the political regime. Nor did modernization succeed economically. However, the Medvedev interlude did give birth to the largest popular protest movement yet experienced in post-Soviet Russia, further accentuating the association the regime had cultivated between democratization, instability, and foreign influence.

PUTIN III: THE CONSERVATIVE TURN

Putin's third term (2012–2018) promised to be difficult. It started with the biggest protests the country had seen in twenty years. When Putin and Medvedev revealed, in September 2011, that they were about to exchange their respective offices and had decided to do so as early as 2008, the active segment of public opinion ignited. Critics denounced the contempt for voters displayed by the presidential "couple," the sham of elections with predetermined outcomes, and the widespread corruption of the system. Between the December 2011 parliamentary elections and the March 2012 presidential elections, tens of thousands of people took to the streets almost every week, in Moscow as well as other major cities. At the height of protests, in late February, over a hundred thousand people were on the streets chanting anti-Putin slogans, demanding the resignation of the Electoral Commission and members of the government, and calling for transparent elections.[35]

The protesters belonged mainly to the urban middle class. They were employed in the service industry and/or the private sector that had emerged in the 2000s, and communicated using social media channels such as Facebook and its Russian equivalent, Vkontakte. These new middle classes rarely thought of themselves as politicized and did not identify with any party. However, they shared a number of values and commitment mechanisms, as well as self-help communities that were ready to take to the streets to defend ethical slogans. During the huge forest fires of summer 2010, which threatened several cities and semi-rural areas around Moscow, volunteer groups were formed to help the firefighters and overcome the obvious disruption of public services. These often-spontaneous voluntary actions were publicized via Facebook and LiveJournal. Surveys of anti-Putin protesters showed that many who took to the streets in 2011/12 were involved in social networks that dated back to the forest fires of the previous year.[36] The same pattern was noted with the Khimki movement, named for a forest near Moscow that was going to be destroyed by the construction of a highway. Many involved in the environmental movement found themselves protesting against the regime a few months later.[37]

The demonstrators mostly presented themselves as unaffiliated to a party but wanting to live in a less corrupt and freer society in which the authorities did not so obviously violate citizens' rights. Dignity, respect, honesty, and transparency were their key slogans, and the color white symbolized the movement. Alexei Navalny, the lawyer and blogger who emerged as the charismatic leader of the movement, invented the anti-Putin "party of crooks and thieves" slogan that was used to denounce United Russia. In his heyday, his blogs—among the most widely read in Russia—punctuated the protests.[38] Other personalities also emerged as the old liberals were joined by a new generation, including economist Vladimir Milov, and gathered together in a new (and quickly banned) liberal party, the Russian People's Party (PARNAS). Even the oligarch Mikhail Prokhorov ventured to become involved in liberal politics, a path that had been closed to the super-rich since the beginning of the Khodorkovsky case, and temporarily received support from Navalny.

The liberals were not the only ones in the streets. They shared the pavement with some nationalist circles that tied the corruption of state bodies to the migration issue and the threat migrants supposedly posed to the Russian nation. Navalny himself embodies this ambivalence, espousing a liberal discourse that invites Russia to move closer to the European model while clearly sympathizing with the positions of the French National Front and other European populist parties.[39] In September 2013, after a complicated judicial drama, Navalny was allowed to stand in the Moscow mayoral election against the official candidate, Sergey Sobyanin, and won 27 percent of the vote, a good result that confirms the mistrust of ruling elites felt by part of the capital city's middle class. Another outcome of the protests was the emergence of a "new left." In Russia, the term refers to all those who claim progressive leftist values and refuse to recognize the two symbols of the post-Soviet nationalist left: the Communist Party, led by Gennady Zyuganov, and Eduard Limonov's National-Bolshevik Party, which combines heavy Soviet nostalgia with Russian nationalism. This new countercultural left shares values with the European and American left and seeks the intellectual rehabilitation of Marxism. Some read Noam Chomsky and Slavoj Žižek; others revisited Bolshevik art or engaged alongside the "Left Front" of Sergey Udaltsov, who was very visible during the 2011 demonstrations and was subsequently placed under house arrest; he served a three-year sentence in a penal colony from 2014 to summer 2017.

The scale of the demonstrations took the Kremlin by surprise, but the response was fairly swift. The main leaders of the protests were detained under house arrest to await what the press called "Bolotnaya trials" after the name of the place not far from the Kremlin where the protesters gathered. The authorities' main response was to quickly tighten the legal apparatus, including by introducing new legislation on "foreign agents" and NGOs accused of accepting foreign funding. The most famous case is probably that of Memorial, a leading Russian NGO active since perestroika, which focused on rehabilitating the victims of Soviet repression. Higher education institutions (the Higher Economic School in Moscow and the European University at St. Petersburg) and independent research centers (the Independent Sociological Research Center in St. Petersburg) that were seen as liberal were subjected to more red tape and threats and placed under the supervision of meddlesome judicial organs. Several professors with liberal views were pushed to resign or were dismissed from the country's leading universities; others preferred to emigrate.[40]

The online realm, hitherto largely left alone, also saw the imposition of greater restrictions. Since 2012, new laws have been passed that require the most popular bloggers to declare themselves to be "independent media" and thus subject to a range of procedures related to that status. Internet services such as Google are being pressured to store information on Russian territory, rather than abroad, and to agree to provide user information upon the request of judicial entities. Officially, the purpose of these measures is to protect the Russian digital system, Runet, from the risk of cyberattacks or information leaks that would benefit foreign powers, but they are also intended to control the flow of ideas.[41]

The regime also reformed and recentralized its security apparatus. The creation, in 2016, of a Russian National Guard aimed to group the different security agencies—all interior troops, including OMON (Special Purpose Mobility Unit) and SOBR (Special Rapid Response Unit)—into a giant force numbering around 250,000 people.[42] Institutions that formerly depended on the regional branches of the Ministry of the Interior now find themselves answering directly to the president and to the guard's director, Putin's former bodyguard Viktor Zolotov. The creation of this new federal institution points to the ongoing restructuring of the power ministries and circles around Putin, with the implicit mission of protecting the regime and potentially suppressing internal dissidents.[43]

As a more comprehensive response to the ideological challenges of 2011/12, the Kremlin undertook to marginalize the middle classes and their liberal convictions by turning its attention to the silent and more conservative majority of the population, which still formed the backbone of the regime's electoral support. This "conservative turn" was signaled by the trial of Pussy Riot, a feminist performance group responsible for staging an anti-Putin "punk prayer" in the Moscow Cathedral of Christ the Savior in 2012. The authorities hyped this news story to denounce "hooliganism," the immorality of liberal thought, and the need to protect authentic values and the church. The conservative turn has been also notable in several other areas. The terms "morality" (*nravstvennost*) and "spiritual" (*dukhovnyi*) became pervasive in Putin's discourse.[44] The president has championed the defense of Christian values, accusing the West of forgetting its historical roots. The authorities, led by Minister of Culture Vladimir Medinsky, have further sought to sanctify everything identified as a symbol of Russian culture. On an annual basis, Putin meets with descendants of Pushkin, Tolstoy, Dostoevsky, Sholokhov, Pasternak, and Solzhenitsyn to celebrate Russia's contribution to world culture. Conversely, any attempt to treat religious symbols with irreverence—such as the *Icons* exhibition organized by gallery owner

Marat Gelman, a staging of Wagner's opera *Tannhäuser* in Novosibirsk, or Uchitel's film *Matilda*, which portrays the relationship between the late Tsar Nicholas II and a young dancer—is quickly labeled blasphemous and incites hostile activity by nationalists and ultra-Orthodox activists.[45]

The regime has become progressively more explicit in terms of its ideology and offers increasingly normative frameworks. Yet these new ideological projects have been less successful than those launched in the 2000s. Their implementation is more complex, because they assume a greater degree of coercion against all those who oppose or are indifferent to them and thus entail a more obviously repressive will. They also give rise to increasingly diversified resistance, ranging from open political opposition (the minority) and regular street protests (for instance the March 2017 protests, mostly of very young people) to people "voting with their feet"—as we already mentioned, emigration rates spiked after 2012.

The war with Ukraine has temporarily changed the game: The masterstroke of annexing Crimea and the constant media focus on the reactivation of the "fascist" enemy in Ukraine consolidated the political legitimacy of Putin, whose approval ratings soared to over 80 percent.[46] Citizens set aside their dissatisfaction with the lack of reforms and the malfunctioning of the Russian state. Even anti-migrant xenophobia eased in the face of conflict with the West.

In practice, the presidential administration's promotion of "conservatism" has two aims: one defensive, one offensive. The defensive aim is to present the status quo of the Putin regime as the best possible choice for the country and thus to delegitimize the liberal opposition and Western influences. This objective has largely been attained: The regime enjoys broad public support and Putin continues to be seen as the symbol of the nation and of the state, despite criticisms of the administration's corruption and concerns about economic stagnation. The second, offensive objective is to remodel Russian society so that it is depoliticized and passive in its interactions with the regime, but engaged and active in the public space. The Russian state is no longer a welfare state but a neoliberal one that will massively decrease public expenditure; it requires a society able to take responsibility and to replace the state social services, especially with charity activities. This second goal has partly failed, as the presidential administration does not exert behavioral power over the population. Russian society is resisting the regime's desired remodeling, only selectively believes what the authorities announce, and will not allow itself to be facilely roped in.

PUTINISM: WORLDVIEW, IDEOLOGY, DOCTRINE?

So many words have been written to pin down the ideological characteristics of the Russian regime. Some denounce Putin's "fascism"[47]; others identify two other pillars as structuring his thoughts: "the idea of empire and the glorification of war."[48] The inflation of terms used to describe the ideological content of the Putin regime is a fascinating example of media self-intoxication, as for instance in the depiction of the neo-Eurasianist and New Right geopolitician Alexander Dugin as "Putin's brain" or his "guru."[49] Yet contrary to Western pundits' declarations, in today's Russia, there is no new official ideology in the Soviet sense. There is no doctrine, no clearly defined corpus of mandatory texts to study at school or promote publicly. Nothing has replaced Marxism-Leninism, and it seems obvious that in Putin's inner circle, very few believe in the virtues of such indoctrination, which would require the establishment of immense enforcement mechanisms and force elites to apply this new jargon and its ideological limits to themselves as well.

While ideology in the sense of a doctrine is absent, there has been a gradual structuring of a certain worldview, or *Weltanschauung*, broadcast primarily through the media. Its objective can be summarized as follows: to be sufficiently offensive to marginalize and delegitimize all those who question the Putin regime, in particular the liberals, but remain sufficiently vague so that the majority of the population can adhere to it. The Kremlin-backed *Weltanschauung* thus plays the role of the lowest common denominator, confirming the flexible nature of this worldview and the instrumental character of "ideology." The Russian authorities want to avoid locking themselves into anything too rigid that would limit their own discretion and their ability to move from one register to another without having to justify themselves. Another virtue of flexibility is that it consolidates popular consensus around the regime, since almost everyone can internalize the major proposed guidelines, which tend to be implicit, symbolic, and even allegorical.

There is a common core to this *Weltanschauung*, a minimum requirement for everyone: express patriotism, demonstrate pride in the country's recovery since the fall of the Soviet Union, cultivate a certain Soviet nostalgia, and criticize the unbridled liberalism of the Yeltsin years that led the country to the brink of civil war. One should support the idea that Russia cannot afford another revolution or shock therapy and should be reformed gradually, at its own pace, and reject all those who still advocate for the outright adoption of the Western model. One has to consider Russia's view of its "near abroad" to be legitimate and welcome the re-emergence of a Russian voice in the world, defend a cynical view of the international community as manipulated by the interests of the strongest under the guise of great idealistic principles, and share a culture of conspiracy.[50]

Once this base is accepted, several ideological products are offered for collective consumption, none of which appears to dominate. One can choose between nostalgia for the Soviet Union or for the Tsarist Empire. One may consider Ivan the Terrible, Nicholas II, Pyotr Stolypin, Vladimir Lenin, Josef Stalin, Yuri Gagarin, or Vladimir Putin himself to be the most important hero of national history. One might hope that Orthodoxy becomes the state religion or welcome the secularity of state institutions and take pride in Russia's religious diversity. One may see Russia as a country of ethnic Russians in permanent struggle for survival against minorities or celebrate the country's multicultural harmony. One can advocate for complete isolationism or exalt Russia's commitment to creating a multipolar world with its allies. One may express the wish to update pan-Slavism to embrace brother Orthodox Slavs, promote Eurasianism with reference to the Turkic-Mongol world, give preference to the "Russian world" and Russia's diasporas, or look for a model in the Byzantine Empire . . . or present-day China.

Who commands and concocts these ideological products? The amount of ideological doctrine directly subsidized by the presidential administration is minimal, and it prefers to use the media, mostly television, to shape the population's worldview. Alexander Voloshin and Vladislav Surkov, the two main figures in charge of ideological issues, are masters at creating slogans, brands, and symbols to support the Kremlin.[51] The official marketing of Putin's personality has successfully created glamour around the image of a strong man with an impeccably patriotic past and a healthy lifestyle, a man sensitive to religion and culture but who embodies traditional male values and enjoys sports, military technology, and nature.[52]

Doctrinal diversity is primarily expressed not in the presidential administration itself, but in the influence groups that revolve around it.[53] The powerful military-industrial complex finances ideological movements that advocate for an aggressive foreign policy and cultivate the Soviet past and the concept of Russia as an empire, such as the Izborsky Club, which includes thirty major conservative and nationalist figures under the leadership of Alexander Prokhanov, editor-in-chief of the weekly *Zavtra* (Tomorrow).[54] Those who prefer imperial and Orthodox references—such as film director Nikita Mikhalkov, who has played a central role in the return and reburial in Russia of the remains of White Army general Anton Denikin (1872–1947) and reactionary Russian émigré philosopher Ivan Ilyin (1883–1954)—are financed by businessmen who made a fortune in the transport sector, such as Vladimir Yakunin, or communications, such as Konstantin Malofeev. This diversity of memory is representative of that of Russian society as a whole, deepened by the discovery of the works of many authors overshadowed by Soviet censorship, including the thinkers and philosophers of the late imperial period, the White émigrés of the 1920s–1930s, and dissidents from different eras.

There are genuine ideological differences between these groups, but thus far none has managed to win a more official status than the others. We saw this during the celebrations of the hundredth anniversary of the 1917 revolutions. The regime decided to go for a non-celebration, with Putin remaining silent at all the key dates for both the February and the October revolutions. Based as it is on a firm counterrevolutionary ideology, the Kremlin considers that any kind of revolution, whatever its "color," is harmful for the country. Yet it let other political actors take the stage: the Communist Party celebrated the Bolshevik Revolution, while the Orthodox Church mourned the collapse of Tsarism. The latter narrative is becoming more powerful and visible, its efforts to conquer the public space benefiting from the state's silence. Former prosecutor of the Republic of Crimea and now Duma MP Natalia Poklonskaya took the lead in rehabilitating the Tsarist past, especially Nicholas II, and the street demonstrations of August 2017 against the film *Matilda* showcased the existence of an Orthodox fundamentalist realm prepared to engage in street violence.

The Kremlin has allowed competition to develop among these ideological groups and their financial backers. For a while, as Putin advanced his Eurasian Union projects, it seemed that the Eurasianists were ascendant, until they appeared to have been overtaken by the "Russian World" concept.[55] But the notion of Novorossiya (designating Ukrainian territories that would prospectively join the Russian "motherland"), put forward in the first months of the 2014 Ukrainian crisis, quickly disappeared from official discourse and is now nothing more than the rallying cry of the most radical nationalists.[56] It is thus essential to note the fluidity of the concepts the Kremlin uses in order not to take them for granted and to distinguish the vocabulary used by the presidential administration and the government from what is being said in the multiple circles that revolve around them in the hope of acquiring the Machiavelli-inspired status of "adviser to the prince."

Yet an increasing trend toward a stiffening of the ideological references used by the regime around the idea of a separate Russian civilization can also be observed, even as the content remains fuzzy. "Civilization" has become a catchall term in Russia, used and abused by the media as well as the government. Putin and Medvedev have spoken repeatedly of Russia's "civilizational codes," of Russia as a separate civilization with its own cultural and moral foundations, but the terminology is deliberately blurry. References to Russia—whether as a European civilization, a distinct Orthodox civilization, or a Eurasian civilization oriented toward a Euro-Asian equilibrium—can be found scattered through Russian official discourse as both context and reference point.[57] Still, allusions to Europe predominate, namely, the theme of Russia as the authentic, Christian Europe charged with remembering the continent's genuine identity in contrast to a Western Europe that would have forgotten its roots. This is one of the threads that has run through discussions of Russian identity since the Slavophiles in the nineteenth century; the same leitmotif, almost word for word, is now found in the state narrative on Russia's conservative values and in the growing number of parallels drawn between present-day Russia and Byzantium.[58]

PUTIN IV: CONTINUITIES AND CHANGES

Thanks to Crimea's annexation, the regime was able to secure a rallying-around-the-flag movement that calmed down the dissatisfaction expressed in 2011/12 and offered a few more years in favor of the status quo. The Western sanctions did not serve to make the state-society consensus more fragile; on the contrary, even in the face of declining living standards, Russian public opinion stood by its president and showed a high level of resilience to changes in everyday life.[59]

More importantly to understand the resilience of the regime is the fact that the Kremlin remains a highly adaptive body, able to improvise and adjust to new contexts. This was evidenced by the reintegration, in 2016, of some figures with a more liberal economic agenda, such as former finance minister Alexei Kudrin, whom Putin has named deputy head of the president's economic council and asked to draw up a new economic strategy for Russia, and Sergei Kirienko, who, after ten years as the head of Rosatom, became deputy head of the presidential administration. With Kirienko's arrival, the pendulum shifted somewhat away from the most conservative/reactionary positions toward more centrist positions. In 2017, the presidential administration decided to give grants to associations registered as foreign agents, halted direct funding of Putin's Night Wolves patriotic motorcycle club, and repressed Orthodox fundamentalists who crossed the line with their anti-*Matilda* demonstrations. During the 2018 presidential campaign, the Moscow Patriarchate remained quite discreet and the official discursive line put aside previous narratives on religious and moral values to advance a more pragmatic agenda of classic great power security and economic consolidation. Even if Ksenia Sobchak's (the daughter of the former St. Petersburg mayor and Putin mentor Anatoly Sobchak) role during the elections was to divert attention from Navalny and represent the "co-opted" liberal opposition, she nevertheless remains a potential figure around whom a new opposition might take shape. Her presence in the political arena and her access to mainstream media confirmed that the presidential administration was willing to reopen some space to liberal voices.

Over more than fifteen years, Putin's regime has managed the feat of reconstructing a political language that the population widely accepts and internalizes, based on a broad consensus around some Soviet symbols. The ideological equilibrium was destabilized by the 1917 centenary commemorations and the rise of a church-backed, pro-Tsarist narrative, yet the broad frame of reference remains that of the late Soviet Union. The balance around Stalinism memory has been also preserved, with dissident institutions such as Memorial being repressed but Putin inaugurating a new monument to the victims of Stalinist purges in late 2017 in order to offer memorial diversity to Russian society.

The regime is also trying to prolong itself by integrating new forces into its realm. For decades, it secured full impunity for its members. Even as some of those close to the president have been openly criticized in various corruption cases (e.g., Anatoly Serdyukov, the minister of defense from 2007 to 2012, who was dismissed from his post but not charged) or repeated scandals related to the mismanagement of a sector (Rashid Nurgaliyev, the minister of the interior from 2004 to 2012, who was subsequently appointed deputy secretary of the security council), no leading figure has yet been tried for his actions. They have received, at worst, a new appointment or a golden exile (as happened to former Moscow mayor Yuri Luzhkov).

Things seem to have slowly begun to change, with Putin deciding to "clean up" his old team by displacing previously immovable figures, including the *silovik* and former chief of staff of the presidential executive office Sergey Ivanov and the head of Russian Railways Vladimir Yakunin. Yet the regime continues to function by finding a balance between different "clans": for instance, economy minister Aleksey Ulyukayev, who was in open conflict with Igor Sechin, was arrested in November 2016 for alleged corruption and condemned to eight years of prison.

Several governors had to resign or got fired, while a new generation of techno-crats—well trained in managing a modern and neoliberal state, totally unknown to the public, and not directly connected to Putin and therefore loyal to the system as a whole—got promoted. Putin's regime is therefore anything but static: It demon-strates enough flexibility to partly—though modestly, compared to China's massive turnover of elites—replace older generations with younger ones and reintegrate liberal figures after having cultivated a nationalist atmosphere. The two are indeed compatible, and one could imagine a neoliberal economy functioning hand in hand with a more nationalist ideology.

The 2018 presidential elections proved the regime's success at managing public opinion. Putin was able to obtain his highest score ever, 76.6 percent of voters at the first round, and for the first time a little bit more than half of the registered voters (51.7 percent). This feat was made possible by securing the votes of Rus-sia's big cities: Usually with a low voting turnout, they massively voted, and voted for him this time. There are several explanations for this, but it is probable that the feeling of a lack of choice and the notion that, aside from its flaws, no one else but the current regime can attempt to reform the country played a critical role. Interestingly, and contrary to what the Western punditry supposed, younger generations appear as the most pro-Putin of all age cohorts: They may mock the president, joke about the regime's excessive features, but they see Putin as the genuine embodiment of the nation.

Yet the regime is now arriving at a point where its "natural death" by inertia ap-pears a plausible scenario, symbolized by Putin's probable last mandate. What will the elite choose to do in the face of this new challenge: Will it become more repres-sive or engage in a new expansionist battle with the—limited—hope of achieving a new rally-around-the-flag effect? Everybody at the Kremlin knows that the triumph over Crimea cannot easily be repeated. Alternatively, will the regime decide to move forward, even if timidly, with reforms, in order to prepare a post-Putin era? Many hope for a smooth evolution that will allow current elites to stay in power and enable the country to avoid any major new political or societal trauma. Putin himself seems to dream not of an individual successor but of a collective successor, represented by the new technocratic generations that have been bottle-fed the values of his regime: a Putinism without Putin. The core elements to be reformed are well known, with the judicial system chief among them. But the future of the regime is also intrinsically linked to its management of the economic challenges Russia faces.

5

The Economy

Is There a Russian Disease?

Russia's mineral raw materials complex plays an important role in all spheres of the life of the state. . . . In the near term, this strategic factor in Russia's economic growth must be restructuring the national economy on the basis of the available mineral raw materials resources with the goal of significantly increasing its effectiveness. . . . Regardless of whose property the natural resources and in particular the mineral resources might be, the state has the right to regulate the process of their development and use.

—V. V. Putin in his thesis, 1997[1]

Russia and its economy are passing through a new period of turbulence. The late effects of the global crisis and the reversal in oil prices have been compounded by the effects of the Ukraine crisis and the sanctions applied by Western countries following the annexation of Crimea and the Donbas insurgency. As with each of the recent crises, pessimistic comments have multiplied—both in the Russian press, which is prone to dramatic interpretations, and in the Western media, where there has been some Schadenfreude over the country's difficulties. Yet the need for objective analysis is even more urgent now that Russia is largely integrated into the global economy and its crises and decisions have a significant impact on Europe as well.

TENSE DEBATES ON RUSSIA'S ECONOMIC DIRECTION

Russia's recent history has been punctuated by incessant debates on macroeconomic policy and budgetary authority—often between members of the presidential administration, the government, and the Central Bank over the need for more rigor in the state budget, the relaxation of exchange controls, and guidelines for investment and social spending.[2] Since the early 2000s, the presidency has dictated that increasing military spending and developing significant social programs are the top priorities, but slower growth, rising inflation, and ruble devaluation in the post-2008 period have created tensions in setting the agenda. The 2014 crisis exacerbated these conditions: The sharp fall in the value of the national currency and the prospect of lasting stagflation (sustained growth and deflation exceeding 10 percent) forced the government to develop an anti-crisis plan and slow down projects in many areas.

In these debates, several nagging issues returned. The first, already discussed in the context of the Soviet era, took the form of a paradox. Russia's proverbial natural resource wealth makes it one of the few states in the world to consider itself nearly self-sufficient in primary goods (as the Soviet Union did). The question was whether this wealth would become a curse. The significance of the fiscal and commercial revenues gained from that real income had negative effects on several occasions during the twentieth century, in that the situation allowed Soviet leaders to postpone necessary reforms. Several authors have mentioned the notorious "Dutch disease," a financial trend—observed for the first time in the Netherlands in the 1960s—that consists of an influx of foreign currency to primary industries, followed by a crisis in other industrial sectors subject to inflationary pressure.[3] Yet scholars are far from unanimous about the presence of such a trend in Russia, and several authors now prefer to speak of a specific "Russian disease."[4]

Diversifying industrial output and increasing productivity to an internationally competitive level have been two of the main challenges facing the Russian leadership since the collapse of the Soviet Union. The raw materials extractive sectors, though they represent a limited share of the total value added to the economy and employment (9.4 and 1.6 percent, respectively, in 2016, according to official data), account for 59.2 percent of total exports,[5] as well as about one-third of budget revenues.[6] It is understandable that a sharp decline in hydrocarbon prices, such as that observed since the beginning of 2014, generates tension and inspires pessimism about the potential for the economy to rebound. Despite the fact that Russia successfully overcame the effects of global crises in 1998 and 2008, there is talk of collapse, stalemate, and inevitable decline.

Since the end of the Soviet Union, foreign capital has found its way to Russia, encouraged by the conclusion of a limited agreement on the infamous "Russian loans,"[7] the legacy of another period of intense investment in infrastructure and industry in the country at the end of the nineteenth century. The liberal reforms under Yeltsin and expanding privatization, including the ability to create 100 percent foreign-capital-controlled companies in various sectors, appeared to be encouraging signs of a Russia on its way to finally becoming a "normal country," as the president himself put it in a 1992 speech.[8]

But Russia has been in no way a model student. It did not fit easily into the analytical models offered to it, as evidenced by the eighteen years of negotiations it took for Moscow to enter the World Trade Organization (WTO).[9] While most analysts, Russian and Western alike, thought in terms of deepening market reforms, integration into the global market, technological cooperation, and interlinking of financial systems, the Putin leadership had another priority: defending national sovereignty and security, since the country was being threatened with losing control of strategic sectors of its economy. Most deviations from the Western model were interpreted as warning signs of the weakness of an economy where some Soviet practices never really disappeared. Some authors indicated that changes had brought about a new mafia state, a kleptocracy,[10] the sole purpose of which was the enrichment of the president's inner circle, whether his name was Yeltsin or Putin.

As in the political and social spheres, challenges and fears became inextricably mixed. The main challenge was clearly stated by candidate Putin in the earliest declarations of his first election campaign: bridging the massive inequality that had grown in recent decades, which, according to World Bank data, placed Russia between Algeria and Venezuela in terms of GDP per capita. Putin indicated that it would take fifteen years of 8 percent average annual growth to reach the level of Portugal and Spain, or fifteen years at a 10 percent growth rate to reach the level of France and Great Britain.[11] This would also require remobilizing the whole country—its elite and its human and financial resources—while accepting the infusion of foreign capital, technology, and experience. Since then, however, Putin has changed course, expressing fear about what he sees as the imposition of external models unsuited to Russia's specific characteristics: "The modernization of our country cannot be achieved only by the simple transfer to Russian soil of abstract models and diagrams drawn in foreign textbooks."[12] This view is in line with longstanding Russian fears regarding the hoarding of natural resources and the takeover of strategic sectors or decisions for the benefit of foreign actors (corporate or state) in a new context where a liberalized Russia is subject to legal frameworks and international standards over which local leaders have no influence.

It is the intermingling of the desire for modernization and fears about loss of control that has shaped Russia's new economic policy. Lying at the crossroads of financial and industrial strategies, it is deeply marked by a vision of an economic balance of power the main aim of which is to strengthen national sovereignty. It is certainly in this context that one should interpret Putin's turn toward state takeover of a range of strategic sectors when he came to power in 2000. The main question then becomes to what extent such practices may actually contribute to the initial goal of making Russia a modern industrial nation and restoring the decisive and autonomous position it claims.

LESSONS FROM THE 1990s–2000s: GROWTH AND IMBALANCE

There is something contradictory about the Russian economy. This huge state, with its wealth of natural resources, has always drawn fascination, attracting travelers, traders, and entrepreneurs. In the nineteenth century, Russia, which lay on the periphery of industrial Europe, began to make up for some of its infrastructural deficiencies and began its own industrialization process, which was intensified by the Soviet regime. After recovering from the damages incurred during the Second World War at great human and financial cost, the Soviet Union took its place as the world's second largest economy—and a large part of its industrial strength was found in Russia.

Although the last Soviet leaders praised this achievement as a success of the political system, it was based on precarious grounds. The Soviet economy functioned largely outside global markets; hence, it developed excess self-sufficiency and autarky, which were considered the main guarantees of national security. Soviet industry could certainly operate within a protected economy, organized on a closed circuit, and enjoy its monopoly in a continent-size state of 250 million people plus some Socialist partners. The shortcomings of this economic model were to be revealed as soon as Gorbachev and Yeltsin introduced market mechanisms and opened the country to global trade.

AN UNPRECEDENTED CRISIS

The crisis in Russia in the 1990s has been described as more dramatic than the 1929 crisis in the West.[13] The value of industrial production fell by over 60 percent on average as the consequences of the Soviet collapse (the breakup of extensive technical cooperation within integrated enterprises and political and monetary disorder) combined with the sudden application of new economic practices, the beginnings of privatization, and the careless opening of the country to the global market. Whole industrial sectors disappeared, precipitating a crisis in cities and entire regions, with social consequences we have already described. Incomplete reforms created uncertainty that led to the collapse of agriculture as investment and state aid dried up (the law on the privatization of agricultural land was only enacted in 2002). This profound crisis also affected other sectors of the economy, chiefly light industries producing household and electronic consumer goods. Products made in Soviet factories did not correspond at all, in quality or appearance, to the goods from Asian or European producers. The variety of imported household appliances, textiles, and leather goods drove such brutal and overwhelming competition that domestic production collapsed within a few years, and sometimes in only a few months. Consumers were stunned to discover the variety of packaged products offered by the large distribution networks that were beginning to take root in the country, from fast food to supermarkets.

Conversely, the extractive industries and primary processing of raw materials—oil, ferrous and nonferrous metals, and basic chemicals—found even more profitable export substitution possibilities when deprived of part of their tumbling domestic market, leading to a period of sustained growth from the late 1990s. This success was by no means immediate, however: Though gas production remained virtually unchanged, oil, coal, and iron all saw significant drops in production before slowly

Table 5.1.   Evolution of Russian output between 1990 and 2017

	1990	*1997*	*2017*
Oil *(million tonnes)*	516	306	547
Gas *(billion m³)*	641	571	690
Electricity *(10.9 kWh)*	1,082	834	1,091
Steel *(million tonnes)*	89.6	48.5	71.3
Fertilizers *(million tonnes)*	16	9.5	20.8*
Synthetic fibers *(thousand tonnes)*	673.5	128.9	183*
Plastics *(thousand tonnes)*	3,258	1,578	7,597*
Cement *(million tonnes)*	83	26.7	54.9*
Turbines *(million kWh)*	12.5	3.6	3.3
Metal-cutting machines *(thousands)*	74.2	9.4	4.4*
Tractors *(thousands)*	214	12.4	6.3*
Combine harvesters *(thousands)*	65.7	2.3	6.5*
Bulldozers *(thousands)*	14.1	2.4	0.5*
Trucks *(thousands)*	665	146	139*
Cars *(thousands)*	1,103	840	1,120*
Freight wagons *(thousands)*	25.1	5	36,440*
Washing machines *(thousands)*	5,419	800	4,000
Refrigerators *(thousands)*	3,774	1,186	3,300*
Televisions *(thousands)*	4,717	327	5,000
Shoes *(millions of pairs)*	385	33	95.2*
Textiles *(million square meters)*	8,449	1,565	5,407*
Cereals (all grains) *(million tonnes)*	116.7	88.6	134
Potatoes *(million tonnes)*	36.8	37.0	31.2*
Milk *(million tonnes)*	55.7	34.1	30.7*

*2016

Sources: Goskomstat, *Statist.* Ezegodnik 2017; *Promyslennost,* 1998 and 2016. *Sel'skoe khoziaistvo,* 2004

regaining their output levels from the late Soviet period (see table 5.1). As in many developed countries, production sectors tended to lag simultaneously. In current prices, industry fell from 38 percent of GDP in 1990 to 30.5 percent in 2011, while agriculture saw its share drop from 16.5 percent to 4.3 percent, and construction from 9.5 percent to 6.5 percent. A similar contraction occurred in industrial employment during the same period, from 22.8 million workers to 13.3 million; its share of the labor force fell from 30.3 percent to 19.5 percent. Manufacturing industries saw the deepest erosion, declining from 14.8 million workers to 7.7 million.[14]

Those dark years were ones of profound and accelerating transformation of the country's economic fabric. While some sectors disappeared, others emerged from almost nothing—for example, banking, insurance, differentiated commercial networks, and services of all kinds. The share of services reached 60 percent of GDP in 2011, and the number of jobs in the sector rose from 33 million in 1990 to 42 million, or 62.3 percent of total employment. This major transformation of the Russian economy had a commensurate effect on society and urban landscapes, with service enterprises taking over ground floors or whole buildings, and large commercial complexes mushrooming on the periphery of all cities. Millions of Russians of all backgrounds left their previous, often state-paid positions to try their luck in tertiary services. When commodity prices rose, the growth of these new types of jobs was one of the factors that allowed the country to bounce back from its 1998 monetary crisis and launch a strong recovery (over 6 percent on average between 1999 and 2008) that more than made up for the losses of the 1990s and mostly reversed the widening of the gap between Russia and the rest of Europe that had occurred during the early post-Soviet period.

There were multiple factors behind this rebound. Adaptation to new economic rules was facilitated by the high level of average education among managers; the implementation of sound monetary and fiscal policies that enabled Russia, in 2006, to repay Soviet debts to the Paris Club group of international creditors ahead of schedule; and high returns on foreign investment. However, this performance would not have been possible without a long period of rising prices for commodities, particularly oil,[15] which ensured Russia a dramatic increase in its trade surplus and budget revenues (see figure 5.1). In some sense, the proportion of extractive and raw materials primary-processing industries as a share of Russia's economy, unusually high for a large industrial country, should be regarded as normal in the Russian case, given the size of its territory and the vast natural wealth it possesses. However, if the country aspires to play a leading role among major economies, it must also fill a number of gaps in its industrial fabric, which remains deeply marked by the end of the Soviet system.

Without covering all sectors, it is notable that among intermediate goods (machine tools, heavy electrical equipment, and transport), particular situations remain highly variable. The most frequently cited factors are the level of obsolete equipment

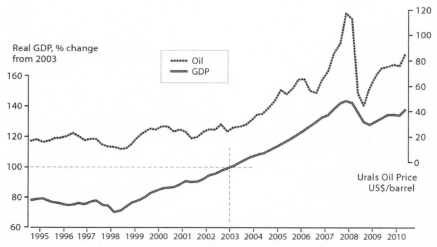

Figure 5.1.   Russian growth and crude oil prices (1995–2010). *Source:* M. Kuboniwa, *Comparative Economic Studies*, 2012, 564, p. 125.

still in place (it is officially estimated at between 35 percent and 65 percent, depending on the sector); the terms of privatization; whether state controls were maintained (e.g., for some military hardware); and leaders' capacity to maintain some market share. Acclaimed industries from the Soviet era, such as shipbuilding and civil aviation, practically ceased to exist and remain in critical condition today. Others—such as parts of the military-industrial complex, civilian and military nuclear, the space industry, and the production of railway equipment—have been buoyed by a combination of investment and state subsidies, the purchase of foreign technology, and protectionist measures, without which deep cuts would be required in each of these areas, causing severe local crises.

The automobile sector is a good example of Russian industry's capacity to rebound in a key area of domestic consumption. Households were subject to a significant car shortage at the end of the Soviet period. The sudden opening of the internal market to foreign models (including a considerable influx of foreign used vehicles) placed Russian manufacturers in a difficult position. National production collapsed, while annual sales figures exploded to the benefit of imported cars. The rescue of this at-risk sector, fully privatized in the early 1990s, was achieved only after the adoption of radical measures that mixed protectionism (the application of more onerous import tariffs and technical standards to limit the influx of used vehicles) with incentives for foreign investment in Russia. Specifically, from 2002, foreign auto manufacturers that wished to sell their models in the country were invited to invest a minimum of US$250 million in the country, either in existing plants or in new plants that they would build, and to ensure that within five years more than 50 percent of the parts used in their manufacturing process would be produced in Russia.[16] Given their great interest in this growing market, Western manufacturers agreed to the new rules, which entailed a transfer of investment, technology, and know-how analogous to Fiat's collaboration with the Soviet government in establishing the VAZ/Volga factory in Togliatti in 1966. Russian manufacturers took advantage of this momentum to start introducing new practices in the fields of management and quality control, as well as reforming sales channels to adapt to changing customer expectations regarding post-purchase services (all of which were sorely lacking). Significantly, in the 2000s, similar rebounds occurred in consumer goods (refrigerators, washing machines, and televisions), again with a major opening to large foreign firms that allowed them to produce under license in various parts of the country.

Conversely, civil aviation is an example of a leading Soviet industry that has not found ways to grow due to the inertia of its organization. This sector—which, according to official figures, still represented some five hundred thousand jobs in 2002—was one of the highlights of the Soviet system. However, the fully closed-circuit manufacturers took no account of the evolution of international standards for noise or fuel consumption, such that after 1991, many foreign countries threatened to ban the entire Russian fleet. This was compounded by the dispersion of production among multiple competing firms (Ilyushin, Tupolev, Antonov, and Yakovlev for civil aviation, MiG and Sukhoi for the military, and Mil and Kamov for helicopters) spread over more than 20 sites from Moscow to Komsomolsk-on-Amur. Production fell from around 150 short- and long-haul aircraft and 300 civilian helicopters per year during the Soviet era to three planes and one civilian helicopter in 2000.[17]

Several explanations have been provided for this industrial disaster, which led Russian companies to buy dozens of Airbus and Boeing aircraft, including for domestic flights, as passenger demand resumed after 1998. One of the first responses, which reveals an obsessive Russian fear, was to blame the U.S. firm Pratt & Whitney, which, at the height of the industrial crisis in 1992, had acquired 25 percent of the shares of the Perm engine factory, a leading supplier of civilian and military aircraft engines. The press stirred up suspicions that the Americans had made the purchase to recover some patents and prevent the firm from developing a new generation of engines adapted to international standards.[18] More fundamentally, under pressure from major manufacturers and regional leaders who wanted to save all of "their" factories, the authorities soon began to weigh in on decisions.

In 2005, for example, the European Aeronautic Defence and Space Company (EADS), future Airbus Group, acquired 10 percent of Irkut, which manufactured the Sukhoi fighter, while Vneshtorgbank purchased 5 percent of EADS. In 2006, Russia's Unified Aircraft Corporation (OAK), a consortium of general aviation companies, was formed in close cooperation with Rosoboronexport (the state holding company for the military-industrial complex) and all major civil and military aviation manufacturers. In a sign of the times, Russian aviation finally ended its isolation and started to engage in various forms of cooperation. Although the government maintained strict control over the military part of the sector, even that opened somewhat. Civil aviation has evolved the most. The only major completed project is the manufacture of the ninety-eight-seat Superjet 100 regional aircraft, available since 2010, which was the fruit of cooperation between Sukhoi and several foreign manufacturers. The planes are assembled in Komsomolsk-on-Amur, but more than 70 percent of the parts (including the engines) are imported, and the ultramodern factory in Komsomolsk is entirely equipped with computer-assisted design and manufacturing systems of French, German, and Japanese origin.[19] The next step in this direction is already announced: the formation of a consortium between OAK and the Chinese COMAC to manufacture a long-haul aircraft capable of competing with Boeing and Airbus. The engine will be Russian and the final assembly will be done near Shanghai.[20]

This reorganization plan came to be used in almost all critical industries, with mixed results. After multiple "protection" plans for Russian machine tools, each as ineffective as the one before, in 2007 the government proposed a recovery program that involved the creation of a Union of Russian Machine Builders, directed (not by chance) by the head of Rosoboronexport.

PERSISTENT IMBALANCES IN FOREIGN TRADE

The return to growth was not enough to reverse one of the most commonly cited shortcomings of the Russian economy: its foreign trade imbalance. It was not in deficit;

quite the contrary. During these years, the external balance remained positive, which was fundamental to the resumption of overall economic growth. But this is mainly due to two related factors: the dominance of low-value-added products, raw materials (especially oil), and basic products (metals and chemicals) among Russia's exports; and second, the significant increase in their prices. The balance is thus very sensitive to price fluctuations. Meanwhile, the country continues to buy equipment and consumer goods on a massive scale, while the range of export products remains limited. Outside of commodities, Russia is among the world's top three weapons exporters, and also exports some large industrial equipment and equipment for power stations.

The notable recovery of many products during the 2000s, including the examples in table 5.1, had little impact on the nature of exports, since these sectors are oriented toward the domestic market and struggled to find external buyers. This is crucial, however, because it goes against the theory of Dutch disease, which is typically accompanied by lasting weakness in processing sectors. In the Russian case, several authors insist instead that they observe a complementarity in this period between the growth in income generated by oil exports and the growth and diversification of domestic industry.[21]

It is in light of these trends, and assessing the portion of capital goods in imports, that some observers are optimistic about the future of Russian manufacturing, noting that encouraging productivity gains have been seen in several sectors, especially the manufacturing industry, which benefited from foreign capital and technology despite insufficient levels of investment.[22] However, real progress in productivity in many sectors should not mask the continued existence of structural obstacles that were already present in Soviet times: the partitioning between military and civilian industries; the weakness of SMEs (small and medium enterprises), which are known to play a key role in innovation; and low interest in innovation among large commodities groups with majority state ownership.

Considering the significant foreign direct investment (FDI) flows into Russia in the early 2000s, it is notable that only one-quarter went to the manufacturing sector. Coming largely from places such as Cyprus and Barbados, FDI flows often reflected the return of Russian capital from offshore centers. The flows were mainly directed toward the services sector (commerce and communication), and to a lesser degree the industrial sector (mining) and construction. The Ukrainian crisis and Western sanctions in 2014 led to contradictory effects: On the one hand, the government reacted by systematizing its development aid to Russian manufacturers for import substitution—agribusiness is a good example of these successes; while on the other, the process of innovation and productivity gains from technology imports suffered.[23] Even many companies that were not directly affected by the sanctions had to restrict imports because the fall in the value of the ruble made such purchases too expensive. Moreover, the foreign trade imbalance between sectors further widened (see table 5.2), increasing the fragility of the whole economy when commodity prices suddenly dropped. This trend may be related to the fundamental changes seen in the organization of large Russian businesses, the evolution of which is guided by political authorities at the highest level.

Table 5.2.   Structure of Russian foreign trade by product (%), 1995 and 2016

	Import		Export	
Products	*1995*	*2016*	*1995*	*2016*
Minerals	6.4	1.8	42.5	59.2
Woods	2.4	1.9	5.6	3.4
Metals and precious stones	8.5	6.5	26.7	13.2
Chemicals	10.9	18.6	10.0	7.3
Machinery, equipment, and transport	33.6	47.2	10.2	8.6
Textiles, leather, and fur	6.0	6.4	1.9	0.4
Agriculture and food	28.1	13.7	1.8	6.0
Miscellaneous	4.1	3.9	1.3	1.9
Total in billion dollars	60.9	182.3	81.1	285.6

Source: Goskomstat, *Statist. Ezegodnik* 1996 and 2017

FROM OLIGARCHS TO "NATIONAL CHAMPIONS": THE REINFORCEMENT OF STATE CONTROL

Over two decades, the organizational structure of the Russian economy was deeply disrupted. The first Yeltsin government decided early in 1992 to throw open the domestic market to the global economy and accelerate the application of market rules that had begun under Gorbachev. Following the precepts of Western advisers on "shock therapy," the government took the controversial decision to liberalize prices on January 1, 1992, one of the first tremors that would substantially change the country's economic mechanisms.

SHOCK THERAPY: CRISIS AND REORGANIZATION

Privatization made most Russian citizens homeowners almost overnight. Yet the movement launched by the government was far broader. The details of the two main phases of this process have been described in detail in other works.[24] The first step carried out privatization through vouchers given to each citizen and auction sales for most small businesses, shops, services, and small factories, which were usually scooped up by local leaders, former party officials, managers, or chief engineers. In the second step, in 1995/96, the government let go the jewels of Russian industry (oil and metallurgical, chemical, civil, and mechanical engineering) under the so-called "loans for shares" system, whereby, as collateral for loans, the state gave a dozen major Muscovite banks shares in the largest national companies for a period of three years. Everyone knew that the state would not be able to repay the loans, making the initiative a concerted redistribution of some of Russia's most successful companies to the financial groups controlled by the oligarchs, on the understanding that they, in turn, would support Yeltsin in the 1996 presidential election.[25] Some key strategic sectors (the core of the military-industrial complex, nuclear, space, electricity, gas, and parts of the transport infrastructure) escaped this process by remaining totally or partially under state control.

The oligarchs of the Yeltsin era were often former Komsomol or Communist Party leaders, who benefited from relationships that allowed them to accumulate initial capital in import-export. By creating their own banks, they could buy vouchers from the population and use them to diversify their activities in industry, services, insurance, and communications. In 1995, the most powerful already had a solid footing in finance, industry, and media, as many of them had purchased publishing and broadcasting groups. This was the heart of the agreement they made with Yeltsin, the first version of the new bargain that bound together the highest echelons of political power and the new masters of the economy. In exchange for financial assistance and favorable media coverage that would ensure the reelection of a weakened president, the oligarchs bought the crown jewels of the Russian economy—those sectors that offered the best export opportunities—at bargain basement prices.

Groups such as Oleg Deripaska's Bazovy Element and Mikhail Prokhorov's Onexim-Bank specialized in non-ferrous metallurgy, aluminum, nickel, and rare metals; Alexei Mordashov's Severstal focused on the steel industry; and Mikhail Khodorkovsky's Yukos centered on oil. The oligarchs also ensured the adoption of favorable administrative and fiscal rules that allowed them to locate much of their business outside Russia in order to minimize their taxes while better protecting their capital and profits. In this respect, as in many others, Russian financial and industrial operations fully embraced the rules of Western multinationals in applying a practice euphemistically called "tax optimization." Their systematic offshore investments explain, in part, what the press has described as capital flight. However, unlike Western multinationals, the desire to avoid taxes was not their only motivation. The country remained extremely chaotic and new laws increasingly uncertain. Supported by competing groups, state or regional administrations and law enforcement organs (police, security forces, and judges) often challenged the ownership of a thriving business.

Besides their assets in Russia, most of these oligarchs invested part of their capital abroad, acquiring properties in various countries and inserting themselves into the economic and cultural life of those places by buying football clubs or publishers. The most advanced started to list their companies on Western stock exchanges (London in particular), both to protect their assets from the rough and tumble of Russian political life and to more easily obtain loans from Western partners. The Western media may have criticized Boris Yeltsin's management of the Chechen crisis and various failures to uphold democratic standards, but they never failed to congratulate the Russian authorities for their accelerated integration into the global system, which seemed to confirm the continuation of the "transition"—Russia's adoption of the main rules and mechanisms of the Western liberal system, as propounded by large international financial institutions such as the World Bank, the International Monetary Fund, and the Organization for Economic Cooperation and Development.

PUTIN'S REASSERTION OF NATIONAL SOVEREIGNTY

However, the prospect of rapid internationalization raised serious concerns among some of the country's elite, who saw in this transition the risk of permanently weakening Russia by abandoning entire segments of the economy in favor of large foreign groups. A few symbolic examples of privatization, such as the sale of a famous porcelain factory in St. Petersburg, had already hit the headlines under Yeltsin, mobilizing public opinion.[26] Putin's election as president in March 2000 led to a significant turn in the country's economic strategy.

One of the first signals the new president sent to the economic elite was a speech he gave on July 28, 2000, to a group of twenty-one major oligarchs he had invited to the Kremlin. Reportedly,[27] he spoke bluntly to them: The authorities knew that the oligarchs had become rich by taking advantage of the weaknesses of the previous regime. They would be ready to forgive them on two conditions: that the oligarchs now use their economic power to support the country's recovery, and that they end any interference in politics, whether directly or through the media they controlled. Some complied. Others, realizing that the tide was turning, gave up parts of their empires and settled in Israel (Vladimir Gusinsky) or the UK (Boris Berezovsky). One, Mikhail Khodorkovsky, believed he could resist and defy the new president; he announced his intention to sell a large part of his oil group to Exxon Mobil, therefore openly challenging the new president's economic strategy, and to use his resources to support an opposition group in which he could take an active role. The authorities decided to break his resistance and make an example of him, sending him to jail for more than a decade.[28]

In addition to the return to an authoritarian phase, described in chapter 4, the Kremlin wanted to regain control of the real levers of economic sovereignty, which it perceived as being under serious threat. The severe strengthening of state control closely combined economic and political measures. This critical phase for the country (recall the simultaneous reform of relations between the center and periphery, with the new regional policy) first of all involved ensuring control of the political image that the mainstream media disseminated to the public. The fact that the major oligarchs were also owners of large media groups was not without consequence as the new president decided whom and what to target first.[29] Second, the authorities decided what could and could not be privatized. The threshold for foreign participation was lowered in forty-two sectors deemed sensitive. Putin also did not hesitate to resort to pure intimidation, increasing the number of arrests and show trials of those who were resistant to his new injunctions. Public opinion believed that no oligarch could have built his fortune legally and therefore tended to support these discretionary measures.

Quickly, foreign investors came to understand that the proposed measures were not just about the Russian stakeholders. Aside from the hit to Khodorkovsky's projects, two other cases demonstrated the Russian authorities' desire to regain control of the hydrocarbons sector, considered one of the keys of sovereignty, to the point of breaking contracts. In 2005, the government undermined the conditions under which one of the emblematic examples of Western involvement had developed. The Sakhalin-2 oil and gas field, initially controlled by a consortium made up entirely of foreign companies—Royal Dutch Shell (55 percent) and Japan's Mitsui (25 percent) and Mitsubishi (20 percent)—became subject to various pressures. In late 2006, the consortium had to sell half of its stake (50 percent plus one share) to a subsidiary of Gazprom, which became the majority shareholder.[30] It was followed by TNK–BP, which began in 2003 as a 50-50 joint venture between the British oil company and a private Russian oil major (Company Tyumen), but came under political pressure in 2008, a trend that culminated with the sale of its exploitation rights to the Russian oil giant Rosneft in 2012.[31]

Within this logic of state control of key strategic sectors, Putin generalized a new type of organization with the formation of a series of integrated state holding companies covering all the research and development institutes or firms in a sector. These "national champions," created to revive the sectors considered vital to sovereignty, were placed in the care of individuals close to the president. Besides the examples already mentioned in aviation (OAK) and machine tools, this approach was taken in the space sector (Roskosmos, established in 1992 to take over for the Soviet-era Glavkosmos), and extended in 2007 to nuclear power (Rosatom), nanotechnology (Rosnano), and shipbuilding (OSK). Some of these state holdings are entirely national, especially in the military field (Rosoboronexport); others are mixed or try to attract some foreign investors (Rostekhnologii). Most Western experts, as well as former finance minister Alexei Kudrin, have criticized these large administrative machines as inflexible and overly opaque. However, they bear a resemblance to some great French postwar entities, such as the Atomic Energy Commission (CEA) and Aerospatiale, and may indeed be effective at a certain point in a country's history.

SHARING AND CONTROLLING RENT

As discussed in chapter 4, an analysis of Putin's inner circle, the so-called "Russia, Inc.," reveals that it covers virtually all the strategic sectors of the economy. It is not a question of simple nationalization, as pointed out in the small excerpt from Putin's thesis highlighted at the beginning of this chapter. Many of the undertakings concerned are private (petroleum, metallurgy, and construction) or mixed, with varying proportions of public and private participation. In fact, what is expected of this system is more complex, because it is responding to a mobilization of resources meant to consolidate a certain approach to national development. This practice is based on a singular system of managing the cash distribution from the commodities sector.[32]

Schematically, the product of rent is divided into four portions that meet specific needs. The first part is intended, as in any capitalist enterprise, to cover production costs, wages, fixed assets, and depreciation, as well as investments needed to continue and develop the business. The second part is the payment of taxes and levies, which have substantially increased in the commodities sector since Putin came to power. In addition to the normal taxes on business revenue, there are now special taxes on raw materials extraction (NDPI) and the export of petroleum products; these two new taxes have helped fill the coffers of the Reserve Fund, established in 2008 following the model of Norway's petroleum fund. In his memoirs, then prime minister Mikhail Kasyanov described the opposition of oil barons, including Khodorkovsky, to these new taxes, which were designed to deduct profits on a sliding scale that increased as oil prices exceeded certain levels.[33]

The third, most opaque, part concerns what Gaddy and Ickes call "informal taxes," which they believe to be more sizable than those taxes required by law. Informal taxes include the widespread phenomenon of corruption, often in the form of kickbacks (*otkaty*). In the Russian case, Gaddy and Ickes also mention other forms of hidden subsidies, which are significant to the operation of many companies. The two main subsidies consist of the share of their production that large businesses (oil companies and metallurgy firms) sell on the domestic market, often at the behest of the state and at prices well below market value. According to Shinichiro Tabata, the domestic price of gas was set at one-fifth of the world price in 2000 and, after initial adjustments, remained at less than one-third of the world price in 2007, a practice that was regularly denounced during the negotiations for Russia's accession to the WTO.[34] Companies are also directed to purchase goods and services (equipment, transport, etc.) at inflated rates, constituting a hidden subsidy to companies whose low productivity or quality would make them uncompetitive in a truly open and transparent market. This kind of indirect support is especially vital for the many subsidiaries, or subcontractors of large companies, created in the Soviet era. They are an important part of the urban and industrial fabric, particularly in *monogorody*, single-industry towns with fragile social situations.

Another variant of these informal taxes can be defined as "obliged patronage." It is observed in Russia, as in many other countries, when oligarchs use a part of their wealth to fund various social activities, museums, and cultural endeavors, building on the established Soviet-era practice of giving aid to the municipalities where their businesses are located in order to finance various public facilities. Under Putin, these actions took a slightly different turn, with industrial magnates practically obligated to co-fund various major events, such as the Sochi Olympics, or to invest in a particularly disadvantaged region, as when oligarch Roman Abramovich was appointed governor of Chukotka, one of the most deprived regions of the country, from 2000 to 2008.[35]

Finally, the fourth part is constituted by the legitimate profits expected of a thriving business. In the current Russian context, these profits are obviously extensive. The Russian press has given detailed accounts of the rise of those close to Putin in the *Forbes* ranking of the richest men in Russia. The most talked-about examples— purchases of yachts, lavish residences on the French Riviera, and English football clubs—came from the first-generation oligarchs. The beneficiaries of the Putin "consortium" have, like their predecessors, invested heavily abroad, which explains the sanctions that Americans and Europeans have targeted against them since 2014, such as denial of visas and the freezing of assets deemed illegitimate.[36] The latest (April 2018) new sanction list targets directly some of Putin's close oligarchs in forbidding any commercial activities with their societies.

It is very difficult to assess the impact of these indirect subsidies, but according to various authors, it is far from negligible. In fact, the growth sectors of the economy contribute decisively to the state budget—and, therefore, to any social policy, defense effort, or infrastructure project. At the same time, the practices help a market system constrained by non-competitive businesses to keep many firms throughout the country afloat. Several authors have attempted to assess these indirect subsidies in different sectors. The Russian press has sought to explain the oft-cited anomaly of the country's roads and the cost of construction or renovating the road network. Comparing the cost of roadworks in the Moscow region and Canada, which have similar climates, analysts from *Argumenty i fakty* concluded that the cost in Russia is thirty-eight times higher than in Canada.[37] This is the direct result of an opaque procurement system, high levels of corruption, and retro-commissions that enable an entire sector and its agents at various levels to squeeze out any economic rationality. The proliferation of articles on this topic led Putin to criticize these abuses, though not actually end them. We will return to the issue of the economic efficiency of such a system.

A POWER VERTICAL OF UNCERTAIN EFFICACY

Economic actors and the government are pitted against one another in a veritable battle over the level of taxes, legal and informal, which cannot be reduced to a simple accounting calculation. To take the example of oil, the leaders of the Russian majors are constantly complaining that the government's tax system is too burdensome, excessively reduces their profit margins, and keeps them from properly funding exploration research and drilling for the new deposits that will ensure sustained production levels five or ten years from now. Several U.S. researchers have made a warhorse from this weakness of investment, believing that this is a strategic dead end in the system.[38]

At the same time, it is clear that the importance of these informal flows causes a sharp decrease in the efficiency of officially announced investments. Some of the funding allocated in the budgets at different levels of government—for example, for infrastructure spending—never reaches the intended recipients. Instead, it is taken in passing, whether in financial form (offshore investments and money laundering to facilitate corruption) or in kind (diversion of materials and equipment for private construction or parallel companies).

Another fundamental point is that the whole system of informal taxes is based on the trust established between the true principals, who ensure that this complex rent sharing is actually observed at different levels. Several researchers point out that this is one of the crucial elements of the political consensus Putin reached. Securing systematic participation of the state and the companies it directly controls (such as Gazprom and the major banks) in the shareholding of many companies across all strategic sectors has resulted in the multiplication of consortium officials in the leadership of each group or subsidiary. These trusted individuals are responsible for enforcing the presidency's policy decisions. In exchange, they receive legal compensation ("attendance fees" and allocated dividend shares); they also have ample opportunity to take a share of the kickbacks in place.

Note that this phase of reorganization and takeover by Putin's inner circles is not, as has often been written, re-nationalization or a return to Soviet management. This is a mistaken view of the actual operation of Putin's economic system. Undoubtedly, the campaign to reaffirm sovereignty coincided with the state's acquisition of shares in many companies.[39] However, the objective is not a general re-nationalization of companies. According to official data provided by the state statistics agency, Rosstat, the share of private or mixed-ownership companies increased from less than 10 percent of fixed assets in 1991 to 70 percent in 2000, 77 percent in 2006, and 82 percent in 2013. As Sergei Guriev pointed out in 2013, Putin has repeatedly affirmed his commitment to the preponderance of private property and liberal management.[40] The system he has in place is an original mixture of statism (direct control of strategic sectors and pervasive state intervention in all major economic decisions) and neo-liberalism (private management in many sectors, with "American-style" liberalization of the health sector and education).

Upon his return to power in 2012, Putin signed a presidential decree on long-term state economic policy, in which he called on the government to "complete, before the year 2016, the withdrawal of the state from the capital of companies except those in the natural resources sector, natural monopolies, or the military complex."[41] Clearly, the 2014 crisis has upset this timeline. Potential Russian investors have been hit hard by the fall of the ruble, while some potential foreign investors have been spooked by the threat of Western sanctions and the implied suspicion of the new patriotic discourse. Yet the Russian budget needs revenue now more than ever, and government asset sales in the near future cannot be excluded.

NECESSARY MODERNIZATION
AND STRUCTURAL BOTTLENECKS

Although they express it in different ways, the highest-ranking Russian authorities are acutely aware of the weaknesses of the economy. Boris Yeltsin, who probably had a sincere belief in the educational effect of the rapid adoption of liberal practices, referred to the need to finally join the "normal" path of Western democracies. His successor, Vladimir Putin, very quickly demonstrated his misgivings about the adoption of foreign models. In developing his sovereignty strategy for strategic sectors, he appeared to trust Russia's internal capacity to gradually make its economy a world leader. The brief tenure of Dmitry Medvedev—to the extent he ever had actual autonomous power—was marked by a more flexible discourse, which offered a closer link between modernization (a term that Putin uses only infrequently) and several necessary conditions for its implementation: greater transparency, reinforced institutional mechanisms, a more independent judiciary, and increased role for civil society, and external resources (foreign investment, expertise sharing, and technology purchases).

The major issue on which to focus is how the Russian leadership planned to carry out modernization and the associated structural upgrades, regardless of what it was called. One of the key issues in this regard is certainly the level, nature, and evolution of investments introduced into the economy. According to most experts, such investments were notoriously weak at the end of the Soviet period and during the 1990s, then gradually increased as the country saw progress in its hard currency earnings. Gross capital formation today stands at about 23 percent of GDP—a little higher than levels in Germany, France, or the United States, but lower than in India (30 percent) or in China (45 percent)—yet this is not enough to catch up economically. In his March 2018 address to the nation, Putin promised to bring investments at a level of 25 and then 27 percent of the country's GDP.[42] Despite the diversification of public and private actors and the creation of management arrangements for major state investments, the heart of the modernization-diversification policy debate remains unresolved.

STATE PROGRAMS, MEGAPROJECTS, AND INCUBATORS: MODERNIZATION BY DECREE?

Whatever the country, it is probably impossible to sufficiently account for the influence of inertia on the structures and attitudes at play in the development of management systems. Since the early 1990s, one of the main ways that Russian state resources are engaged remains the launch of major federal programs, which can be regional (see examples in the Caucasus and the Far East), national (pro-natalist programs), or sector-specific in nature. Each of the main strategic sectors—machine tools, aviation, shipbuilding, and pharmaceuticals—has a set of decrees, programs, and committees that are meant to promote its development. These were standard procedures of Soviet planning, intended to coordinate different ministries, regional party committees, and *soviets*. While central planning may be gone, the desire to coordinate the action of new players is not, as shown by the proliferation of these coordinating bodies: departments of the all-powerful presidential administration, interdepartmental committees, and holdings of a particular sector. The systematic use of these programs is an unmistakable sign that administrative decisions still largely outweigh economic mechanisms. However, this form of management is also related to the distribution mode discussed above, which involves constant trade-offs by the real decision-makers: the presidency and those in the trusted inner circle in charge of the various "national champions" that have been established in all strategic sectors.

In recent years, the authorities have established new forms of support for modernization, including wider use of foreign cooperation. In 2009, President Medvedev

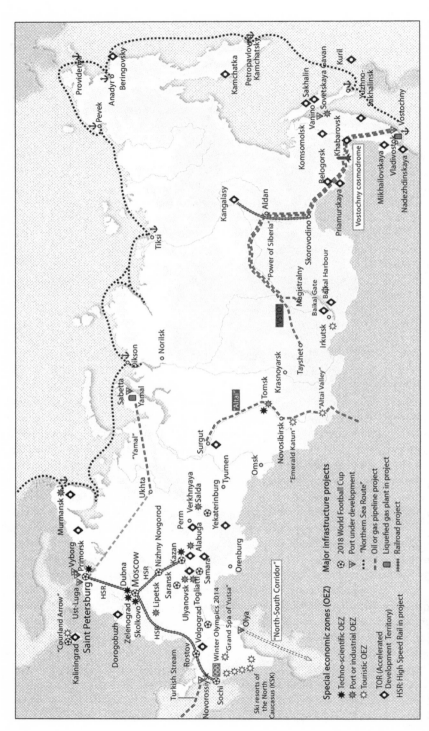

Map 5.1. Russia's main regional economic projects

launched the Skolkovo project, a kind of scientific and applied innovation mega-incubator created with explicit reference to Silicon Valley. The initial focus areas (telecommunications, biomedical and information technologies, new forms of energy, and nuclear technologies) are all sectors where the Russians feel they have theoretical skills but lack technology transfer and applications, which they hoped to increase through cooperation with large foreign firms and laboratories. This interesting initiative was followed by the creation of several technology parks, such as the Kazan IT Park and Innopolis in Tatarstan, and scientific clusters in Tomsk and Novosibirsk.[43]

Another good example is that of the TOR (a Russian acronym for "accelerated development territories") projects, archetypal free economic zones. For three decades, the Russian press praised the Chinese version of these zones as a successful model that could close some of the structural gaps affecting the country. Created by law in December 2014, these areas offer tax and customs breaks to attract foreign investors and diversify exports. Yet this new initiative, initially proposed for the Far East, was met with skepticism in the Russian press. Outside of the Kaliningrad "amber zone," federal authorities questioned the initial promises of relief. Of course, we have already mentioned the example of Sochi as a success with regard to building infrastructure and attracting various investors. However, the president had a personal stake in that exceptional project, which enjoyed virtually unlimited access to credit, as well as other special attention.[44] By contrast, the North Caucasus ski development project (*Kurorty Severnogo Kavkaza*, or KSK), which has not received the same attention, has been delayed.

The issue of regional budgets and investments outside Moscow is also crucial and complex for regions not benefiting from priority federal programs. In the growth period of the 2000s, many cities and regions borrowed heavily to improve their infrastructure and attract investors. Although there are a few success stories—such as Kaluga, Ulyanovsk, and Voronezh—many regions have found themselves with significant amounts of dollar-denominated debt and "toxic" credits, and are now hoping for federal government assistance to get them out of this situation.

The exceptional procedures that create these federal programs all present the same paradox: They are based on tax and regulatory exceptions that seek to bypass various bureaucratic obstacles, which are clearly identified as potential levels of corruption and roadblocks for "normal" companies, and introduce circuits that run parallel to the ministerial bodies in a particular sector. As such, they underscore the same criticism as they seek to address: If the government can identify these roadblocks and unnecessary administrative measures, why not eliminate them across the entire economy? This circles back to an old debate on business climate.

THE SERPENTINE NATURE OF "BUSINESS CLIMATE" AND THE SUPPOSED FIGHT AGAINST CORRUPTION

Since Vladimir Putin came to power, the Russian authorities have stepped up discussions with business circles. These interactions were formalized in the form of the president and prime minister's interventions at the Congress of the Union of Industrialists and Entrepreneurs of Russia (RSPP) and in the presence of many foreign guests at annual forums in St. Petersburg and Sochi. This is both to promote the investment opportunities available to Russian and foreign actors and to discuss the "investment climate" with them. These exchanges are often somewhat surreal, since the barriers they identify are—with the exception of new issues related to the current economic situation—endemic. For years, actors have denounced the same defects, some of which are similar to those found in the West. A first set of criticisms involves the complexity of the bureaucratic procedures necessary to register a new business, which entail inordinately long delays. While there is nothing specifically Russian about this paperwork, a second persistent theme is added: the harassment and widespread corruption that surround the acquisition of the proper paperwork and weigh constantly on companies.

Although corruption exists in all countries, Russia suffers from it to a greater degree than most. The country occupies an unenviable position in the international corruption indexes. In 2014, Transparency International ranked Russia 136th (between Nigeria and Uganda); despite political elites' regular promises to fight against corruption, this indicator has only deteriorated since the early 2000s.[45] This phenomenon is present in different forms in various situations. In everyday life, any citizen may have to pay a bribe during a routine traffic stop or for simple administrative paperwork; in some regions, bribes have even been assessed on the payment of "maternal benefits" to families. According to a Transparency International survey, 34 percent of Russian households that came into contact with any of a set of government organs (traffic police, bureaucrats from whom documents were needed, public education, healthcare, and the social security bureaucracy) paid a bribe to at least one of them—including 29 percent for lower education and 26 percent for healthcare. The only European countries with a higher rate of bribery were Moldova and Ukraine. This compares to rates in the low single digits in Western Europe and a mere 7 percent and 10 percent in famously corrupt Italy and Greece, respectively.

All businesses, large and small, have been confronted with the obligation to pay a "commission" in order to obtain an authorization or avoid an excessive fine during an inspection. The Swedish head of IKEA Russia once created a scandal by denouncing the kickbacks that the Moscow authorities demanded to obtain land and connect the store to the regional road network.[46] In two notorious cases—in Moscow in 2010 and Kushchevskaya, a small town in the Krasnodar region, in 2011—the press denounced the way the agencies of the Interior Ministry systematically fleeced all companies and businesses in their territory, with local governments and judges complicit in the extortion.[47] At the same time, the case of Sergei Magnitsky shed light on another aspect of these abuses: the brutal capture of businesses from competitors with the covert support of the judiciary, the Ministry of Interior, or the FSB.[48] This case took on an international dimension, as U.S. investors held some shares in the firm that Magnitsky, a lawyer, had been defending. The Russian government's refusal to clarify the reasons for Magnitsky's imprisonment or the circumstances of his death in jail drove a new wave of sanctions passed by the U.S. Congress.

In Russia itself, the denunciation of these abuses saw the formation of several critical initiatives. In several explicitly titled brochures[49] that mixed historical facts and unverifiable rumors, Boris Nemtsov denounced what he saw as President Putin's direct responsibility for the perpetuation of this system. But the most effective attack was Alexei Navalny's decision to launch a new anti-corruption initiative. In 2010, he created with some associates a dedicated website, RosPil, where all citizens have been invited to bear witness to the corruption they face. The site sparked an obsession with some of the special economic zones, including the one in Krasnodar, which was notable for its role in the personal enrichment of Governor Alexander Tkachev's family, its concentration of significant public investments in the run-up to the Sochi Olympics, and major agriculture and infrastructure development projects (the Port of Novorossiisk and new oil and gas terminals on the Black Sea). The authorities' reaction was swift: They compiled a series of criminal charges against this "whistle-blower" and his family.[50] But Putin did not react when, in 2017, Navalny attacked Prime Minister Medvedev—nicknamed Demon—and his wealthy properties, in a video accumulating evidence against him.

To all observers, the eradication of these abuses is one of the keys to cleansing Russia's notorious business climate. While both Russian and foreign investors have become used to adapting to corruption and aspects of the informal economy in many countries, the extent of these practices in Russia has become a real roadblock. Uncertainty over business sustainability, benefits, property rights, and patents, as well as raiding (*raiderstvo*), are a leading cause of capital flight and reluctance to invest in certain sensitive areas. Russia leapt from 124th place in the Doing Business index in 2010 to 36th place in 2015, but was ranked 53rd out of 190 countries for its protection of minority investors in 2017.[51] It is difficult to imagine that a genuine fight against these scourges can be undertaken without reforming other crucial segments of society—the judiciary, the media, the role of NGOs, and public opinion. The judiciary is probably the central piece of the puzzle, and it has been tightly controlled by the regime: In 2011, Putin put the Investigation Committee under his direct supervision and named Alexander Bastrykin its head, while in 2014 he merged the relatively independent Supreme Court of Arbitration with the Supreme Court.[52]

Since the death of the former prime minister of Singapore, Lee Kuan Yew, in March 2015, there has been a resurgence in the Russian press of another old hypothesis: that a decisive anti-corruption campaign mandated by President Putin himself could address the issue. However, while the president has long railed against these abuses at a discursive level, on-the-ground practices have not actually changed. That being said, it cannot be ruled out that Putin might choose to take more decisive action were there to be another crisis. The 2017 wave of firing and hiring governors and high-level administration officials has been seen by some as a potential sign of renewed attention to corruption on the part of the leadership. Still, this anti-corruption campaign remains surface-deep compared to those regularly carried out by the Chinese regime to purge its administration. The sanctions crisis of 2014 prompted the authorities to change some rules of the game. After some banks and members of Putin's inner circle had their assets frozen, the government introduced a requirement for officials to declare their holdings abroad, and now encourages the repatriation of all offshore assets.[53] Yet at the same time, the government provided various forms of assistance to Russian companies to compensate for sanctions-related losses and the unavailability of credit.

All these practices and excesses are ways of adapting to the specificities of the Russian system; they comprise a particular way of managing a perpetually dysfunctional system, which can be described as the "Russian disease."

REDEFINING THE "RUSSIAN DISEASE"

The Ukrainian crisis, with its attendant sanctions and countersanctions, has had profound effects on the Russian economy. But contrary to the intentions of the United States and the EU, which thought these measures would influence the Kremlin's foreign policy, sanctions appear to have proved the value of Russian leaders' autarkic strategy amid a world economy in turmoil.

The quarantine of several major state-owned banks, prohibitions on loans, embargoes on technology deliveries in some strategic sectors (oil exploration in particular), and the freezing of the accounts of some members of Putin's inner circle had immediate effects on the economy, especially by deterring investment. GDP grew by a mere 0.6 percent in 2014 and then shrunk by 3.7 percent in 2015 and 0.2 percent in 2016. This de-growth is likely to have been primarily the result of the collapse in world oil prices more than of sanctions, and is in any case far from the result that was probably hoped for.

The Russian Central Bank, by spending about one-third of its international reserves on ruble purchases in 2014 and maintaining a high key interest rate thereafter, managed to limit the ruble's devaluation (50 percent devaluation in Q3–Q4 2014, and more or less steady thereafter) and consequent inflation (11.4 percent in 2014, 12.9 percent in 2015, 5.4 percent in 2016, and even a record low 2.2 percent in 2017)[54] brought on primarily by the oil collapse. Beginning in 2015, the Central Bank's reserves resumed modest growth,[55] and Russian officials are now mainly concerned that the ruble might regain too *much* value, as its lower price—settled on by the free float begun in 2014—increases the competitiveness of exports, reduces that of foreign imports, and increases revenues from the sale of oil and gas, which are priced in dollars.

Meanwhile, industry suffered only a few points of decline, from which it began recovering in 2016,[56] while the crisis's effect on agriculture appears to have been downright positive: Production of grain and other main agricultural products in 2016 and 2017 reached a level unmatched since the best Soviet years.[57] Crisis's main damage was done via stagnating wages and reduced real income, which at the end of 2016 stood 9 percent below its level two years earlier, and which only began what may or may not prove to be a sustained recovery in 2017.[58]

Once again, the Russian economy's resilience was, on the whole, underestimated; moreover, the proponents of sanctions certainly did not anticipate all of its consequences. With GDP growth reaching 2 percent in 2017, the main international financial organizations have had to readjust their forecasts for Russia, even if structural bottlenecks have not been addressed. Besides the successful mobilization of Russian public opinion around the theme of defending the country against Western actions, the president used these challenges to accelerate what now amounts to a strategic turning point in several critical areas. Citing the U.S.-imposed sanctions, the Russian authorities have pursued a series of new measures to significantly reduce the importance of offshore investments in the national economy, prohibiting officials from owning foreign accounts and considerably reducing the allowable foreign investment thresholds in all strategic areas, which should eventually encourage large Russian investors to relocate their businesses and sources of funding back home.

The technology embargo will likely have only limited effects, as was the case with the sanctions imposed in 1979/80 during the SS-20 crisis with NATO. Some projects may become more expensive due to the necessity of producing equipment and developing technology domestically, while others, such as Rosneft's exploitation of its Arctic fields, may be delayed—though it is unclear to what degree this is a result of the global oil collapse, which has prompted energy companies the world over to put expansion on hold. One illuminating example is that of one of the most sensitive Arctic projects, the Sabetta LNG plant on Yamal Peninsula, which was spared the impact of sanctions by acquiring Chinese investment, including a loan in yuan. However, Russia is pressing ahead with the development of domestic supply chains and technology, directing government funds to projects, and attracting Asian and even European investment. The ultimate cost and results of this approach remain uncertain, but success would mean the development of Russian industry and technology, more energy revenues kept at home, and reinforced autarky.[59]

However, these major changes will not modify the organizational foundations of the Russian economy, and one can continue to question its ability to effectively reduce the development gap that then future president Putin identified in the late 1990s. In 2015, according to data from the World Bank, Russia ranked sixth in GDP (after Germany), but only fifty-fourth in GDP per capita (behind Latvia),[60] indicating that the ambitious program Putin set at the end of 1999 is far from complete. In this regard, it is tempting to join the observers who have diagnosed a "Russian disease" arising from a particular set of structural defects that hamper the country's growth. For Marshall I. Goldman, an economist who has used the term "Russian disease," it is essentially the pernicious effects of corruption that distort overall economic and political practices.[61] Although it is true that corruption is unusually widespread, it is also a very common illness in the world at large, meaning that corruption alone does not seem like an adequate explanation. Gaddy and Ickes see the causes of "Russian disease" in the peculiarities of rent sharing, which sets the Russian case apart from countries affected by "Dutch disease."

According to these two authors, one of the specificities of the Russian case is that most of the rent from the commodity sectors is picked up by a few large companies and holdings that are directly or indirectly led by entrepreneurs close to the state. The rent is then redistributed under the close supervision of the presidential administration, which seeks to ensure that the funds are directed toward national security, major social commitments, federal priority programs, and regional equilibrium. It is through this mechanism that Russia, while overcoming the effects of two major crises, has managed to preserve some of its productive apparatus and, since the early 2000s, to engage in a new diversification of its industry. The fact that it has sought international cooperation (the purchase of licenses and foreign production in Russia) is not at all abnormal. This ability to rebound also has to do with the significance of the consumer market, which continues to attract investors, and the perception of the importance of the industrial sector for the future and security of the country, which remains an important part of the mentality of leaders and population alike.

We thus join French economist Julien Vercueil in considering that the "Russian disease" is specific insofar as it combines economic realities (the disproportionate share of raw materials in the country's export mix and constraints on the modernization of manufacturing industries related to low investment) in an institutional and policy setting itself underpinned by the management of commodity rents.[62] The real problem is not only the primary sectors' dominant role in the overall economy, but also their leaders' position in decision-making structures, the lack of judicial independence, difficulties in protecting property rights, etc. By giving them priority in the takeover of sectors considered strategic to the stability of the country, Putin has promoted the rise of these lobbies. But the nature of the output of these sectors is such that innovative research is of marginal concern to them. Their needs for research and development and qualified professionals are relatively low.

In addition, the average size of firms in these industries has strengthened the Soviet-era tendency to favor large organizations to the detriment of SMEs, where the innovative capabilities that are important to new industry and service fields are concentrated. The issue of support for Russian SMEs is another serpentine issue. In a revealing study of the five hundred most important Russian firms, the economic newspaper *RBK* shows the level of inertia in the SME realm, which has a particularly low level of renewal. Very few new enterprises have been created in recent years, another sign of the difficulties of modernizing and diversifying the Russian economy.[63]

Another aspect of this problem is the inertia at play in the decision-making structures themselves. The priority given to major federal programs is probably necessary in a period of infrastructure catch-up and upgrading of major industrial sectors. But the lack of real control mechanisms from society (parliament, media, NGOs, and autonomous public opinion) opens the door to all kinds of abuses that reduce efficiency. Such weak social control has yet another daunting consequence: Innovative entrepreneurs receive no reliable protection and are often pushed out, constituting a particular form of "brain drain" that is very damaging to economic equilibrium. Such practices, which former finance minister Alexei Kudrin regularly denounced, also eventually push out foreign investors who are not involved in the primary sectors, while specific operating rules exclude many useful areas of cooperation.

It is this set of structural defects at the intersection of economic and political practices that we define as the "Russian disease." From it flow inefficient investment decisions and mismanagement of huge profits generated in periods of growth. The current period of policy stiffening accompanied by patriotic rhetoric, with increasingly vehement denunciation of the influence of "foreign agents," is certainly not conducive to the questioning of these aberrations. It accentuates even more significant defects that can only weigh on already weak growth. Capital flight for instance peaked, reaching a record US$150 billion in 2014—it has since decreased but remains structurally high. Well beyond issues of corruption, it is these excesses that constitute the most serious curbs on Russian growth.

But aside from the specifics of economic operations, there are issues that go far beyond management approaches and structures. The Russian authorities are effectively questioning some of the international institutions that govern all global balances, in monetary and financial terms, as well as arbitration rules, ratings, and credit instruments. Reaffirming their strong conception of national sovereignty and security, Russian leaders are redefining a substantial part of the balance of their foreign policy. We will return to this subject in the next chapter.

6

Between Europe and Asia

The Double-Headed Eagle

> Russia is one of the largest countries in the world and a major nuclear power. [Its president] must restore its prestige and its major role in the world.
>
> —Vladimir Putin, televised speech, March 24, 2000

> We know that Russia is a European and Asian country. We respect both European pragmatism and Eastern wisdom. That is why Russia's foreign policy will be balanced.
>
> —Vladimir Putin, interview with Chinese media, June 12, 2000

Just eighteen months after the Ukrainian crisis began, Russia launched an armed intervention in Syria, its first major engagement outside the post-Soviet space since the Soviet adventure in Afghanistan in 1979.[1] This action significantly changed the West's perception of Moscow's role in the world. For a long time, a weakened Russia intervened only in its immediate post-Soviet vicinity. The Russian air raids in Syria and the Kalibr cruise-missile attacks (or SSN30, according to the NATO designation) from ships in the Caspian Sea aimed at Syrian targets on Putin's birthday, all designed to demonstrate Moscow's support for the Bashar al-Assad regime, confirm that Russia is again a major actor on the international scene. It is able to carry out military actions on two operational fronts—thinly veiled in the eastern Donbas, and openly in the Middle East—and asks other major world powers to take its interests and proposals more into account. While some commentators see in these renewed tensions a return to the Cold War, it seems to us a much more complex interaction process that necessitates full acknowledgement of the global structural changes that have occurred since the dissolution of the Soviet Union.

During the Ukrainian crisis of 2014, foreign policy analysts took note of Russia's "Asian pivot," particularly the spectacular rapprochement between Moscow and Beijing, which was billed as a major strategic change for the Kremlin. But if there was a real break in Russian diplomacy, it occurred with the West. Accelerating exchanges with its neighbor China and seeking partnerships in the Asia-Pacific region have been two tenets of Russian policy since Mikhail Gorbachev. The U.S. sanctions initiated in March 2014 and intensified in the summer of 2015, and the similar measures undertaken by the European Union and key U.S. allies, dramatically changed the nature of the relationship between Moscow and the West. Even if the countersanctions then imposed by the Russian authorities (including banning imports of EU agricultural products and establishing a list of individuals forbidden from visiting Russia) were the only official responses to Western measures, one is struck by the magnitude of the political signals sent from the Russian authorities of their deep distrust of the global liberal international order. On the U.S. side, the current anti-Russian atmosphere around "Russiagate" is very toxic, as it conflates genuine domestic polarization with a foreign actor largely external to the current crisis, and does not offer any short- or medium-term prospect of rebuilding trust on both sides. The coordinated expulsion of 151 Russian diplomats by twenty-seven Western countries to protest against Russia's supposed poisoning attempt of a former double spy, Sergey Skrypal, in the UK is a revealing sign of the high level of tensions, to which should be added the escalation in Syria, with the April 2018 Western strikes against the Assad regime—and its Russian ally.

Russia's real foreign policy break thus appears not in the search for a more balanced policy between the West and Asia—a classic issue for the country—but in the decision to follow through on all the consequences of the absolute distrust the Kremlin now feels toward U.S. policy, leading to questioning of all the instruments that have governed the global balance of power since 1945, as discussed in the following chapter. Yet worrying about a new Cold War does not adequately reflect this major turning point in Russian foreign policy. It is too often considered the manifestation of Russia's supposed determination to reclaim its former subjects in an imperial logic that has never really come to pass. Besides Russia's legitimate national interests, it raises the question of whether it is possible to understand this policy without taking into account two indispensable complementary factors: the actions of other actors in the international system and the mutual perception by Russia and the United States that the other is behind the major ongoing events in the post–Cold War world.

RUSSIA AND THE WEST: A MUTUAL MISUNDERSTANDING?

The Russian perception is undoubtedly marked by a sense of a threat that is moving ever closer to its borders. After the negotiations that led to the reunification of Germany (1990) and the dissolution of the Warsaw Pact under Gorbachev, Russia witnessed the accession of the three Baltic states to NATO and the EU in 2004 and the "color revolutions" in Georgia and Ukraine, both seen as products of Western pressure in what Moscow has always considered to be its strategic security zone. From the late 1980s to the mid-2000s, Russia was weak. Its lack of diplomatic weight was demonstrated in March 1999, when its only visible response to the Western bombing of Belgrade was Prime Minister Evgeny Primakov having his plane turn back and abandon a visit to the United States. As the country dealt with internal issues, it saw NATO's spectacular progress toward Russian territory as one of a succession of humiliations made possible by the country's temporary weakness. Since then, however, Russia has regained some of its power and confidence and now challenges the status of second-tier actor that has been attributed to it.

THE EAST-WEST RAPPROCHEMENT AND ITS LIMITS

Even before the dissolution of the Soviet Union, Boris Yeltsin made plain his desire for closer ties with key Western countries. This Western axis remained a foreign policy priority in the first years of the new Russia. In some regards, it was echoed in the support Putin expressed to President George W. Bush following the September 11, 2001, attacks and in Putin's and Medvedev's proposals for greater EU-Russia strategic partnership. However, it would be simplistic to interpret these gestures, symbolic though they are, as guarantees of Russia's "return" to the Western path.

The first Russian president and the group of figures around him were sincere in their declarations of interest and their desire to move away from the Soviet development path as quickly as possible. Imbued with European culture (a point that Mikhail Gorbachev had repeatedly stressed), Russian elites naturally thought to draw on various Western practices, whether German, French, or American, political or economic. Trade exchanges, already widely initiated under Gorbachev, were reinforced by a full complement of Western advisers ready to offer guidance for the writing of a new constitution, the development of various regulations, and the privatization of the banking system. Europeans and Americans saw these reforms, which they cheered, as signs of Russia's "normalization" and "transition."

But in the minds of Russian leaders, there was no necessary link between the technical and policy practices borrowed from the West and a re-conceptualization of the country's foreign policy. The apparent geopolitical rapprochement actually obscured deep differences and a double misunderstanding. On the Russian side, although the desire for reform was real, the new government had not abandoned its major role in what it considered its almost exclusive zone of influence in the "near abroad." The creation of the CIS on December 8, 1991, met this objective, even as the proposal Yeltsin made at the United Nations—that Russia should continue to act as the guarantor of the security of the whole region—was wholly rejected by his Western partners. However, it would take years for the Russian authorities to fully comprehend this difference in perspective.

Meanwhile, the West, especially the United States, sought to leverage the Russian leadership's initial goodwill, the opening of the country, and the new opportunities it presented to implement a policy that went beyond simple assistance to democracy promotion. After their surprise at the sudden collapse of the Soviet system, U.S. and European officials gradually established a strategy of systematic actions on multiple scales, tailored to the different circles that constituted Russia's strategic environment. The old "people's democracies" that had been part of the Warsaw Pact and had constituted a kind of buffer to Soviet borders were offered different stages of accession to the European Union and NATO. A groundswell of pro-Western public opinion in the states of Eastern Europe transformed this part of the continent into one that Moscow could no longer influence. In fact, within a few years, what had been the Socialist bloc had become an anti-Russian buffer—it would be Poland and the Baltic states that led the campaign against the "Russian threat" within the EU.[2]

Successive Kremlin leaders tried to preserve some of Russia's economic and geo-political influence. Issues related to EU accession aside, integration into NATO remained the most controversial subject. When he succeeded Yeltsin, Putin picked up the discourse of reproaching Gorbachev for having too easily given in to Westerners on essential points, such as German reunification, and the repatriation of Soviet soldiers, without negotiating anything substantial (funding for the withdrawal of the Russian military, for example). NATO's expansion to Eastern Europe would become a fundamental and enduring point of contention in East-West relations, with Kremlin leaders accusing the United States of non-compliance with the oral commitment James Baker had made to Gorbachev that NATO would not move closer to Russian borders.[3]

With the exception of the Baltic states, which very quickly refused to join any post-Soviet structure and expressed their desire to enter EU and NATO, the publics and elites of the former Soviet republics and CIS members were divided between supporters of a clean break and defenders of maintaining close ties with Moscow. After a period of hesitation, Europe put a number of institutional and financial instruments in place (such as TACIS [Technical Assistance to the Commonwealth of Independent States]). Initially, these tools were intended to foster the development of democratic and liberal practices and increase cooperation. Under the influence of conservative U.S. advisers such as Zbigniew Brzezinski, however, a concerted policy relatively quickly took shape, with the explicit aim of "decoupling" these states from their former metropolis and decisively "rolling back" Russian influence.[4] In all the new capitals, the U.S. embassies insisted on the uselessness and even harmfulness of instruments developed within the CIS, and offered massive assistance to government teams that criticized various Kremlin decisions. After NATO launched its Partnership for Peace program in 1994, Europe implemented a "Neighborhood Policy" (2003) and then the Eastern Partnership (2009), which instituted association agreements for post-Soviet states that were driven by the hostility of the new EU members (particularly Poland and the Baltic states) to any concessions to Moscow. The Americans became particularly involved in some key post-Soviet countries that

Brzezinski called "pivots": Georgia (gateway to the Caucasus), Uzbekistan (the only Central Asian state bordering the four others and claiming its right to play a regional role), and of course Ukraine. They promoted the rise of pro-Western sentiment in these countries' public opinion, a process that would contribute to the color revolutions of 2003–2005.

Finally, Western action became evident in the heart of Russia itself, with the establishment of networks of influence in many realms. These networks' focus areas included the political sphere, with systematic financial and technical support for liberal democratic organizations, and the religious realm (American Protestant-funded congregations appeared in even the smallest cities, as discussed earlier). Specific mention must be made of activities in the academic and scientific realms, where the Russian government was compelled to withdraw financial support, plunging researchers and engineers into real distress. Although U.S. government programs did not reach the level of George Soros's activity in Georgia, for instance, the proliferation of Western aid and scholarship funds had a double effect: It helped to support whole areas of research and Russian culture at a very difficult time, but it also contributed to brain drain.[5] The whole approach was a classic demonstration of the exercise of soft power, and indeed contained the elements of a strategy of societal penetration and influence that would eventually elicit strong reactions from the Russian elite. Significantly, it was the Moscow Patriarchate that delivered the first warning: In 1997, it convinced Yeltsin to change the law on religion in order to reduce the influence of "foreign" churches.

Formally, Russia and the West maintained the appearance of a constructive dialogue, even developing a range of instruments of cooperation. Along with other post-Soviet states, Russia joined the NATO Partnership for Peace (1994) and the Council of Europe (1996). Moscow played an active role within the Organization for Security and Co-operation in Europe (OSCE) even as it became increasingly critical of the organization's mission, since Moscow hoped to make the OSCE the pivot of a new pan-European security architecture—a plan that would be definitively buried. Relations with the EU were formalized by a partnership agreement signed in 1994. During the 1990s, Moscow and NATO officials discussed cooperation on topics of common interest, such as the fight against terrorism and trafficking in drugs and weapons. The joint NATO-Russia Council, established in 1997, was reinforced in 2002 under the leadership of President Putin, although, as leaks at the Lisbon Council later revealed, U.S. officials were simultaneously reassuring their allies that transatlantic firmness toward Russian policy would remain unchanged. In sum, there were critical topics on all sides, and mutual accusations proliferated.

RUSSIA PLAYS WITH EURASIA'S SMOLDERING CONFLICTS

One aspect of Russian foreign policy especially alarmed Western countries and would drive them to intervene more openly among its immediate neighbors. Upon coming to power, Yeltsin interfered in the tensions emerging between some ethnic minorities and governments in the post-Soviet region. Moscow was not behind these conflicts; their sources were much older, dating back to Stalin-era geopolitical calculations or even earlier,[6] and they were the natural consequence of the rise of nationalism in the late 1980s. However, the Kremlin exploited these frictions by openly supporting secessionist movements in Transnistria, Crimea, and the South Caucasus[7] to pressure Moldova, Ukraine, and Georgia, respectively, to join the CIS and follow Russia's directions. After the first wave of eastward NATO enlargement, support for secessionist movements was also a way to prevent certain states (namely Georgia and Ukraine) from joining the alliance, as having an ongoing territorial dispute makes a country ineligible to join NATO. Of a different nature, because the conflict involved took place within Russia's borders, was Yeltsin's decision to take control of Chechnya by force in late 1994; the catastrophic consequences of that intervention marked a turnaround in Western perceptions of the new Russia.

Western leaders and media, though they barely reacted to the brutal suppression of the Russian Parliament in October 1993, were increasingly critical of Moscow's political and military interference in its "near abroad." Although the United States had intervened repeatedly in many parts of the world throughout the twentieth century, it now accused the Kremlin of having neo-imperialist designs. The OSCE, the UN High Commissioner for Refugees (UNHCR), and various NGOs worked to end the active phases of the conflicts in the region, but they never managed to completely resolve any of them politically. Russian interference in these conflicts mobilized public opinion in the states concerned, a process that eventually weakened the CIS itself. The Kremlin was viewed as being responsible for prolonging "frozen conflicts" in order to maintain political pressure on its neighbors. At a summit in Chisinau in 1997, the leaders of several of these states publicly challenged Yeltsin's policy in the CIS.[8] At the time, he agreed to revise his approach, but never kept this promise.

The Americans, for their part, fueled the criticism, and in 1997 supported the creation of a new anti-Russian regional front, the GUAM (named for its members: Georgia, Ukraine, Azerbaijan, and Moldova; Uzbekistan also belonged to it briefly). Several of its member states were affected by a secessionist movement partly fueled by the Kremlin. GUAM never managed to achieve an influential role in the region, but it served as a convenient platform for its members and U.S. leaders to increase their criticism of Russian policy in one of its sensitive areas.[9]

COLLECTIVE SECURITY, GROWING DIVERGENCES

Another area of dispute arose in the 1990s with regard to the negotiations over the control of armaments in Europe. In November 1990, the countries of NATO and the Warsaw Pact signed the Conventional Forces in Europe (CFE) treaty, which established ceilings on various types of weapons. Based on the momentum created by

Gorbachev, in January 1993, Presidents Yeltsin and Bush signed START II (Strategic Arms Reduction Treaty), which limited the number of nuclear warheads the two major powers could deploy. They undertook to continue negotiations for further reductions, but disputes very quickly arose. Western actors were pressing Moscow to close Russian bases in Georgia and Moldova, which would only partially be carried out; meanwhile, the Kremlin was concerned about successive phases of NATO enlargement that brought the alliance ever closer to Russia's borders. Yeltsin fought an uphill battle to try to delay the Baltic states' accession to NATO over the fate of Russian minorities in Estonia and Latvia, who were the objects of discrimination.

For the first time, the Duma invoked a specific action on behalf of these citizens of foreign states and specified the Russian state's responsibility to protect them. Unable to stop the accession, which took effect in 2004, the Russian government tried to carve out specific concessions for Kaliningrad, in the form of a permanent transit visa for all residents of the exclave. (The European Commission limited this to an annual transit permit issued on demand.) Although the Russians and Europeans avoided turning Kaliningrad into a "hot spot" with each major crisis, Moscow did not fail to announce the possible deployment of nuclear missiles to this Russian territory geographically located within the EU and NATO.[10]

The attacks of September 11, 2001, seemed to mark a possible change of direction, as Putin proposed engaging with the United States in the battle against the scourge of international terrorism. But new areas of concern quickly bubbled to the surface, and the idea that Russia was engaged in a fool's game became increasingly prevalent in local media. In December 2001, the U.S. president declared that the ABM (Anti-Ballistic Missile) treaty had no further application and announced plans to deploy a missile defense system in several of the new NATO member states. These missiles were supposed to target "rogue" states (such as Iran), but the Russians believed they would threaten the credibility of their own nuclear deterrent. At the same time, the Pentagon arranged for access to bases in Romania and Bulgaria. Putin and George W. Bush signed SORT (Strategic Offensive Reductions Treaty) in 2002, but as Moscow saw it, U.S. actions had thrown off the balance of power in Europe.[11] The accession to power of Barack Obama in 2008 again seemed to offer the possibility of reducing tensions, as the new president appeared to question some aspects of his predecessor's anti-missile shield. In April 2010 in Prague, Obama and Medvedev signed the New Start Treaty (START III), further reducing the number of warheads and delivery systems in each country.

During the Medvedev presidency, Russians seemed attentive to new proposals, such as the international Global Zero movement, which advocated for a drastic reduction of nuclear arsenals.[12] But Obama's policy of resetting relations between the two countries soon hit a stumbling block. The Kremlin was adamant on the issue of missile defense and even more so on the possibility of further NATO enlargement, particularly to Ukraine. According to the Russians, any new disarmament agreement would have to address the missile defense issue, a ban on deploying weapons in space, and the imbalance in conventional weapons in Europe, in which NATO had a two-to-one advantage, according to U.S. sources.[13] Russian leaders were particularly concerned about American advances in areas such as UAVs (drones) and nonstrategic nuclear missiles; they believed the Pentagon was prepared to further reduce nuclear arsenals because the United States now could count on these other types of weapons. Furthermore, although this was never officially stated, the Kremlin was also concerned about the imbalance with China, whose military budget and armed forces were growing rapidly during this period. This explains the tenet of Russia's military doctrine, published in the 2010 version and maintained in its 2014 successor, that nuclear weapons could be used even in the case of a massive conventional threat ("when the very existence of the state is under threat").[14]

After that, the tension peaked and the doors to negotiations closed. In the early 2010s, the White House questioned the "reset" that had characterized U.S. policy toward Russia during the Medvedev years. The decision of the U.S. Congress to introduce the Magnitsky Act in 2012—named after Sergei Magnitsky, the tax lawyer who died in 2009 while detained in a Russian prison—aroused Moscow's ire.[15] In response, the Russian authorities passed a law to prohibit Americans from adopting Russian children. In 2013, Putin managed to thumb his nose at Washington by granting political asylum to Edward Snowden, whose data leaks revealed massive eavesdropping on global communications by U.S. institutions.[16]

In March 2015, Moscow announced its definitive withdrawal from the CFE treaty (it had suspended its participation in 2007). Russia still wants to discuss its new security proposals for Europe but the conditions for eventual negotiations are particularly difficult given the security context in Eastern Europe. The July 2016 NATO summit in Warsaw decided to deter Russia by strengthening the alliance's military presence on its eastern flank. By 2017, there were four NATO battalions in the region, stationed in Poland, Estonia, Latvia, and Lithuania on a rotational basis. Each of these battalions was provided by a NATO country—the United States, Canada, Germany, or Britain. The 2016 summit also inaugurated NATO's Ballistic Missile Defense, putting a base in Romania. The announced purpose is to counter threats posed by Iran and North Korea, but Russia believes it is also targeted. Montenegro was invited to become NATO's twenty-ninth member and discussions on the status of Georgia and Ukraine were held, angering Moscow.[17] NATO also launched a "Strategic Communication Center" in Latvia and opened a training center in Georgia.[18]

NATO's consolidated presence in Russia's western neighborhood and Russia's responses accelerated a spiral of distrust. Knowing that the gap between the Russian military budget and the U.S. one (about US$60 billion against US$600 billion respectively) could not be bridged, the Kremlin opted for a hybrid strategy to secure its margins. It is now putting in place an A2/AD (Anti-Access / Area-Denial) strategy, seeking to create territorial "bubbles" that are almost impossible for NATO countries to access and protect. Moscow has been deploying various new-generation radar and missile systems, including SS-26 Iskanders (which have nuclear capability), in the Kaliningrad enclave; the only way for NATO to break through there would be by ending Sweden and Finland's long-standing traditions of military non-alignment, a dangerous move. The other "bubbles" are along the Baltic-Arctic axis (the Kola Peninsula, the Franz Josef Land archipelago, and Novaya Zemlya), in Crimea, and in Kamchatka.

At the same time, one may notice an increasing number of finger-pointings by both sides concerning adherence to the INF Treaty for the elimination of intermediate-range and shorter-range missiles. The Americans accuse Moscow of contravening the treaty's clauses by deploying in their "bastions" new P-800 Oniks and "9M729" (SSC-8 in NATO's classification) missiles, new generation S-300 and S-400 missiles, as well as Kalibr-NK rockets, all of which can be either ship-launched (and are thus not subject to the treaty) or made land-mobile in the way of an Iskander missile. Moscow has retorted by making reciprocal accusations that denounce the U.S. ability to mount diverse categories of offensive missiles on the MK41 antimissile complexes at the new American facilities in Romania and in Poland, or at those that, as announced in late 2017, will be built in Japan. On March 1, 2018, during his address to the parliament, Putin presented a new generation of missiles supposedly invulnerable to enemy interception, and therefore able to keep the strategic balance with the United States even with Russia's small military budget compared to its competitor—an answer to the Pentagon's just-released Nuclear Posture Review.

A FAILED STRATEGY IN THE "NEAR ABROAD"

Since 1991, all Russian leaders have claimed that the states of the "near abroad" are the most important element of their country's foreign policy, even if, in reality, priority has often been given to good relations with the West. This enduring ambiguity reflects a form of blindness among Kremlin leaders, who have acted as if the relationship with the former Soviet republics was such a given that no special effort was necessary. It was clear that Moscow would retain a natural influence over these states' futures, given their shared history, geographic proximity, and economic and demographic interconnections. But this task of asserting Russia's domination over its neighbors, now contingent on a multitude of meetings and agreements, would prove much more complicated than expected.

THE CIS: AN AMBITIOUS PROJECT WITH IMMEDIATE DIVERGENCES

The statements signed at the two summits[19] announcing the dissolution of the Soviet Union and the creation of the CIS appeared to fully satisfy Boris Yeltsin. The Soviet system was officially abolished, but—with the exceptions of Georgia and the three Baltic states, which refused any association with Russia—Moscow managed to bring together all the other republics in one organization. The signatories undertook to respect the independence of each state, the integrity of each state's territory as it was at the end of the Soviet Union, and the inviolability of each state's borders. The vague and ambitious final declaration provided for advanced cooperation in a visa-free area, with a common currency (the ruble) and common effort on major economic and trade decisions. A specific statement provided for the denuclearization of the three states—Belarus, Ukraine, and Kazakhstan—where nuclear weapons were deployed by the Soviet Union; the states concerned committed to dismantle the weapons or transfer them to Russia.

Yet signatories' perceptions of the agreements varied. Upon his return to Kiev on December 8, 1991, after participating in the first meeting and the signing of agreements in Minsk, Ukrainian president Leonid Kravchuk made a clear statement that he had not signed any commitment that would restrict the sovereignty of his country, which had just voted in favor of independence in a December 1 referendum. Kravchuk's narrative painted the Minsk agreements as "amicable divorce papers," a label that would stick.[20] In fact, although Moscow pushed many more agreements and instruments intended to govern this new community, which the Russian leadership hoped would be like a European Union for Eastern Europe, virtually none of the successive agreements (forged between 1992 and 1996) were signed by all members. The annual presidents' meetings would come and go, a parliament and many government commissions were created,[21] but parts of the initial commitments were cast aside. Gradually, each state created its own currency and military and charted its own course in policy and external trade.

For the most part, the Kremlin's own strategy was responsible for the failures of the CIS. In January 1992, the Russian government liberalized prices and foreign trade in a unilateral decision taken without the consultation provided for in the agreements, thereby backing its partners into a corner and leaving lasting scars. By the mid-1990s, two groupings of countries had formed within the CIS. For various reasons—the economic dependency and landlocked status of Kazakhstan, Kyrgyzstan, and Tajikistan; the trade and security interests of Belarus; Armenia's quest for an ally in its conflict with Azerbaijan—some member states had adopted virtually all of Moscow's proposals and had become the basis for future alliances. But another group, composed of Ukraine, Moldova, Georgia, Azerbaijan, and to a lesser extent Turkmenistan and Uzbekistan, rejected everything that could be seen as interfering with their sovereignty, especially in matters of security and defense; they constituted a sort of refusal front that depended on the United States and its allies for help and advice.

Moscow put forward a multitude of treaties in various domains. Among the most important was the Collective Security Treaty, signed in Tashkent in May 1992. Another was the framework agreement for an economic union, which provided for a single economic space, free movement of goods, and unification of customs procedures; it was signed by nine states in Moscow in 1993 (Ukraine and Turkmenistan were only associated). The framework was followed in 1994 by an agreement for a free trade area and the creation of the union's first supranational structure, an interstate economic committee headquartered in Moscow, in which Russia would hold

50 percent of the votes and Ukraine 14 percent. But none of these treaties were ratified by all the states, especially in the area of defense, which was the most sensitive issue for the Kremlin. Only ten states signed on to the unified air defense system (Azerbaijan and Moldova did not), and only seven accepted the joint defense treaty for external borders. Uzbekistan, Turkmenistan, Azerbaijan, Moldova, and Ukraine were opposed to the presence of Russian guards on their borders. Georgia's decision to join the Collective Security Treaty in 1994 proved to be an ephemeral victory for Yeltsin. In 1999, Azerbaijan, Georgia, and Uzbekistan decided to leave the Collective Security Treaty Organization (CSTO), which since then has consisted of just six states: Russia, Belarus, Armenia, Kazakhstan, Kyrgyzstan, and Tajikistan. (Uzbekistan would rejoin a few years later before withdrawing again shortly thereafter.)

THE RISE OF CENTRIFUGAL FORCES

Although the appearance of centrifugal forces within the CIS was entirely predictable, Russia did not really anticipate or consider it for several years. Once each state gained independence, it sought to affirm the fundamental elements of its sovereignty: defending its borders, raising an army, adopting a national currency, developing a constitution and a set of laws, and choosing the symbolic pillars of its identity and history, its national heroes, and so forth. Each state also had to define its strategic direction given its specific geopolitical environment. One of the first challenges that each of the newly independent states faced was redefining its relationship with the former imperial power. Although the Kremlin sought to use the full range of tools at its disposal—economic levers, demographic realities, and various military and geostrategic pressures—the obvious quickly became apparent: Moscow had lost its monopoly and was no longer the only capital influencing its neighbors in the "near abroad."

Added to this was Russia's lack of experience with managing a multilateral organization. The Kremlin has always preferred bilateral relations, where it excels at making the most of its partners' weaknesses; it has not been inclined to make the sort of compromises and concessions involved in the patient construction of an organization that brings together a large number of independent states, as does the European Union. As in the case of price liberalization in 1992, the natural tendency of the Russian leadership was always to impose its decisions on its partners, taking advantage of Russia's objective economic, demographic, and military weight. The most difficult issues of the early 1990s were bilaterally negotiated, including the denuclearization of Ukraine (with decisive intervention from the United States) and the leases of the Sevastopol base in Crimea[22] and the Baikonur Cosmodrome in Kazakhstan.

Attempts to capture these centrifugal tendencies quickly appeared within the CIS. Fears that they were seeing the assertion of a "Slavic bloc" centered around Russia[23] led several Central Asian leaders to support the creation of a Central Asian Economic Community in 1994, but due to the strong rivalry between Kazakhstan and

Uzbekistan, this never came to fruition, to Moscow's benefit. Proposals that relied on external support tended to be more prospective. With five new states speaking Turkic languages, Turkey sought to create a federation, in the hope of achieving Ankara's dream of pan-Turkism and becoming a regional player. The establishment in Istanbul in June 1992 of the Black Sea Economic Cooperation area (BSEC) symbolized Turkey's vision. The BSEC brought together eleven states, including Russia, Ukraine, Moldova, Armenia, Azerbaijan, and Georgia; it was modeled on the Council of Baltic Sea States that had been established with ten members, including the three Baltic states and Russia, in March 1992. For its part, even before launching its neighborhood policy, the European Union created a series of euro-regions spanning several states, such as the "Northern Dimension," which included the Scandinavian countries, the Baltic countries and Russia.

The role of the United States, which grew during the mid-1990s, came to be decisive in this process. As already noted, Washington played a role in organizing the "refusal front" and in creating GUAM, born in reaction to Russia's manipulation of local conflicts. The increased U.S. presence was part of the broader strategy of decoupling mentioned above. On the southern flank of Russia, this action would be formalized in 1999 with the adoption by the U.S. Congress of the Silk Road Strategy Act, which offered aid and financial assistance (including for military purposes) to all of the states of the South Caucasus and Central Asia. One aspect of this proactive policy was opening these two regions through the creation of a series of transport routes that bypassed Russia. The U.S. military made its first appearance in the Caucasus in 2002, when, as part of the second Chechen war, Putin threatened to intervene in the Pankisi Gorge, a Georgian region populated by Kists (an ethnic group related to the Chechens) that was hosting fighters from the north. To counter this threat, Georgian president Eduard Shevardnadze invited a group of U.S. instructors to advise his army.[24] As an expression of gratitude, in 2003, Georgia became a member of the "coalition of the willing" that supported the U.S. intervention in Iraq.

EXACERBATING TENSIONS: FROM THE "COLOR REVOLUTIONS" TO THE UKRAINIAN CRISIS

For several reasons, the early 2000s saw a rise in tensions throughout the CIS. The primary causes were the coming to power of Vladimir Putin, who adopted a much more offensive discourse, and the second Chechen war, which caused a surge of criticism of Moscow's policy. Another factor was the shock of the September 11 attacks and their aftermath, including the resurgence of U.S. military activity, which led to a series of swings in the geopolitical orientation of the post-Soviet space. To support their intervention in Afghanistan, the Americans established air bases in Central Asia. In so doing, they relied on the increasing irritation local leaders felt toward Moscow, which was taking advantage of their isolation, and these countries' consequent hopes of diversifying their alliances. Initially, Putin reluctantly accepted the opening of bases in Uzbekistan (Khanabad) and Kyrgyzstan (Manas), but both Moscow and Beijing would later pressure local leaders to renege on those deals.

There was also increased mobilization of "pro-Western" forces in several states in the region, with the undisguised support of the European Union and the United States. This culminated in the "color revolutions," a generic term given to a series of similar street revolts that began with the overthrow of Serbian president Slobodan Milošević in 2000. The Rose Revolution in Georgia between November 2003 and January 2004 led to the resignation of Eduard Shevardnadze and the election of Mikheil Saakashvili, a libertarian and pro-Western politician. After several dramatic twists and turns, the Orange Revolution in Kiev led in December 2004 to the election of Viktor Yushchenko, the purportedly pro-Western opponent of Putin-backed Viktor Yanukovych. Finally, the Tulip Revolution in March 2005 led to the resignation of Kyrgyz president Askar Akayev, who fled to Moscow. Extensive literature has already been devoted to these events, so we will not go into detail here.[25]

Although one may rightly emphasize the significance of the popular movements that led these mobilizations, it would be wrong to underestimate the supporting role played by external organizations. Within the EU, several governments openly assisted: the Baltic states and Poland campaigned for the rapid integration of Georgia and Ukraine into the European Union and NATO, for example. On the U.S. side, a series of official and unofficial channels were used to organize and finance networks that were hostile to Russian influence, favorable to the proposals of President George W. Bush, and supportive of these countries' accession to NATO and integration into the European space.

Nevertheless, it is essential to make several observations. The first concerns the Kremlin's misinterpretation of the nature of these crises. In Moscow's view, "color revolutions" stemmed primarily from the intervention of outside forces manipulated by Washington—whether indirectly via NGOs such as the Soros Foundation or directly with the systematic involvement of diplomats and advisers from various U.S. and European entities. Here we observe the significance of conspiracy theories in Russia, but also a hollow reading of how the Russian leadership perceived the evolution of post-Soviet societies. Moscow largely neglected the genuine democratic aspirations and criticisms of the oligarchic system that had developed in almost all CIS countries, as well as the profound rejection of various aspects of Russian policy in many of these states. Obviously, the "color revolutions" were not a Western conspiracy so much as a concerted effort to influence "sensitive" countries; their decoupling from Moscow was considered key to permanently weakening Russian pretensions, which was Washington's strategic objective. Second, we need to make note, too, of some misinterpretations made by the West, especially the United States. Indeed, U.S. strategists neglected two points that would later prove decisive: the fragility and complexity of these societies after the collapse of the Soviet Union, particularly due to internal ethnic and regional opposition; and Moscow's capacity to respond within its sphere of strategic interest.

Russian leadership first reacted by tightening economic relations with the states that were trying to escape its grip. With Ukraine, this took the form of what were called the "gas wars." The mechanism is quite simple and based on the real interdependence that binds the two countries. In the 1990s, Ukraine depended almost entirely on Russia for its supply of hydrocarbons. In turn, Russia depended on its neighbor for the transit of about 70 percent of the gas it delivered to various European countries. Early on, trouble emerged between the two forced partners. Moscow deliberately offered Kiev a permanent discount on gas as compared to global prices (see table 6.1) but made this "friendly" arrangement contingent, in part, on control over Ukraine's policy decisions. Specifically, the Kremlin not only expected that Kiev would subscribe to the various treaties proposed within the CIS framework, but also that Ukrainians would sell Russia some essential elements of their energy infrastructure (pipeline and gas distribution networks, refineries, and power plants), which Kiev consistently refused to do. In turn, the Ukrainian leadership made the most of their situation by taking a portion of the gas in transit for their own use and exporting a portion of what they received at a discount to pay off substantial debts. One particularly opaque aspect was that these markets were also a major source of enrichment for the Ukrainian oligarchs who were the trading partners of Russian companies.

After the Orange Revolution, relations soured. The first conflict began in March 2005 and peaked in January 2006, as Gazprom refused to supply Ukrainian pipelines due to disagreements over the transit price, causing a knock-on energy crisis in several European countries. Similar conflicts arose in the following years, and Kiev and Moscow each sought to take the other to the European Commission. Moldova and Georgia, the other two states seeking to move closer to the EU and NATO, would in turn suffer from Russian sanctions when Moscow banned two of their main exports, mineral water and wine.

In addition, Moscow reacted in political ways. In a speech that became famous,[26] Putin gave his interpretation of these events. He railed against what he called the "unipolar world" that the United States wanted to impose, citing the "unilateral actions" taken by the country, which were "often illegitimate" (i.e., when not approved

Table 6.1. Price of Russian gas to CIS members (US$ per 1,000 m³)

	2005	2008	2009
Ukraine	50	179.5	201–450**
Belarus	47	119–128*	140–240**
Moldova	80	188–280*	160–260**
Armenia	54	110	165**
Georgia	64	280	280

*Price range over the year
**Price during negotiations

Source: *Kommersant Vlast'*, January 19, 2009

by the UN Security Council). He accused U.S. leaders of breaking the promises given in 1990 by Manfred Werner, then the secretary general of NATO, who reportedly said, "The fact that we are prepared not to deploy a NATO army outside of German territory gives the Soviet Union a firm security guarantee." Putin went on to discuss the role of NGOs, saying their interference "does not contribute at all to the maturation of genuinely democratic states, but makes them dependent, resulting in economic and political instability." President Bush ignored these warnings. At the NATO summit in Bucharest in April 2008, he pressured allies to endorse the procedure for Georgia and Ukraine to join NATO. The vetoes of France and Germany blocked this process, but the perception deteriorated rapidly on both sides.[27]

In Georgia, Western states supported President Mikheil Saakashvili's ultra-liberal reforms and anti-Russian rhetoric without reservation, while ignoring his increasingly frequent meddling in the media and action against opposition forces. Provocations and hostile gestures multiplied, particularly around the two breakaway regions of Abkhazia and South Ossetia. Although the State Department warned the Georgian president about the consequences of direct action, other U.S. entities persuaded him that he could take by force a part of Ossetia where many Georgians still lived. On the night of August 8, 2008, while Putin was in Beijing for the opening of the Olympics, Saakashvili launched what would become a catastrophic military operation. Long prepared for such a scenario, the Russian army intervened and effectively occupied the western third of the country.[28] Following EU intervention the war stopped, but the damage was done. Georgia lost control of the two regions and Moscow recognized their independence on August 26. For the first time, the Kremlin had called into question the territorial integrity of a neighbor, breaking one of the foundations of the 1991 Minsk agreements.

The international community condemned this attack on the sovereignty of an independent state, a gesture that was taken as proof of Moscow's neo-imperialist aims. Significantly, none of the other members of the CIS would recognize the independence of the two Russian-backed regions. But curiously, the European Union did not see all the implications of this event, and several of its members, underestimating Putin's determination, led the European Commission toward further integration of Ukraine into the EU in parallel with considering its accession to NATO. As part of the neighborhood policy put forward in 2003, Poland, the Baltic states, and several Scandinavian countries supported an "Eastern Partnership" in 2009, then pushed for individual EU association agreements with Ukraine, Georgia, and Moldova.[29] The treaty, which included a comprehensive free trade agreement and also opened the door to potential military cooperation with European armies, immediately drew objections from Moscow, which pointed out that its adoption would jeopardize economic agreements within the CIS and trigger a thorough review of agreements with Kiev. Still, the European Commission refused to consider tripartite negotiations on the new agreement, saying it was not Russia's concern.

What followed is well known. Facing an impossible choice between two partnerships that were both essential to the Ukrainian economy, in November 2013,

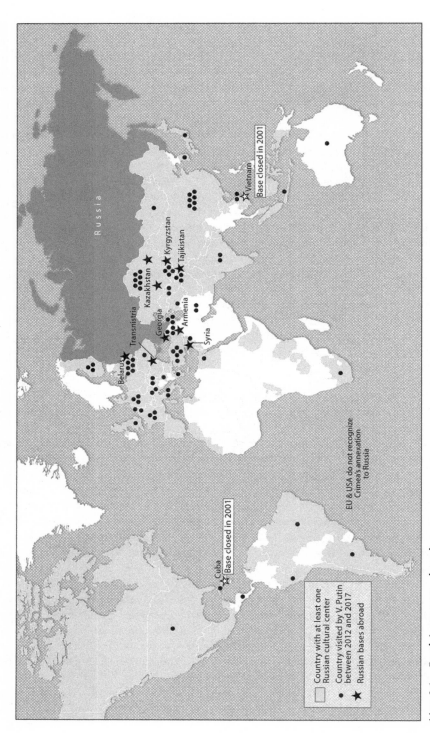

Map 6.1. Russia's presence abroad

President Viktor Yanukovych canceled the signing of the EU agreement in Vilnius. Massive protests in Kiev, led by the pro-Western part of the population and the Ukrainian nationalist movement, and supported by many Western leaders, precipitated his flight to Russia. Putin took advantage of this crisis to seize Crimea in March 2014 and support the separatist forces in eastern Donbas, plunging the country and the whole of Europe into crisis. For the second time, the Kremlin had changed the borders of a sovereign state, while rejecting Western criticism as the manifestation of a double standard in light of its recognition of Croatian and Slovenian independence in 1991, which ended the existence of Yugoslavia, and the independence of Kosovo in 2008.[30] Following Georgia, which had left in September 2008, Ukraine announced its withdrawal from the CIS. An increasing number of voices within Russia itself came to question the value of keeping the organization going, since it was down to ten official members and had never really been effective.

DISORDERLY RUSSIAN ATTEMPTS AT REARRANGEMENT

Aware of the pressures and resistance to reform within their sphere of influence, Russia's leaders did try during this period to respond to the disintegration of the CIS. But the proliferation of parallel and competing proposals left a deep impression of hesitation and weakness. As it oscillated between declarations of intent of a balanced and mutually beneficial partnership and the temptation to impose its own vision, Moscow seemed unable to define a clear strategy in its relations with former Soviet republics. Russian leaders again tried to use the instruments and agreements of the CIS to their advantage, multiplying technical treatises, lengthening the duration of the "leases" on concession bases and trade agreements, and holding a rotating presidency of the organization, none of which measures added to the organization's effectiveness.[31] More paradoxically, they proposed, even within the CIS, different types of nested associations, expanding the nature of reciprocal commitments. There is no need to go into the details of each of these associations, some of which have never existed except on paper; the mere mention of them demonstrates the Kremlin's strategic embarrassment.

The first example seems circumstantial. In April 1996, on the campaign trail for his difficult reelection against a Communist candidate, Yeltsin launched the Union of Sovereign Republics with Belarusian president Alexander Lukashenka. The union's Russian acronym (SSR) brought to mind a draft reconstruction of the Soviet Union (SSSR), suggesting that it might be a purely electoral maneuver. But in April 1997, the two presidents signed a Russian-Belarusian Union Treaty that consisted of a political integration program, ultimately providing for a shared parliament, president, currency, borders, and defense strategy. When he came to power, Putin seemed embarrassed by this union with Belarus and its capricious president, but he maintained this association without developing any commitments. It grew, however, with his attempts to create a real customs union within the CIS. In 2000, the union became the Eurasian Economic Community (EEC). The distribution of voting rights ensured Russia's dominance (40 percent), with the other members sharing the rest (Belarus and Kazakhstan had 20 percent of the votes each, while Kyrgyzstan and Tajikistan received 10 percent each). However, it is clear that, in the Kremlin's view, this type of enhanced economic cooperation—ultimately leading to a single customs and fiscal space and an integrated VAT—could not succeed without Ukraine, which remained a key partner for Russia in many areas, including the military-industrial complex.

It was in this spirit that the creation of a new union of Russia, Ukraine, Belarus, and Kazakhstan—the Common Economic Space—was announced in September 2003. Reflecting on the failure of that effort, in July 2010, Putin revived a version of the customs union—with Russia, Kazakhstan, and Belarus—within the Eurasian Economic Community. Despite considerable pressure, Ukrainian president Viktor Yanukovych refused to enter into this union; following the 2014 crisis, the issue became moot. Russia therefore had to constrain its ambitions and return to an old proposal from Kazakh president Nursultan Nazarbayev. On January 1, 2015, it announced the official launch of the Eurasian Economic Union (EEU), with Belarus, Kazakhstan, Kyrgyzstan, and Armenia (Tajikistan is a prospective member). This new form of intra-CIS cooperation is certainly the best-planned and most elaborate free trade project initiated since 1991.[32] But even setting aside the absence of Ukraine, many Russian experts doubt its effectiveness. Russian leaders simply need to accept that, contrary to their wishes, this union will not become political, as its partners do not wish it to be; it will remain strictly economic. Over the long term, they also need to respect the balance with the other signatories. That they will play the game of reciprocal and shared interdependence is far from settled, given the initial inequality of the members.

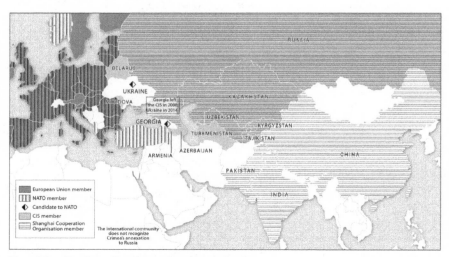

Map 6.2. Russia and major regional organizations

This difficulty in organizing the post-Soviet space in a constructive fashion is one of the major failures of Russia's foreign policy. It indicates a persistent inability to implement a new type of relationship with the former Soviet republics that have become independent states. On this point, the Kremlin remains ambivalent. Although Russian leaders say they recognize the states' independence, they are obviously setting an essential condition: that these neighboring states not enter into any coalitions, particularly NATO, that might undermine Russian security. This indicates that Russia has adopted a version of the U.S. Monroe Doctrine for its immediate environment. Moreover, the recent return of "Eurasian" rhetoric is paradoxical. Putin has been developing the Eurasian Union at a time when the Russian population is rife with xenophobic reflexes and demands—if not for the closing of the eastern and southern borders, at least for greater control of migration flows from several members of the new union.[33]

The series of tensions and crises in the post-Soviet space since 2004 has generated a great deal of commentary. While one can legitimately be impressed by the peaceful nature of the breakup of the Soviet Union, especially compared to that of Yugoslavia, it is now clear that the echoes of this explosion are far from over. The crises in Georgia in 2008 and more recently in Ukraine indicate a dual failure in which responsibility is shared.[34] The Western side certainly underestimated the consequences of the temporary weakening of Russia, and some states thought they could use it to permanently reduce Russia's influence. The Western policy of accelerating the democratic transition of several post-Soviet states without truly analyzing their internal complexity or the lessons of history and geography raises questions about the limits of the interference strategy as a whole. But this series of crises also highlights Russia's failure to establish constructive relations with its immediate neighbors. The political and economic costs of the war with Georgia and the Ukrainian crisis, beyond the annexation of Crimea, have been heavy; they have raised questions about the instruments of Russian power and their use.

RUSSIA'S NEW INSTRUMENTS OF POWER: A DIFFICULT LEARNING CURVE

Like any state that claims to play a major international role, Russia, like the Soviet Union before it, uses the full range of tools available to it to project power. The Soviet authorities never hesitated to deploy military means to defend strategically important areas of the empire, as seen in Eastern Europe (Budapest in 1956 and Prague in 1968) and Asia (the Soviet-Chinese conflict over the Amur in 1969, and the invasion of Afghanistan in 1979). The Soviet leaders also excelled in the use of propaganda, carefully presenting their achievements in all areas in order to attract foreign sympathies well beyond Communist circles, and mastering a kind of soft power long before the term came into common usage. In this sense, the 1990s marked a break. Preoccupied with other internal and external concerns, and with their resources reduced by the crisis, the new Russian leaders seemed to abandon the previously vaunted merits of having a foreign plan. To consolidate its leading role in the post-Soviet space, Moscow had to return to the exercise of these tools of power.

EXERCISING POWER IN A
NARROWED SPHERE OF INFLUENCE

Even before the Soviet Union collapsed in late 1991, Moscow had had to abandon some of the symbols of its power. The fall of the Berlin Wall in 1989 and the dissolution of the Warsaw Pact in 1991 followed other setbacks. The repatriation of Soviet troops from East Germany and other Socialist states, the loss of the Baltic states, and the closure of bases at Lourdes in Cuba and Cam Ranh in Vietnam in 2001 are milestones that mark the loss of a strategic system that had been organized over the course of the twentieth century, as well as the weakening of Moscow's role as a global superpower. For over twenty-five years, from Gorbachev to Medvedev, Moscow's policy was almost exclusively oriented toward Europe and the Atlantic, but its direct scope was singularly limited to the post-Soviet space.

Notwithstanding its willingness to organize an integrated defense space under Russian command, the Kremlin had to perform a drastic reset of its own armed forces. The two Chechen wars and the Russian-Georgian conflict in 2008 highlighted the weaknesses of a bloated army often equipped with obsolete weapons. Its structural defects have long been known: a command imbalance with a lack of junior officers that facilitates the mistreatment of conscripts (*dedovshchina*); and units plagued by corruption and irresponsibility, causing the proliferation of serious incidents such as explosions on military bases.[35] Even the nuclear forces are implicated, as proven by the Kursk submarine accident in 2000 and repeated failures in the development of the Bulava missile and the GLONASS program (intended to compete with the American GPS). From 2008, Putin undertook comprehensive reforms to upgrade the entire Russian military. He greatly increased the defense budget and brought order to the military-industrial complex to secure his country's place in the international arms trade. He also fundamentally changed the territorial and operational organization of the troops, to the end of a more professional, better-paid, and better-equipped army.[36] In some ways, the demonstration of force in Syria is intended to show NATO leaders that this effort has already partially reached its goal: The Russian military is ready to fulfill commitments beyond the post-Soviet space. Russia's recent military expenditures have been slowing down with the economic downturn and the country continues to lag well behind in areas such as surface ships and automated control systems. Yet it remains ahead of NATO in anti-ship missiles, electronic warfare, and air defenses, and is narrowing the gap in areas such as drones and precision-guided munitions.[37]

Beyond strictly military responses, Moscow uses a range of methods to exert pressure. All relations within the CIS are marked by constant bilateral negotiations in which each country tries to obtain this concession or that exchange. As already mentioned in the case of gas prices, Russia negotiates on a case-by-case basis, rewarding "good allies" and punishing the recalcitrant. Numerous industrial cooperation agreements show how Russian negotiators deal with individual partners, always striving to obtain the transfer of elements of strategic interest in exchange for debt forgiveness or assistance. Thus, after years of pressure, large Russian companies own all or large parts of the gas and power-generation networks in Belarus and Armenia, chemical and metallurgical plants in Central Asia, and shares in many other companies.[38] Some of these acquisitions are based on pure industrial and commercial logic and should not call for special attention. Others generate ample controversy in the countries concerned, given the often-opaque conditions of acquisition or the new owners' non-compliance with their investment commitments. These battles sometimes lead to the eruption of anti-Russian demonstrations, as happened in Armenia in 2015, when the population rebelled against the mismanagement of the country's power grid by its Russian owner.[39]

PIPELINE WARS AND THE NEW "GREAT GAME"

The post-1991 reorganization of the main lines of communication on the margins of Russia's territory became a major issue for all CIS states. As previously observed, the situation resulted from the initial isolation of nine of the fifteen states, as well as Russia's dependence on certain transit states for its exports to Europe. Very quickly, two battlefronts opened. To the east, Moscow tried to preserve its monopoly over the transit of exports from Central Asia. To the west, transit countries (the Baltic states, Belarus, and Ukraine) sought to take advantage of their location in bitter negotiations over the passage of Russian energy. Meanwhile, several external actors quickly stepped in to challenge Moscow's efforts to preserve its influence in this strategic space.

In 1993, the European Union, with U.S. support, launched TRACECA (the Europe-Caucasus-Asia Transport Corridor), an ambitious project that aimed to create a major alternative transportation channel that would circumvent Russia and Iran; modernize the roads, railways, and ports of the three states of the South Caucasus and the five Central Asian countries; and boost extra-CIS cooperation between all the countries on Russia's southern border. It was open mainly to the non-Russian areas of the Caspian Sea, a highly strategic region where the Western oil giants had returned after seventy years of absence during the Soviet era. It is precisely within this context of privileged relations that, in 1999, U.S. president Bill Clinton and Azerbaijani president Heydar Aliev managed to launch BTC (Baku-Tbilisi-Ceyhan, the third city being a Turkish port on the Mediterranean Sea), an expensive pipeline to export Azeri oil while avoiding passage through Russia, the Turkish straits, or Istanbul. It was completed in 2005, and was soon joined by a parallel gas pipeline, Baku-Tbilisi-Erzurum, to export the gas discovered in the early 2000s near Baku. The Europeans, who also wanted to enjoy the benefits of these new deposits, proposed the Nabucco project, a large pipeline that would import Azeri and Turkmen gas via a pipeline constructed under the Caspian, then routed through Turkey and the Balkans.[40] Ultimately, however, EU hesitation and Russian opposition scuppered the project.

Russian leaders were quick to react to these initiatives, which reduced the virtual monopoly that had benefited Moscow during the imperial and Soviet periods. At summits in the Caspian states, the Kremlin (with implicit support from Tehran, which challenged the division of the seabed proposed by Azerbaijan and Turkmenistan) managed to block any construction of a trans-Caspian pipeline, preventing Kazakhstan and Turkmenistan from connecting to any Western-funded pipelines in the Caucasus. Simultaneously and in record time, the Russians built a series of pipelines connecting deposits in northern Kazakhstan to the new oil and gas terminals they had opened between Novorossiisk and Tuapse on the Black Sea. Moscow signed special agreements with Kazakhstan to ensure the routing of a large proportion of Caspian crude exports through its territory. Finally, to counter Nabucco, in 2003 Moscow completed the Blue Stream underwater gas pipeline between Russia and Turkey, the culmination of Russia's long struggle to maintain its share of gas exports to all of southern Europe.[41]

Meanwhile, the Russian authorities were not inactive on their western borders. Upon taking office in 2000, Putin began to speed up construction projects at the Vysotsk and Ust-Luga ports outside St. Petersburg in order to reduce transit through the Baltic states to a minimum—and, later, to punish these states for their NATO membership. The rise of these new facilities, particularly the Vyborg gas terminal and, in 2011, the inauguration of the Nord Stream undersea pipeline to Germany (negotiated with then-chancellor Gerhard Schroeder, now chairman of the board of Gazprom subsidiary Nord Stream AG), fulfilled a strategic Kremlin objective: enabling Russian gas exports to the EU to avoid transit states. An agreement to double these exports was signed in June 2015, despite the Ukrainian crisis.[42]

A similar project was planned to the south, with the South Stream natural gas pipeline from Russia to Bulgaria under the Black Sea to supply the southern European Union. In the face of Bulgaria's hesitation and under pressure from the European Commission, which sought to break Gazprom's monopoly, Putin finally decided to abandon the project in December 2014. It was replaced with Turkish Stream (another Russia-Turkey pipeline), while Ankara and Moscow maintained privileged relations based on their common irritation with EU policy and their partial overlapping interests on the Syrian theater. The completion of this pipeline would represent a crucial chip in the ongoing tug-of-war between the EU and Moscow over Ukraine. Given the decline in EU purchases of Russian gas, it would eventually allow the Russians to completely avoid transit through Ukraine.[43] Deprived of this asset, the importance of which was seen during the "gas wars," Kiev would either have to comply with future tariff conditions imposed by Gazprom or look for other suppliers, which would push the country's already weakened economy into an even more critical situation.

Meanwhile, another actor became involved in this battle of pipelines and export routes that quickly became known as the "new Great Game."[44] Long absent from regional interactions except for some trade with the Central Asian states, China made a notable entrance by negotiating purchases of oil, the construction of the first oil pipeline with Kazakhstan (opened in 2005), and a gas pipeline with Turkmenistan (2009).[45] This was a decisive step for these countries, which were offered an alternative export route that allowed them to overcome Moscow's hitherto near-monopoly. This continental competition is just beginning: In 2013, Beijing launched its own "New Silk Road" project, now renamed Belt and Road Initiative, which aims to completely reshape the transport links between the Asia-Pacific region and Europe. Russia, which has for more than twenty years emphasized its desire to revive the Trans-Siberian Railway and the Northern Sea Route, will have to work even harder if it wants to overcome this competition, which could intensify with Iran's potential return to the regional fold.[46]

THE PIVOT TO ASIA AND THE BRICS: A NEW GLOBAL PRESENCE?

Presented as a byproduct of the 2014 Ukrainian crisis, Russia's "Asia pivot" has in fact been one of the strategic pillars of Russian policy since Gorbachev's speech in Vladivostok in 1986. The anomaly was the earlier situation, in which Soviet Russia virtually abandoned any policy on its Pacific coast despite the economic and strategic issues in this region. On behalf of the Soviet Union, Gorbachev began talks with Chinese leaders to normalize diplomatic and commercial relations, reopen border crossings for trade, and resume negotiations on the border dispute along the Amur River. Yeltsin concluded a new border treaty in 1996, which Putin finalized in 2004 by handing over half of Bolshoi Ussuriisk Island, near Khabarovsk, thus putting an end to the forty-year conflict. Relations between the two great Asian neighbors were finally able to expand in a significant way, and by 2010, China had become Russia's largest single trading partner. Altogether, however, the European Union still dominates Russia's trade, accounting for 41 percent of its exports and 36 percent of its imports in 2016, versus levels of 29 percent and 34 percent for Asia, and Oceania combined (see table 6.2).[47]

Although relations with Beijing are now an essential component of the Kremlin's foreign policy, Moscow is being careful not to trap itself in a bilateral relationship that still arouses many fears. While accelerating the reconciliation, Putin sought to develop relations with other Asian countries and to involve Russia as much as possible in all the Asia-Pacific regional structures. Finally, the attention the Russian leadership has paid to the BRICS phenomenon[48] has the advantage of detaching Russia from Eurasian issues sensu stricto and facilitating the country's integration into a truly global economy.

Table 6.2. Russia's main trading partners (% of total volume) from 1995 to 2016

	1995		2000		2006		2013		2016	
1	Ukraine	11.0	Germany	9.6	Germany	9.8	China	10.5	China	14.1
2	Germany	10.2	Belarus	6.6	Netherlands	8.8	Netherlands	9.0	Germany	8.7
3	United States	5.6	Ukraine	6.4	Italy	7	Germany	8.9	Netherlands	6.9
4	Kazakhstan	4.2	Italy	6.2	China	6.5	Italy	6.4	Belarus	5
5	Italy	4.2	United States	5.6	Ukraine	5.5	Ukraine	4.7	United States	4.3
6	Belarus	4.1	China	4.5	Belarus	4.5	Belarus	4.0	Italy	4.2
7	Netherlands	3.9	United Kingdom	4	Turkey	3.9	Japan	3.9	Japan	3.4
8	Finland	3.5	Poland	3.8	United States	3.5	Turkey	3.8	Turkey	3.4
9	China	3.4	Netherlands	3.7	Poland	3.4	Poland	3.3	South Korea	3.2
10	Switzerland	3.4	Kazakhstan	3.4	United Kingdom	3.2	United States	3.2	France	2.8
11	United Kingdom	3.3	Switzerland	3	France	3	Kazakhstan	3.1	Poland	2.8
12	Poland	2.4	Finland	3	Switzerland	3	South Korea	3.0	Kazakhstan	2.8
13	France	2.1	Turkey	2.5	Finland	3	United Kingdom	2.9	United Kingdom	2.9
14	Turkey	1.7	Japan	2.4	Kazakhstan	2.9	France	2.6	Ukraine	2.2

Source: Goskomstat, Statist. Ezegodnik 1996 to 2017

FROM "YELLOW PERIL" TO STRATEGIC ALLIANCE: THE CHALLENGES OF RAPPROCHEMENT WITH CHINA

Since the conclusion of the first bilateral agreements to open the border, trade relations with China have expanded rapidly. The first to benefit were the "shuttle traders," who carried consumer goods that soon flooded markets in Siberia and the rest of Russia. Chinese merchants appeared in most Siberian cities (in Irkutsk, part of the market was called Shanghai) as well as in Moscow, where they dominated the huge Cherkizov wholesale market that closed in 2009. This sudden influx of Chinese shoes, leather goods, clothing, and household appliances was one of the causes of the collapse of Russian light industry. The new presence of Chinese, the significance of which was exaggerated by the media, also drove the resurgence of the old Russian fear of "yellow peril," the alleged invasion of the country by Asian migrants. Some Siberian leaders invoked this discourse in complaining about the federal center's lack of attention to their concerns. These fears, also found in Moscow, have not prevented bilateral relations from developing in all directions.[49]

The border regions of Siberia and the Far East have increasingly resorted to using Chinese workers and companies, which are given contracts to develop farms, logging, and various other undertakings. Russia has long eyed the Asian market as a destination for its raw materials and hoped to attract investors to develop deposits in the Far East. Given their desire not to depend on any single buyer of oil and gas to the east of Russia, Russian policymakers ensured, at least initially, that new pipelines were built not only toward China, but also to Russia's eastern coast, so as to meet the demands of other customers, such as South Korea and Japan. By the late 2000s, the Kremlin had made this a point of pressure on Europe, indicating that if the EU asked for conditions that would limit its purchases of gas, Russia could replace its European customers with new Asian partners. But negotiations proved particularly difficult, with the Chinese seeking to obtain lower prices and the Russians undoubtedly seeking to impose their usual clauses, long-term delivery contracts, and "take or pay" formula, which requires payment even in the case of non-purchase.[50]

Developments in both states have resulted in the acceleration of their rapprochement. Heightened tensions with the EU and NATO have convinced Russian leaders, now more than ever, to quickly conclude agreements with Beijing. On the Chinese side, the ambitions of the new leader, Xi Jinping, have facilitated this rapprochement, which has resulted in a record number of bilateral summits since 2013. In May 2014, the parties finally announced their major gas deal, with China pledging to buy more than thirty-eight billion cubic meters per year over thirty years.[51] Meanwhile, some projects, such as the "Western option," the shortest route between the Ob Plain and China via the valleys of the Altai, may be delayed by the current slowdown of Chinese growth.

It is notable that these projects now go well beyond the simple commercial exchange of commodities for consumer products. This was something Russia wanted; it sought to rebalance its trade with China, one of the few countries with which it had a negative trade balance. Chinese investors have been invited to intervene in many sectors, including infrastructure (roads, bridges, and tourism) in the European area of Russia. More recently, the two countries seem to have entered into more in-depth technical cooperation in the energy, aerospace, automotive, and military-industrial sectors, allowing Russia to partially mitigate the effects of Western sanctions and the decline in trade with Ukraine, although doubts remain about the quality of Chinese technology in these fields.[52]

Beyond economic exchanges, there has been a deepening of political cooperation that is striking for its novelty, especially in criticizing the current liberal world order. Yet Beijing has also refused to fully align itself with Russia in the Ukraine conflict, such as by abstaining—along with the vast majority of non-members of NATO—from General Assembly Resolution 68/262, which condemned and declared illegitimate Crimea's independence referendum and subsequent annexation by Russia.[53] Ultimately, the complex debates surrounding the conditions of these foreign interventions in different regions, often with tragic consequences for the peoples concerned, fuel the fire of Russian leaders, who are increasingly active in their advocacy for a more comprehensive review of how security is exercised on a global level. In addition, Russia and China are actively cooperating on many other issues—Internet control, credit ratings and associated agencies, and monetary policy—where the two states consider it necessary to counterbalance the excessive weight of American and European players, a point that will be revisited in the next chapter.

ADDRESSING REGIONAL ISSUES: THE SHANGHAI COOPERATION ORGANIZATION

In 1996, Russia and China created the "Shanghai Group" with three of the new Central Asian states: Kazakhstan, Kyrgyzstan, and Tajikistan. With the accession of Uzbekistan in 2001, this became the Shanghai Cooperation Organisation (SCO). While the SCO rejects the label of a military organization, its primary objective is to ensure the safety of all members and protect them from three major risks (the "three evils" in Chinese newspeak): terrorism, separatism, and extremism.

In these years full of strategic decisions for the Soviet successor states, each of the first signatories saw advantages in this configuration. All the Central Asian states generally wanted to emerge from the burdensome tutelage of their former metropolis, but were also afraid of falling under the domination of their powerful eastern neighbor. Bringing together these two actors in one organization created the conditions for a reassuring balance. For Russia, this choice allowed the country to anticipate the expected rise of Chinese influence while preserving what it considered essential: maintaining trade and special security relations with Central Asia. For Beijing, which had other priorities in the Pacific region, the SCO allowed it to formally establish high-level relations with its new neighbors while reassuring a suspicious Moscow that while China would assert a rising economic presence in the region, it would not call into question Russia's role in organizing security as provided for within the CSTO.[54] The emphasis on security issues also fits within the logic of a period that saw the rise of secessionist movements in Xinjiang (Beijing absolutely wants to prevent Uyghur nationalists from finding refuge with their compatriots in Central Asia) and recurring issues in the majority-Muslim member states, which border Afghanistan and were threatened by incursions from al-Qaeda-influenced groups such as the Islamic Movement of Uzbekistan. These concerns led to the establishment, in 2002, of the SCO's Regional Anti-Terrorism Structure, headquartered in Tashkent, and, since then, some modest joint maneuvers.

At the same time, economic concerns were not absent. The SCO format has served as a convenient base for the growing presence of Chinese interests in what would, a decade later, become the "New Silk Road." Although Western experts have disparaged the SCO as a mere talking shop, commentary on the organization has somehow changed as new members have joined, first as observers and then, in the case of India and Pakistan in 2015, as full members.[55] The SCO currently unites eighteen states in a highly strategic area stretching from Turkey to China. They are all sensitive to the rise of extremist and terrorist movements, as well as to trafficking in arms and drugs. Although the Kremlin is broadly satisfied with the actions of the SCO, it shows some signs of concern regarding the slow but noticeable move of China toward increasing military agreements with the Central Asian states. Moreover, the organization has not helped address the tensions that have emerged between Russia and some Central Asian states, such as Uzbekistan, which left the Collective Security Treaty in 1999. It is only with the change of president that occurred in Uzbekistan in 2016 that Tashkent and Moscow have been reopening a new era of bilateral security and economic cooperation.

THE BRICS AND THE SEARCH FOR A NEW GLOBAL ORDER

Given their desire not to be constricted by their relationship with China, Russia's leaders have sought to develop cooperative arrangements with other Asian countries, increasing their trade, technical, and (where possible) military agreements with countries such as India and Vietnam. An end to the conflict over the Kuril Islands and the signing of a peace treaty with Japan (pending since 1945) would probably prove to be a decisive opening for this strategy. However, Japan has for decades insisted on the return of all disputed islands, while Russia—which has at times proposed some form of compromise—has only hardened its position over the last decade.[56] In 2016, however, a joint commission on the economic development and exploitation of the islands was established.[57] The resolution of the conflict would facilitate Russia's acceptance into Asian regional associations, in which Moscow is already playing a growing role, as demonstrated by the convening of the 2012 APEC (Asia-Pacific Economic Cooperation) summit in Vladivostok.

But it is primarily through its active participation in the BRICS that Moscow intends to play a major international role. Taking into account their rapid growth, the combined GDP of these "emerging" countries (originally Brazil, Russia, India, and

China, joined by South Africa in 2011) is supposed to equal that of the G7 by 2050, with two of them, China and India, on track to surpass the United States in the global economy.[58] The first formal summit of the original BRIC members was held in Yekaterinburg in Russia in 2009. Beyond economic cooperation, the five leaders agreed to make the BRICS "a large-scale mechanism for intervention on the main issues of the global economy and politics," as formulated by Dmitry Medvedev at the New Delhi summit in 2012. The five member states seek to mobilize the "other world" that is excluded from the G7 and to challenge Western global hegemony.[59]

Although recent economic turmoil has reduced the BRICS's relative intervention capacity, the agenda they have proposed is vast, and Russian leaders, in cooperation with China, are particularly active in promoting it. Russia is now isolated in Europe, but its BRICS policy framework is generally popular in both domestic and global public opinion. If many of the BRICS's declarations will probably never become realities, long-term global battles are already visible, as demonstrated by Beijing's head-on opposition to the Trans-Pacific Partnership and Asian Development Bank projects Washington sought to secure while excluding China and Russia. China's counter-proposal, the Asian Infrastructure Investment Bank, received support not only from Moscow, but also from several European states—France, Britain, and Germany—despite U.S. opposition.[60]

Unquestionably, Russia's foreign policy has become more brittle due to the effects of the Ukrainian crisis. However, the claim that the Kremlin now finds itself isolated seems questionable, because the issues at stake remain in flux. Russia may be at odds with the West, but its global outreach has undoubtedly increased.[61]

The world is becoming less centered on the Atlantic Ocean, and Moscow's "pivot to Asia," although still in its early days, is in sync with a wider global shift. Perhaps even more important for its relationship with Europe, Russia has regained influence on a wide array of pressing and timely issues in the Middle East. Its military intervention has changed the game in Syria, thus far allowing Bashar al-Assad to stay in power and defeat the Islamic State, as well as the rest of the opposition. Despite divergent agendas, for instance on Kurdish issues, Moscow has strengthened its ties with Ankara. The rapid turnover of Russian-Turkish relations, from the near rupture of links after the Turks shot down a Russian Sukhoi Su-24M bomber aircraft in November 2015 to President Recep Tayyip Erdoğan's apology in July 2016 and the resumption of economic and diplomatic interactions show both countries' adaptability to a fast-evolving context. Russia has also reinforced coordination with Tehran in Syria as well as in Afghanistan, and secured good relations with the majority of Sunni conservative regimes, as well as with Israel. Russia's refusal to move its embassy to Jerusalem until the Palestinian question has been solved[62] has strengthened the country's position in the Muslim world.

Yet one of the core issues for the sustainability of Russia's global outreach will be its ability to display soft/smart power and to show consistency and logic in its proposals for an alternative world order.

7

Russia in the World

Besieged Fortress or New Crusader?

Western perspectives on Russian foreign policy can be roughly divided into two points of view. Some see a country in decline, one that has failed to integrate into the Western world and has missed the chance to fundamentally reform. Such a country has no choice but to take refuge in militarist and nationalist withdrawal and engage in aggression toward its neighbors. Its only way to have its great status recognized is by acting as a "spoiler" in the international order, brandishing its "nuisance value." Others—among whom we stand—see a changing country that is still battling with its past and managing thirty years of unprecedented societal ruptures. Seeking its place in the world, this country is not satisfied with following rules that it believes others have developed to serve their own interests, and dreams of shifting the operational mode of the international community, without knowing if it will fail, succeed, or just change path such that this binary opposition disappears.

This double image of Russia, produced in the West, is symmetrical to the frame the Russian media and the Kremlin themselves produce. Sometimes they present Russia to their public as a besieged fortress that has no other choice but to defend itself against the coordinated attacks of its internal and external enemies, and would otherwise want nothing more than to be left in peace. At the same time, they show Russia as a conquering country, taking steps that wreak havoc on the "political correctness" of the international community, offering alternatives to the failures of the West, and building a "new world" that will rebalance power in favor of emerging players. It is interesting to note that Western and Russian discourses, ignorant of one another, still mirror each other—a mirroring game inflated to an unexpected level with the new U.S. obsession with "Russiagate."

Another critical component to add to the discussion is the interaction between Russia and the rest of the world, in particular the West. Russia's trajectory on the international scene is not the product of a predestined path, but has been developing in tenuous interaction with the way the Russian leadership interpreted the West's own actions. Upon coming to power in 2000, Putin stated in a BBC interview: "Russia is a part of European culture. I cannot imagine my country isolated from Europe and the so-called civilized world. So it is hard for me to see NATO as the enemy."[1] Read today, these lines seem to belong to a bygone era. Granted, Putin is no longer the same man, but the Europe and NATO of which he speaks have also changed. Could it be that decisions made *outside* Russia were more important than any predestination of the regime? The two key moments when Russia directly questioned the sacrosanct principle of respecting the borders inherited from the Soviet Union, in 2008 and in 2014, can likewise be explained by developments outside Russia: The Georgian authorities wanted to regain control of the breakaway regions and the "Euro-Maidan" opened the way for Ukraine to leave the Russian fold. The Russian leadership is not simply following its own internally predetermined path, but is reacting to a fast-changing world and to what it sees as the challenges to the post-Soviet status quo it has agreed to.

THE REACTIVATION OF RUSSIAN SOFT POWER

Putin and his inner circle do not aspire to a restoration of the Soviet Union. In 2000, the Russian president was very explicit on this point: "Anyone who does not regret the passing of the Soviet Union has no heart. But anyone who wants to restore it has no brains."[2] Fifteen years later, the diagnosis has not changed. The rehabilitation of Soviet symbols does not mean seeking outright reconstruction of the Soviet Union; rather, Soviet nostalgia is primarily a social and cultural tactic to rebuild society's unity. Relations between Russia and its "near abroad," and the place of Russia in the world, are now perceived in a different way, using modern tools that combine hard power and soft power.

The abrupt weakening of the Russian state's institutions and finances in the early 1990s disrupted the powerful public diplomacy that the Soviet Union had conducted. Fraternal nations such as Cuba saw assistance from Russia reduced to a trickle; Communist parties around the world lost funding and logistical support; associations promoting world peace and other "fellow travelers" of socialism disappeared from the international scene or had to reinvent themselves, often as anti-globalization movements. Tools such as Moscow Radio, translated editions of Soviet publications from Progress Publishers, and art tours organized by the USSR Ministry of Culture became obsolete; many of the cultural events that continued to be exported relied on support from their host countries. Even the influence of the Russian language was left in the rearview mirror, with no institutions supervising the important network of Russian-language universities and programs that operated in many countries, in the CIS as well as in the "far abroad."

During the 1990s, Russia had no voice on the international scene or was silent by virtue of sharing the Western point of view. It was not until the Yugoslav wars and the bombing of Belgrade in 1999 that a Russian voice re-emerged in protest. Yet from the early 1990s, many "political technologists"—the term used to describe the new specialists in political communication—began to surround the Kremlin, supporting Yeltsin in his 1995/96 re-election campaign and selling their services to other Russian politicians. Gleb Pavlovsky, an adviser to the presidential administration until 2011, was the iconic figure among these public relations specialists—Russian speakers internalized the term PR so much that they russified it as *piar*. Within a few years, Russia would take marketing techniques designed for private firms and apply them to the political sector and to the country's own branding.

It took a few years for these marketing techniques to find a place in Russia's foreign policy toolkit and become part of Putin's narrative. During his election campaign in 2012, the Russian president openly invoked soft power, mentioning the "set of tools and methods to achieve foreign policy objectives without use of weapons."[3] It was the crop of color revolutions, especially the Orange Revolution in Ukraine in 2004, which pushed the Kremlin to re-invest in its soft power aimed at the "near abroad." A presidential directorate for interregional and cultural relations was created, charged with rethinking Moscow's relationship to its "near abroad" and developing new tools of influence. It required boosting the new multilateral institutions and avoiding bilateral relationships with colonial overtones; developing academic, cultural, and linguistic cooperation; and financing media, NGOs, and local political parties with pro-Russian interests. The Kremlin also implemented a policy of "passportization"—the issuing of Russian passports to secessionist or potentially secessionist ethnic minorities in neighboring countries—to further Russia's legal right to protect "compatriots."[4]

The Kremlin also wanted to reach the international community, especially Western public opinion. In 2004, at the peak of his international popularity, Putin launched the Valdai Club, an annual meeting of global experts on Russia, based on the Davos model, to build the image of a globalized Russia dialoguing with the West, Asia, and the world, and displaying a diversity of political perspectives. In 2007, Moscow founded two chapters of the Institute for Democracy and Cooperation, one in Paris and one in New York (the latter closed its doors in 2015 on the grounds that "its mission of monitoring human rights in the United States had been accomplished"). The institute promoted the Russian concept of "sovereign democracy"—a then-in-vogue term developed by Kremlin power broker Vladislav Surkov that signified Russia's right to reject Western interference. In 2010, the Kremlin created the Alexander Gorchakov Public Diplomacy Fund, which funds projects to promote Russia and Russian culture abroad, and the Russian Council on International Affairs, in charge of international cooperation between scholars. That same year, Moscow started the Rossotrudnichestvo International Cooperation Agency, whose mission is to oversee the soft power projects Russia funds in the "near abroad," Latin America, and the Middle East, complemented by the launch of RosAid, a Russian humanitarian aid agency modeled after the U.S. Agency for International Development (USAID), which oversees the humanitarian and emergency aid that

Russia delivers worldwide.[5] As part of this new soft power toolkit, the Kremlin also invested massively in mega-events: In 2007, the selection of Sochi to host the 2014 Winter Olympics fit perfectly with the objective of rehabilitating Russia's image as a modern and attractive country, even if the results have been overshadowed by the Ukrainian crisis. The 2018 FIFA World Cup has been unable to reach the same level of impact, happening at a time of renewed tensions between Russia and the West around the Syrian war theater and the Salisbury poisoning affair, which resulted in the biggest collective expulsion of diplomats in history.

Russia has also drawn upon the legacy of Soviet-era soft power. Contacts with Communist or former Communist political parties have been reactivated in Europe. The most striking example is probably Die Linke, the German extreme-left party, but there is a similar strategy at play with leftist circles in Greece, for instance around Syriza, or in France, with the pro-Russian positions of Jean-Luc Mélenchon and Jean-Pierre Chevènement.[6] Although Russia no longer represents the ideals of the left, its stance in favor of national, economic, and cultural sovereignty, its anti-American and anti-NATO geopolitical positioning, and its rejection of excessive multilateralism in favor of traditional nation-states are convincing elements for many anti-globalization movements. Moscow has rebuilt ties with countries that identify or used to identify as socialist in various ways, including Cuba, Vietnam, North Korea, Egypt, Syria, and Venezuela. Russia is also innovating by building strong relationships with countries that were traditional allies of Washington during the Cold War, such as the Gulf monarchies. (See Map 6.1 for an illustration of Putin's impressive array of trips abroad.) Finally, as discussed in chapter 6, Moscow plays on the concept of the BRICS; though artificial in many respects, it is a valuable calling card for Russia because it anchors a country that is actually declining in many ways to a group that symbolizes a non-American future for the twenty-first century.

The increasing importance of world public opinion and nation branding was another lesson that Russian leaders learned from the "color revolutions" and the conflict with Georgia. They became seriously concerned that the deterioration of their country's image had become an overall source of weakness. At the peak of the Orange Revolution, Sergei Markov, a professor at MGIMO University in Moscow known for his pro-Kremlin positions, verbalized what the Russian political establishment had been thinking: Russia had lost its control over Georgia and Ukraine because its political communication technologies were inferior to those of the West.[7] Since then, the topic of an information war organized by the West against Russia has come up in almost all debates about the country's interaction with the rest of the world. Moscow considers that it lost its influence in the world due to its inability to master new information technologies capable of guiding public opinion by providing only one side of the story. The Russian authorities therefore decided to invest massive sums in catching up with the latest information technologies, taking advantage of the arrival on the labor market of a generation of young Russians bottle-fed from the Internet and social media.

In 2005, Russia launched its own television channel, Russia Today (today renamed the more neutral RT), modeled on CNN and Al-Jazeera and broadcasting in Russian, English, Arabic, Spanish, and French. RT's strategy, as expressed by Putin himself, is to "break the Anglo-Saxon monopoly on information flows"[8]—that is, not only to promote the Russian worldview, but also (and more importantly) to give voice to the "dissidents" in Western societies. All the evils of the West are put in the spotlight—racist violence and social inequality in the United States, Europe's failure to integrate migrants, and dissonant voices that do not find expression in mainstream Western media. RT has an impressive budget, increased from US$30 million in 2005 to $300 million in 2015, approaching the budget of the BBC's World Service ($376 million), the largest news agency in the world.[9] These funds allow the Russian channel to recruit famous international journalists and open national sections tailored to each audience; these sections were launched in the United States in 2010, where over two million people are said to regularly watch, in Britain in 2015, and in France in 2017. RT has also broken into the Argentinian market, where it has been included in the package of public channels accessible to everyone. RT is only the tip of the iceberg. The former Voice of Russia, now renamed Sputnik, is developing a similar strategy on the Internet and social media. In the press, *Russia beyond the Headlines* is published as a supplement in well-known, respectable newspapers in more than twenty countries, including the *Washington Post*, the *Daily Telegraph*, *Le Figaro*, and *La Repubblica*.

While from one perspective, Russia is simply modernizing the tools of influence that were created during the Soviet era, the Kremlin sees itself as replicating the influence strategies that the United States has built. The media outlets of Voice of America and Radio Free Europe / Radio Liberty, along with the financial support of USAID, the National Endowment for Democracy, and other state-sponsored institutions and NGOs are among the mechanisms of U.S. influence that, from Moscow's perspective, were used to weaken Russia, create internal dissent, and shape information to advance the American point of view. Russia believes it must turn these tools to its advantage, offering an alternative version that denounces Western lies and double standards—an element well explained by Putin himself in the Oliver Stone interviews.[10]

This information war, a war for the "hearts and minds" of public opinion, has reached unprecedented levels with the Ukrainian crisis. It has also been characterized by the use of all the instruments of power, to the point that some observers have created a model of a new type of conflict, "hybrid war," to take account of all the means of modern propaganda brought to bear on a conflict, with significant downsides. Indeed, Russian leaders have given broad support to the secessionist forces in Crimea and eastern Donbas—from sending volunteers and advisers to delivering weapons and equipment—as well as reinforced their presence on social media and developed more cyber activities. The perception of a powerful Russia mastering hybrid war reached a new level in the United States with the "Russiagate," a complex, heated, and overinflated mix of accusations of collusion with the main figures of the Trump campaign, meddling in the U.S. election, hacking the Democratic National Committee, and Russian social media presence in the United States. This frenzy is reinforced by the fact that Republicans and Democrats now share a relatively similar anti-Russia agenda, inspired by the Cold War "Red Scare" rhetoric.

RUSSIA AS THE STANDARD-BEARER OF CONSERVATIVE VALUES

As discussed in chapter 4, the Kremlin has gradually built up policy tools that allow it to marginalize the liberal opposition and structure a "silent majority" supporting the regime around some key unifying themes: the defense of Russia's status in the world and the promotion of "healthy" patriotism, morality, and spirituality. The Russian authorities and the Orthodox Church have worked hand in hand to promote "morality" (*nravstennost*) through both domestic and foreign policy. Russia's positions on several hot topics concerning sexuality, gender, and family have allowed it to build a new international brand as the standard-bearer of conservative values and the last defender of Europe's Christian heritage. Although this framing has been more widely used in recent years, it has been part of Russia's foreign policy toolkit since the mid-2000s. Moscow became aware of this untapped soft power potential during the reconciliation process between the Moscow Patriarchate and the Russian Orthodox Church Outside of Russia (ROCOR), born during the White emigration, which resulted in the canonical communion between the two churches in 2007.[11]

While debates rage around gay marriage in several European countries, and Catholic and Protestant churches face many questions on whether to accept societal changes (divorce, homosexuality, etc.), the Kremlin has built up the image of Russia as the preeminent defender of so-called traditional values by means of anti-homosexual laws, police violence during gay pride parades, and judgmental and pro-natalist propaganda. Russia's representatives in international bodies such as the UN, Council of Europe, and OSCE now vote alongside the Vatican on these issues.

The Moscow Patriarchate is at the forefront of this strategy. One of its main representatives, Hilarion Alfeev, was sent to discuss Russia's perspectives with Pope Francis, as well as with the American religious right. In 2010, he gave a speech in front of thousands of evangelicals in Dallas, calling for a strategic alliance between all those who defend Christian values, and met in person with George W. Bush.[12] A part of the American evangelical right suddenly recognized Vladimir Putin as an ally in its war against what it saw as Obama's overly liberal presidency. Leading Republicans such as Pat Buchanan, Tea Party members, and pro-life activists have celebrated the Russian president and his defense of Christian values. The World Congress of Families, which includes all the radical associations on the right that defend the "traditional family," praised Russia and even planned to hold its global meeting in Moscow in 2014 before the Ukrainian crisis caused it to cancel.[13] The issue of connections between Russia and part of the U.S. far right became a critical one with the election of Donald Trump, especially during the few months Steve Bannon, the editor of the far-right news portal Breitbart, worked as White House chief strategist (January–August 2017). The U.S. alt-right, or alternative right, does not hide its admiration for Russia, but contacts on both sides are tenuous and revolve around a few marginal figures, not impacting "high politics."[14]

In Europe, Russia's ideological successes are even more visible. Putin has cultivated his image as a European leader with the courage of his convictions, expressing out loud what many European citizens think, but do not dare to say in the face of the political correctness of European institutions. At the Valdai Club's 2013 summit, Putin offered a long ideological statement on what authentic European values should be:

> We can see how many of the Euro-Atlantic countries are rejecting their roots, including Christian values, which form the basis of Western civilization. They are trying to deny moral principles and their traditional identity: national, cultural, religious, and even sexual. They put in place policies that equate large families with homosexual families, and make faith in God equal to belief in Satan. . . . In many European countries, people are embarrassed to talk about their religion. . . . I believe that this opens a direct path to degradation and primitivism, leading to a profound demographic and moral crisis. What else but the loss of the capacity to reproduce could be the best evidence of this moral crisis? Today, almost all developed nations are no longer capable of assuring their demographic renewal, even with the assistance of immigration. Without the values present in Christianity and the other religions of the world, without the moral standards that have formed over thousands of years, people inevitably lose their human dignity. We see it as right and natural to defend these values. It is necessary to respect the right of each minority to be different, but the rights of the majority should not be called into question.[15]

This positioning won Putin the support of traditional religious circles and populist and extreme right groups, as well as some of the more mainstream conservative parties in Europe. The most exemplary case is probably the connection between the French National Front, and especially Marine Le Pen, and Putin, in whom Le Pen says she sees "a patriot. He is committed to the sovereignty of his people. He is aware that we defend common values. These are the values of European civilization."[16] Besides the National Front in France, Russia's greatest supporters in Europe include far right and populist parties such as Jobbik in Hungary, Forza Italia, Lega Nord and many figures close to Silvio Berlusconi in Italy, the openly neo-Nazi Greek party Golden Dawn, the Austrian FPÖ (which is now part of a coalition government), and an array of smaller parties in Belgium, Germany, Netherlands, and Britain. Victor Orban's Hungary positions itself as a pro-Russian country inside the EU structure, as do many political forces in Slovakia and Bulgaria. This alliance between Moscow and the European populists and radical right first came to light during the Ukrainian crisis, with these groups' almost unanimous support for the Russian position on Crimea. The committee of European observers who visited Crimea to validate the March 16, 2014, "referendum" on joining Russia was, for instance, composed of representatives of the European extreme right.[17]

Russia's soft power with the European right does not rely solely on the "conserva-tive values" agenda; it also banks on other, equally important elements that are more geopolitical than moral. Moscow criticizes European integration and holds Brussels' supranational institutions responsible for Europe's "submission" to U.S. interests. Putin has called for a Europe of nations that would pursue a "continentalist" rather than an "Atlanticist" policy. Moscow also plays an ambiguous game on questions of national identity and immigration. The Russian media highlight the alleged failure of multiculturalism in Europe and advance a racial interpretation of social tensions related to immigrants and their descendants while calling for the protection of Eu-rope's "white" and Christian identity against an uncontrolled invasion of migrants.[18] All these components constitute a genuinely shared vision between Russia and several European actors on the right—and, for its geopolitical component, on the left—of the political spectrum.

The revival of a certain Russian messianism, now under the guise of conservative values, is driving the Russian authorities to pull off a delicate balancing act. The Kremlin has denounced the "fascist junta" that supposedly came to power in Kiev and complains that Europe has purposely forgotten the Soviet Union's role in the victory in 1945. At the same time, Moscow openly sympathizes ideologically with—and even sometimes supports financially—the far-right groups that are the direct or indirect heirs of the former enemies of the Soviet Union. This apparent contradic-tion is explained by Russia's desire to work on a new "world order" in which all the enemies of the "liberal order," whatever their convictions, are rediscovered as allies.

RUSSIA IN SEARCH OF A NEW "WORLD ORDER"

Both the Georgian war and, to an even greater extent, the Ukrainian one were ac-companied by unusually active propaganda, both within Russia—to mobilize people around the president and his objectives—and outside it, to denounce what the Russians call the West's double standard: From the Russian perspective, the United States is allowed to intervene abroad in the name of protecting human rights, while Russia is forbidden to intervene in its own backyard. In 2008, during the Medvedev presidency, the Duma adopted a new foreign policy doctrine; for the first time, an official text stated, "The world arena has acquired a civilizational dimension that sug-gests competition between different value systems and development models in the context of universal democratic principles and the market economy."[19] The Russian establishment has an acute vision of this supposed competition between civilizations, and the authorities are working to formulate a Russian position that would challenge the current liberal world order and propose alternatives.

In the Russian view, the world order as it stands is directly subject to Washing-ton's decisions. This is particularly the case for the large financial structures of the "Washington consensus" (the Bretton Woods accords in 1944), such as the World Bank and the International Monetary Fund, where Westerners refuse to modify operations and voting rights in favor of emerging powers. U.S. supremacy over European interests in transatlantic institutions such as NATO and the OSCE is likewise rejected. Russia condemns the United States' repeated breaches of this world order that they themselves created and now police with a double standard: America's friends are supported by their protector even when they violate international norms (Israel) and are exempted from U.S. activism in the cause of human rights (the Gulf states, particularly Saudi Arabia). Moscow has called for a reading of the international scene based on old Realpolitik—the theory that, by nature, states are selfish organizations that defend their own strategic interests. According to the Russian discursive line, the United States has used idealistic and moralistic rhetoric to assert an illusory regime of human rights and a concept of international governance embodied by the right to intervene, when in reality Washington is simply pursuing its strategic interests as a great power.

Russia's distrust of the world order is reflected in its gradual questioning of all the instruments that have governed the global balance since 1945, with the exception of the UN General Assembly (based on the principle of "one state, one vote"), which Russia considers the only legitimate body representing world opinion. In many international institutions, representatives of Russia propose amendments that would introduce formulas calling for respecting every state's legislation and traditions, rather than the supremacy of human rights that they feel paves the way for foreign intervention. Russia calls for a return to a Westphalian international community, in which the sovereignty of each state is established as the supreme principle. In Moscow's view, states are the ultimate players on the international scene; non-state actors—transnational corporations, anti-globalization movements, and civil society—are regarded as instruments of dominant states. This explains Russia's firm refusal to acknowledge popular street movements, which it sees as inevitably manipulated by foreign interests and not expressing genuine support for democracy. Of course, one can argue that this position suits the Russian authorities, who are concerned about their own survival and who have sometimes, even if infrequently, welcomed the overthrow of leaders with whom they are unhappy—as in the case of Kyrgyz president Kurmanbek Bakiyev, who was forced out of office in April 2010.

On many occasions and often in association with Beijing, Moscow has used its veto at the UN Security Council to oppose Western resolutions to intervene in any country—as noted in Iraq and in Syria, where the Kremlin is engaged as Assad's last defender. Several reasons have been invoked to explain this policy, which the West denounces as a conservative blocking strategy. Russian and Chinese leaders have always pointed out to Westerners that their countries are much closer to these sources of tension and therefore more likely to suffer the effects of contagion. However, it is also clear that in defending regimes embroiled in internal conflict, Moscow and Beijing are disputing the very principle of foreign interference in the internal affairs of states. They see a risk that this principle could one day be applied to their own countries during a global or regional political crisis, for example in the North Caucasus for Russia, or Tibet or Xinjiang for China. Moscow and Beijing accuse the United States of double-talk and overuse of its dominant position to ignore the UN Security Council (e.g., Kosovo and Iraq) or twist its resolutions to suit Washington's will (e.g., Libya).[20]

Russia's position goes beyond criticism or rejection of the world order. Since the second half of the 2000s, and more actively since the Ukrainian crisis, Moscow has worked to institute collective resistance, or more or less credible alternatives. Hence the Kremlin's assertive promotion of the BRICS, as it knows that Russia alone lacks credibility: It remains a twentieth-century power whose economy cannot challenge the world order without more powerful allies. In the financial sector, Russia is reliant on China, and the BRICS as a whole, to advance alternatives to U.S.-led financial capitalism. The launch of the BRICS New Development Bank and the creation of a BRICS Reserve Fund (Contingent Reserve Arrangement) in 2014 were intended to openly challenge the roles of the International Monetary Fund and the World Bank. Although both institutions depend on China's financial power and are based in Shanghai, all the member states have an equal stake and an equal vote. In January 2015, the BRICS also discussed the creation of their own international rating agency, which could compete with the existing U.S.-based agencies by establishing other methods to assess the health of global economies that would be more respectful of domestic social conditions. Moscow and Beijing have also discussed converting contracts to rubles or yuan, in order to start moving away from the domination of the U.S. dollar—this proposition took a more acute light after the new U.S. sanctions against Russian companies very much involved with Western partners. Added to this is the launch, by Russia alone, of a competitor to the SWIFT interbank transfer system, so that the country will be prepared should Western sanctions disconnect it from the international banking network. The new system would allow Russian banks to operate independently when conducting all internal transfers, rather than being paralyzed by sanctions.

Russia has also become proactive in the digital realm. Moscow criticizes American supremacy in Internet management: The servers of the cloud and major domains (.com, .org, etc.) are based in the United States, and the large U.S. technology companies are accused of sharing information about their users at the behest of Washington. The Snowden and WikiLeaks cases, multiple revelations of illegal eavesdropping conducted by U.S. government bodies such as the National Security Agency, and, more recently, the end of net neutrality have strengthened Russian suspicions that Washington uses the Internet as a weapon to protect U.S. strategic and economic interests. Obviously, the Russian authorities are not themselves without ulterior motives. Like China, though to a lesser extent, Moscow wants to take control over its "national segment" of the Internet in order to protect itself from possible coercive measures, as well as better fight against internal opposition, as evidenced by new laws governing the Internet and social media accounts.[21] This dual strategy of both criticizing the West's stranglehold on globalized instruments and simultaneously building for itself the same autonomous instruments is in evidence in multiple sectors. One example is the decision that all Russian state institutions will stop using

Western software in favor of Russian alternatives, a response to the U.S. decision to forbid the use of Kaspersky antivirus software in U.S. federal institutions.

While it has not yet regained its status as a first-tier power, Russia has again become attractive, but being an economic or military force is not enough for a country to be seen as a role model. Yes, Putin has succeeded in putting Russia firmly back on the world stage. Nonetheless, to quote an observation made by Fyodor Lukyanov, editor-in-chief of the journal *Russia in Global Affairs*, Russia's soft power is "too soft":

> Nearly all discussions about Russia's soft power lead to the conclusion that if a country wants to gain influence in the world, it must have an attractive model to offer other countries. Unlike the Soviet Union, which offered an alternative social model and potentially powerful patronage, Russia lacks an ideological foundation on which to develop a concept that appeals to other countries. It has exhausted the Soviet model and is groping for a replacement, but has so far formulated only traditional ideas based on conservative values, which are by definition incapable of spurring progress.[22]

Yet the world is changing, as seen with the last wave of elections in Europe and the United States. Reacting to the effects of globalization they judge negative, the feeling of losing identity and sovereignty, and declining standards of living, a growing proportion of the electorate supports political parties that call for a return to traditional values—family, religion, and national identity—and the reaffirmation of state sovereignty in terms often isolationist. In this new global configuration embodied by the election of Donald Trump in November 2016, and with many illiberal leaders on the rise, especially in Central Europe, Putin's personality and "brand" may be more attractive than many observers would have imagined a few years ago.

In Europe, the feeling of deadlock over the Syrian crisis, as well as the difficulties of the refugee crisis, has been a strong push factor impelling some mainstream European politicians to call for a reconciliation with Russia, seen as an ally in managing the Middle East. At the 2016 NATO summit, for instance, French president François Hollande stated that "NATO has no right at all to say what Europe's relations with Russia should be" and "For France, Russia is not an adversary, not a threat."[23] New waves of tensions between the West and Russia over the Syrian war theater have since then reactivated tensions. Yet the prospect of progressive U.S. withdrawal from European affairs and the rise of calls, by European leaders such as Emmanuel Macron and Angela Merkel, for the launch of a genuine European defense, as well as new government coalitions with the pro-Russian far right in Austria and Italy, could therefore contribute to reshaping the debate over Russia's role and place in Europe.

Conclusion

Since the annexation of Crimea and the West's imposition of sanctions, it has often been said that Russia is isolated, and its leadership caught in a strategic deadlock. A more realist analysis, however, demonstrates that this is a Western-centric perception. Putin's "conservative values" trademark has been a real success in foreign policy, allowing Russia to find common ground with many non-Western countries and gain soft power among some segments of the European public opinion. The blending of conservative values with distrust of international institutions, the liberal world order, and what is seen as U.S. supremacy seems destined to shape part of the international scene for decades to come. Russia can therefore hope to cultivate influence and recognition by criticizing the liberal West but sympathizing with the conservative West, and by strengthening its global outreach, especially in the Middle East and Asia.

Consideration of Russia's desire to emerge as an alternative power to the current world order still raises several questions. The main one is whether Russia has the capacity to fulfill its ambitions. It seems obvious that without the common will of the BRICS—and especially a partnership with China—Russia cannot credibly seek to modify the international order. Its economic and financial strength is minimal: The country represents less than 2 percent of world GDP and lacks dominance in any innovative sectors. Moreover, even with modest growth projected for 2018 and the rise of oil prices, Russia's economy is unlikely to develop and transform dramatically in the coming decades. The emergence of an alternative economic and financial order could only come from China or from a coalition of emerging countries in which Russia will look like an aging economy based on raw materials exports. It risks being confined to junior status behind Beijing, which will cause knock-on security concerns for Moscow in the coming decades.

Russia has poor prospects as a transformative great power able to modify the structures of the world order. Yet nor are its power prospects somber—it demonstrates authority in at least three realms. First, Russia has the ability to hold its place on the international scene as a status quo power: It still has its veto at the UN Security Council and a revamped nuclear arsenal that remains the only one capable of causing irreversible damage to the United States. It masters cyber technologies that can cause easily, and for quite a cheap price, harm to countries that are victims of it. It also displays strategic initiative that defies Western expectations, as we have seen in Ukraine and Syria. Second, Russia will remain the major power in the Eurasian space. Obviously, this space is progressively losing its geopolitical unity and the resistance of neighboring countries to the overseeing rights Moscow claims will only increase with the passage of time—even among traditionally friendly partners such as Belarus and Kazakhstan. Russia's status in the region will therefore be reasserted both by hard and soft power means, but it will not disappear any time soon, regardless of what many predicted in the 1990s at the time of Russia's greatest weakness.

Last but not least, Russia will remain a key power for Europe. Whether as partner or opponent—or, most likely, a combination of the two—Moscow will continue to make its mark on the many internal and external challenges facing the continent. Hence, it is critical for Moscow to cultivate its new European allies, especially in Central Europe, and consolidate its soft power logic. Its allies are to be found, for the moment, mostly on the far right and the far left of the political landscape, but Russia also has support in mainstream business circles and more centrist conservative groupings who are able to shape genuine pro-Russian stances in Europe.

The balancing act between becoming a second-rate, regional power allied to "Western interests" or the junior partner of younger emerging powers, with China at the helm, will require major changes to the vision Russians have of their place in the world. But Russia will not evolve independent of the global context. The permanence (or not) of its current ideological quest, its hesitation between isolationism and integration, between fortress and new crusade, will largely be shaped by parallel developments in other major international players, especially Western countries. For years, the United States has struggled to define Russia, going from Obama's misjudgment of it as nothing more than a "regional power" to the ongoing hysteria that sees Russia as the United States' main geopolitical foe with the power to interfere in domestic politics. The two countries currently mirror one another's assessments of a supposed threat. As stated by Mathieu Boulegue, "The Atlantic Alliance and the Kremlin are today locked in a self-reinforcing vicious circle of mutually biased perceptions of each other, conflicting narratives, and opposed world visions that have hampered any constructive dialogue."[1]

This negative spiral serves vested interests on both sides—from the two military-industrial complexes to security measures to restrain public freedoms in Russia and continuation of sanctions on the U.S. side, some of which (like the ones passed by the U.S. Congress in July 2017 and April 2018) clearly seek to promote U.S. businesses to the detriment of European and Russian companies. This spiral is a dangerous one, as it accentuates mistrust and therefore delegitimizes established channels of communication that work as a safety net in the case of major crisis—the Ukrainian or Syrian ones, but also a potential nuclear one.

Few countries in the world have experienced as many societal changes as Russia has in the last thirty years. Its borders, political system, economy, worldview, and cultural values have been brutally transformed. And yet the West misread the impact that the collapse of the Soviet Union had had on itself: If Russia is struggling to accept its status of a diminished great power, the United States, too, is in many ways grappling to recognize that it cannot impose its vision and values on the rest of the world and can itself become a "victim" of some globalization patterns. Because both countries were accustomed to deciding Europe's future during the Cold War decades, they find themselves indirect hostages of Europe's current identity crisis. Europe's future in terms of its own collective defense, its internal construction in the face of growing resentment from some segments of the population and illiberal tendencies among the Visegrad countries, and its relationship to its Eastern neighborhood, as well as to Turkey, will not be decided by Washington and Moscow but by Europeans themselves. Bilateral discussions between the White House and the Kremlin will not come up with solutions on the ground for Europe and its neighborhood.

Brexit and Catalonia are good example of the "reopening" of European history, confirming, if such confirmation were necessary, that Fukuyama's "end of history" does not apply even to well-established democracies. In this history-in-the-making, Russia can still see its place and role shifting. Obviously, some elements of this framework will remain quite decisive: both Europe and Russia will for instance have to find a way to negotiate their mutual influences in their shared neighborhood. But contrary to Western pundits' statements, the current tensions and contradictions can still evolve, disappear, and be modified; Russia's future is not written in stone.

Domestically, Russia's future likewise remains quite open. The authorities have succeeded in formalizing the political stability and predictability that Russian society had been demanding since the early 1990s. Yet this quest for stability and consensus is also acting as a weight, slowing down the changes needed to help the country face its own challenges and fears. Indeed, there is no doubt that Russians are going to continue to face major trials in the coming decades. Economic reforms will arrive at some point, whether instigated and guided by the state or going against it. In October 2016, the Ministry of Economic Development admitted that living standards are unlikely to improve until 2035,[2] and that the Russian federal budget will remain strained for years.

Paradoxically, Russia's demographic decline would not be such bad news for a retracting economy, but it would mean investing massively in human capital to maintain a highly skilled workforce, something that does not appear to be happening thus far. Migration, for its part, primarily provides the country with a low-skilled workforce. Spatial reconfigurations within the Federation itself, with dying regions in the East and North contrasting with booming regions in the West and South, will also transform Russian citizens' perceptions of their relationship to Europe. The annexation of Crimea contributed to refocusing Russia toward its Southwest and anchoring it more in the Black Sea region—and, by extension, in the Mediterranean realm. The "Eurasian" vector of Russia toward Asia therefore appears to be a fragile one, while many demographic, economic, and geopolitical structural factors are in fact pushing Russia toward Europe and the Eastern Mediterranean world.

What will be the role played by the political regime in the changes affecting Russia as a state and a nation? How much room for maneuver does the Kremlin have to cope with these structural challenges? It is problematic to answer such a question, since the longevity of the Putin regime has obscured our perceptions of alternate futures for the country. What would they look like? Can Russia reinvent itself with a more democratic regime without reproducing the mistakes of the 1990s and incurring new massive societal traumas? Can the country promote a genuine decentralized federalism without risking secessionism? Even if the political field reopens to a greater diversity of opinions, the desire to promote a "Russian voice" in the world, whatever its content, and to display global outreach, will remain. Many elements of the contemporary ideological toolkit—messianism, conservative values, Russia as an autonomous civilization—could be easily adapted to other political contexts, including more liberal ones. Many political figures currently in opposition, such as Alexei Navalny, might promote a stricter form of Russian nationalism if they came to power. The country could become more liberal economically without being liberal politically. Equally, Russia could become more politically liberal without advancing a pro-Western agenda.

With Putin's successful re-election in March 2018, Russia has entered a new phase of its history—that of preparing for a post-Putin era whose challenge will be to keep abrupt upheaval from happening while dealing with declining legitimacy and a public that is increasingly apathetic toward the regime. The window of time to prepare for change is a maximum of six years—the duration of the presidential term—and probably less if Putin wants to appoint a successor while he holds the reins of power. What is sure is that the successor will be directed to continue the effort undertaken since the second half of the 1990s to consolidate Russia both domestically and on the international scene. Both the society and the regime have demonstrated an incredible level of adaptability and flexibility during the last thirty years. They will need to continue being resourceful to reinvent Russia in the forthcoming decades.

Notes

INTRODUCTION

We are grateful to the reviewers of the French and English versions for their comments, and to Dylan Royce and Ellen Powell for their careful and informed reading and editing of the English version.

1. Philipp Rucker, "Hillary Clinton Says Putin's Actions Are Like 'What Hitler Did Back in the '30s,'" *Washington Post*, March 5, 2014, https://www.washingtonpost.com/news/post-politics/wp/2014/03/05/hillary-clinton-says-putins-action-are-like-what-hitler-did-back-in-the-30s/.

2. Stendhal, letter to Félix Faure, August 24, 1812.

3. Tom Paterson, "Ukraine Crisis: Angry Angela Merkel Questions Whether Putin Is 'In Touch with Reality,'" *Telegraph*, March 3, 2014, http://www.telegraph.co.uk/news/worldnews/europe/ukraine/10673235/Ukraine-crisis-Angry-Angela-Merkel-questions-whether-Putin-is-in-touch-with-reality.html.

CHAPTER 1. TERRITORIAL FATIGUE: NEW STATE, NEW BORDERS

1. Meaning Saint Peter, first bishop of Rome.

2. Including Crimea, the Russian territory amounts to 17,125,407 square kilometers (6,612,157 square miles).

3. Julia Breen, "Russophobie: Un préjugé à la peau dure," *Le Courrier de Russie*, February 11, 2014, https://www.lecourrierderussie.com/societe/gens/2014/02/russophobie-prejuge-dure/.

4. Including in the statistical tables of foreign trade, in which, for several years, the data for CIS states were given in rubles, whereas data for the "far abroad" foreign states were denominated in dollars.

5. See, for example, his letter of January 27, 1992, to the new UN secretary general, Boutros Boutros-Ghali (http://lawru.info/base29/part3/d29ru3539.htm), and his address to the Security Council, on January 31, 1992 (www.unmultimedia.org/radio/russian/archives/60837/).

6. Cited by Marie Mendras in "Russie: le débat sur l'intérêt national," *Problèmes économiques et sociaux*, no. 694 (Paris: La Documentation française, December 1992), 19.

7. Alexander Cooley, "Scripts of Sovereignty: The Freezing of the Russia-Ukraine Crisis and Dilemmas of Governance in Eurasia," Center on Global Interests, Washington, D.C., January 30, 2015.

8. Moldova no longer had access to the Black Sea after Stalin transferred the south of Bessarabia to the Ukraine. In the end, only after an exchange of territory with Kiev did Moldova manage to escape its landlocked status, obtaining a kilometer of shoreline along the Danube and the possibility of opening an international port there.

9. See more in Jeanne Wilson, *Strategic Partners: Russian-Chinese Relations in the Post-Soviet Era* (Armonk, NY: M. E. Sharpe, 2004).

10. Tore Henriksen and Geir Ulfstein, "Maritime Delimitation in the Arctic: The Barents Sea Treaty," *Ocean Development & International Law* 42, no. 1–2 (February 2011): 1–21.

11. Ilias Bantekas, "Bilateral Delimitation of the Caspian Sea and the Exclusion of Third Parties," *International Journal of Marine & Coastal Law* 26, no. 1 (2011): 47–58.

12. Lauri Mälksoo, "Which Continuity? The Tartu Peace Treaty of 2 February 1920, the Estonian-Russian Border Treaties of 2005, and the Legal Debate about Estonia's Status in International Law," *Archiv des Völkerrechts* 43, no. 4 (December 2005): 513–524.

13. Cory Welt, "The Thawing of a Frozen Conflict: The Internal Security Dilemma and the 2004 Prelude to the Russo-Georgian War," *Europe-Asia Studies* 62, no. 1 (2010): 63–97.

14. Mikulas Fabry, "The Contemporary Practice of State Recognition: Kosovo, South Ossetia, Abkhazia, and Their Aftermath," *Nationalities Papers: Journal of Nationalism & Ethnicity* 40, no. 5 (2012): 661–676.

15. Ishaan Tharoor, "Why Putin Says Crimea Is Russia's 'Temple Mount,'" *Washington Post*, December 4, 2014, https://www.washingtonpost.com/news/worldviews/wp/2014/12/04/why-putin-says-crimea-is-russias-temple-mount/.

16. Eva-Maria Stolberg, "The Siberian Frontier between 'White Mission' and 'Yellow Peril,' 1890s–1920s," *Nationalities Papers: Journal of Nationalism & Ethnicity* 32, no. 1 (March 2004): 165–181.

17. Tatiana Nefedova, "Szhatie i poliarizatsiia sel'skogo prostranstva Rossii," *Demoscop*, no. 507–508 (April 16, 2012).

18. *Rossiiskii statisticheskii ezhegodnik–2015* (Moscow: Rosstat, 2015), 399, www.gks.ru/free_doc/doc_2015/year/year15.rar; *Rossiia v tsifrakh–2016* (Moscow: Rosstat, 2016), 282, http://www.gks.ru/free_doc/doc_2016/rusfig/rus16.pdf.

19. Vladimir Kaganskii, *Kul'turnyi landshaft i sovetskoe obytaemoe prostranstvo: sbornik statei* (Moscow: NLO, 2001), 304.

20. Jean Radvanyi, "Quand Vladimir Poutine se fait géographe," in *Géopolitique de la Russie, Hérodote* 166–167 (2017): 113–132.

21. This count of eighty-five federal subjects includes the Republic of Crimea and the Federal City of Sevastopol, whose annexation in March 2014 is not recognized by the international community. As of 2017 there were, in all, forty-six oblasts (regions), one autonomous oblast, nine krais (territories), twenty-two republics, four autonomous okrugs (districts), of which three are simultaneously components of oblasts, and three federal cities (Moscow, St. Petersburg, and Sevastopol).

22. See Vladimir Kolosov and Olga Vendina, eds., *Rossiisko-ukrainskoe pogranich'e. Dvadtsat' let razdelennogo edinstva* (Moscow: Novyi Khronograf, 2011).

23. Nikolay Yadrintsev, *Sibir' kak koloniia: sovremennoe polozhenie Sibiri, eia nuzhdy i potrebnosti, eia proshloe i budushchee* (St. Petersburg: Izd. M. Stasyulevicha, 1882).

24. Ministry of Regional Policy (1998–1999); Ministry of Federation and Nationalities Affairs (1999–2000); Ministry of Federation Affairs and National and Migration Policy (2000–2001); Ministry of Regional Development (2004–2014).

25. See their website: http://www.minkavkaz.gov.ru/ for the North Caucasus, https://minvr.ru/ for the Far East, and the Arctic Governmental Commission, https://arctic.gov.ru/.

26. *Tatar-inform*, October 10, 2001.

27. See "Tatarstan gotov pogovorit' o dogovore," *Kommersant*, August 4, 2017, https://www.kommersant.ru/doc/3374350 or "Rustam Minnikhanov otkazalsia ot dogovora s Rossiei," *Kommersant*, September 22, 2017, https://www.kommersant.ru/doc/3417048.

CHAPTER 2. A TROUBLED IDENTITY: DIVERSITY, DECLINE, AND MIGRATION

1. Oxana Shevel, "Russian Nation-Building from Yeltsin to Medvedev: Ethnic, Civic, or Purposefully Ambiguous?" *Europe-Asia Studies* 63, no. 1 (2011): 179–202.

2. See Riva Kastoryano, ed., *Les codes de la différence. Race, origine, religion. France, Allemagne, États-Unis* (Paris: Presses de Sciences Po, 2005).

3. See Ronald Grigor Suny and Terry Martin, eds., *A State of Nations: Empire and Nation-Making in the Age of Lenin and Stalin* (New York: Oxford University Press, 2001).

4. Lukasz Jurczyszyn, "Russian Radical Nationalist Interpretation of the French Riots of November 2005," *Demokratizatsiya: Journal of Post-Soviet Democratization* 19, no. 3 (Summer 2011): 277–285.

5. See Dmitry Gorenburg, *Minority Ethnic Mobilization in the Russian Federation* (New York: Cambridge University Press, 2003).

6. The Soviet identity card (internal passport, or *vnutrennyi passport*) registered the ethnic origin (*natsionalnost'*) of each individual.

7. Valerii Tishkov, *Rossiiskii narod. Istoriia i smysl natsional'nogo samosoznaniia* (Moscow: Nauka, 2013).

8. All Russian censuses are available from *Demoskop Weekly*, published by the Higher School of Economics, www.demoscope.ru.

9. Yitzhak M. Brudny, *Reinventing Russia: Russian Nationalism and the Soviet State, 1953–1991* (Cambridge, MA: Harvard University Press, 2000); Nikolai Mitrokhin, *"Russkaia partiia": dvizhenie russkikh natsionalistov v SSSR 1953–1985 gg.* (Moscow: NLO, 2003).

10. Oxana Shevel, "The Politics of Citizenship Policy in Post-Soviet Russia," *Post-Soviet Affairs* 28, no. 1 (2012): 111–147.

11. Marlene Laruelle, "Russia as a 'Divided Nation,' from Compatriots to Crimea: A Contribution to the Discussion on Nationalism and Foreign Policy," *Problems of Post-Communism* 62, no. 2 (2015): 88–97.

12. Olga A. Avdeyeva, "Policy Experiment in Russia: Cash-for-Babies and Fertility Change," *Social Politics: International Studies in Gender, State & Society* 18, no. 3 (2011): 361–386.

13. The 2010 census is available at "2010 Vserossiiskaia perepis' naseleniia," *Demoscope Weekly*, http://demoscope.ru/weekly/2011/0491/perep01.php.

14. Michel Guillot, Natalia Gavrilova, and Tetyana Pudrovska, "Understanding the 'Russian Mortality Paradox' in Central Asia: Evidence from Kyrgyzstan," *Demography* 48, no. 3 (August 2011): 1081–1104.

15. See "2010 Vserossiiskaia perepis' naseleniia."

16. More in Nicholas Eberstadt, *Russia's Peacetime Demographic Crisis: Dimensions, Causes, Implications* (Seattle, WA: National Bureau of Asian Research, 2010).

17. "Strategy Report 2015," US Bureau for International Narcotics and Law Enforcement Affairs, International Narcotics Control, 279, www.state.gov/documents/organiza tion/239560.pdf.

18. "Russia's AIDS Epidemic Reaches Crisis Levels," *Vice News*, January 22, 2016, https://news.vice.com/article/russias-aids-epidemic-reaches-crisis-levels.

19. Jean Radvanyi, "Quelques réponses à une question non posée: l'islam et le recensement de la population de Russie en 2002," in *Islam et politique en ex-URSS,* ed. Marlene Laruelle and Sébastien Peyrouse (Paris: L'Harmattan, 2005), 159–169.

20. See the different UN scenarios at United Nations Population Division, "Replacement Migration," http://www.un.org/esa/population/publications/ReplMigED/RusFed.pdf.

21. "Migration Profile: Russia," Migration Policy Centre, Robert Schuman Centre for Advanced Studies, European University Institute, June 2013, www.migrationpolicycentre.eu/docs/migration_profiles/Russia.pdf.

22. Ankit Panda, "Russian Emigration Spikes in 2013–2014," *The Diplomat,* July 25, 2014, http://thediplomat.com/2014/07/russian-emigration-spikes-in-2013-2014/. See also *Rossiia v tsifrakh* (Moscow: Rosstat, 2017), 78.

23. Anne de Tinguy, *La grande migration* (Paris: Plon, 2004).

24. Sébastien Peyrouse, "Former 'Colonists' on the Move? The Migration of Russian-Speaking Populations," in *Migration and Social Upheaval as the Face of Globalization in Central Asia,* ed. Marlene Laruelle (London: Brill, 2013), 215–238; and Julien Thorez, "*Khorosho, gde nas net.* L'émigration des 'Russophones' d'Asie centrale," *EchoGéo,* no. 9 (2009): 1–25.

25. More in Marlene Laruelle, ed., *Migration and Social Upheaval as the Face of Globalization in Central Asia* (London: Brill, 2013).

26. See, for example, Zhanna Zaionchkovskaya, ed., *Migranty v Moskve* (Moscow: Tri kvadrata, 2009).

27. Genesee Keevil, "Tajikistan: Migrant Laborers Dying to Work in Russia," *EurasiaNet,* February 26, 2013, www.eurasianet.org/node/66602.

28. Galina G. Karpova and Maria A. Vorona, "Labour Migration in Russia: Issues and Policies," *International Social Work* 57, no. 5 (September 2014): 535–546.

29. Madeleine Reeves, "Clean Fake: Authenticating Documents and Persons in Migrant Moscow," *American Ethnologist* 40, no. 3 (2013): 508–524.

30. Esther Tetruashvily, "How Did We Become Illegal? Impacts of Post-Soviet Shifting Migration Politics on Labor Migration Law in Russia," *Region* 1, no. 1 (January 2012): 53–74.

31. Caress Schenk, "Controlling Immigration Manually: Lessons from Moscow (Russia)," *Europe-Asia Studies* 65, no. 7 (2013): 1444–1465.

32. Umida Hashimova, "What 2015 Is Promising for Labor Migrants from Central Asia," *Central Asia Policy Brief,* no. 23 (March 2015), http://centralasiaprogram.org/archives/7380.

33. Eberstadt, *Russia's Peacetime Demographic Crisis,* 163.

34. "Levada-Tsentr o natsionalizme i ksenofobii," SOVA-Center, September 1, 2015, http://www.sova-center.ru/racism-xenophobia/discussions/2015/09/d32693/. See also Natalia

Yudina and Vera Al'perovich, *Starye problemy i novye soiuzy. Ksenofobiia i radikal'nyi natsionalizm i protivodeistvie im v 2016 godu v Rossii* (Moscow: SOVA-Center, 2017), http://www.sova-center.ru/racism-xenophobia/publications/2017/03/d36630/.

35. "Mozhet, ikh prosto otgorodit'," *Kommersant Vlast'*, September 21, 1999, http://www.kommersant.ru/doc/15937.

36. For more details, see Marlene Laruelle, *In the Name of the Nation: Nationalism and Politics in Contemporary Russia* (New York: Palgrave Macmillan, 2009), 35–47.

37. Caress Schenk, "Open Borders, Closed Minds: Russia's Changing Migration Policies: Liberalization or Xenophobia?" *Demokratizatsiya: Journal of Post-Soviet Democratization* 18, no. 2 (April 2010): 101–121.

38. Theodore Gerber, "Beyond Putin? Nationalism and Xenophobia in Russian Public Opinion," *Washington Quarterly* 37, no. 3 (2014): 113–134.

39. Edward Holland and Eldar Eldarov, "'Going Away on Foot' Once Again: The Revival of Temporary Labour Migration from Russia's Dagestan," *Central Asian Survey* 31, no. 4 (2012): 379–393.

40. Marlene Laruelle and Natalia Yudina, "Islamophobia in Russia: Trends and Societal Context," in *Religious Violence in Russia*, ed. Olga Oliker and Jeffrey Mankoff (Washington, DC: CSIS, 2018).

41. Hilary Pilkington, Elena Omel'chenko, and Al'bina Garifzianova, *Russia's Skinheads: Exploring and Rethinking Subcultural Lives* (London: Routledge, 2010).

42. See the annual reports by the Moscow-based SOVA-Center, sova-center.ru.

43. On radical violence, see Richard Arnold, "Visions of Hate: Explaining Neo-Nazi Violence in the Russian Federation," *Problems of Post-Communism* 57, no. 2 (2010): 37–59.

44. See Marlene Laruelle, "Alexei Navalny and Challenges in Reconciling 'Nationalism' and 'Liberalism,'" *Post-Soviet Affairs* 30, no. 4 (2014): 276–297; and Pål Kolstø, "Russia's Nationalists Flirt with Democracy," *Journal of Democracy 25, no. 3* (2014): 120–134.

CHAPTER 3. SOCIETY: FRAGMENTED BUT REINVENTED

1. *Obshchestvennoe mnenie – 2014* (Moscow: Levada Center, 2015), 15, http://www.levada.ru/sites/default/files/om14.pdf.

2. *Obshchestvennoe mnenie – 2014*, 14.

3. *Obshchestvennoe mnenie – 2013* (Moscow: Levada Center, 2014), 17, http://www.levada.ru/sites/default/files/om13.pdf; *Obshchestvennoe mnenie – 2014*, 18.

4. *Obshchestvennoe mnenie – 2014*, 22.

5. Il'nur Aminov, "Smertnost' ot samoubiistv v Rossii i v mire," *Demoskop Weekly*, 705–706 (November 14–27, 2016), http://demoscope.ru/weekly/2016/0705/tema03.php.

6. *Rossiia v tsifrakh – 2016* (Moscow: Rosstat, 2016), 129, http://www.gks.ru/free_doc/doc_2016/rusfig/rus16.pdf.

7. *Rossiia v tsifrakh – 2016*, 26.

8. *Rossiiskii statisticheskii ezhegodnik – 2015* (Moscow: Rosstat, 2015), 158, www.gks.ru/free_doc/doc_2015/year/y ear15.rar.

9. "Number of Russians in Poverty Hits Decade-High," RFE/RL, April 6, 2017, https://www.rferl.org/a/recession-sanctions-left-20-million-russians-living-poverty-2016-up-300000-2015/28413387.html.

10. The dollar is considered equivalent to 21.279 rubles, in accordance with "Purchasing power parities (PPP)," OECD, https://data.oecd.org/conversion/purchasing-power-parities-ppp.htm.

11. *Rossiiskii statisticheskii ezhegodnik – 2015*, 146.

12. "200 bogateishikh biznesmenov Rossii," *Forbes*, www.forbes.ru/rating/200-bogatei shikh-biznesmenov-rossii-2014/2014.

13. *Obshchestvennoe mnenie – 2013*, 25.

14. *Rossiiskii statisticheskii ezhegodnik – 2015*, 254.

15. More in Eberstadt, *Russia's Peacetime Demographic Crisis*.

16. "Staff Shortages Cripple Russian Business," *Russia Today*, April 9, 2008, http://rt.com/business/news/staff-shortages-cripple-russian-business/.

17. Marlene Laruelle and Sophie Hohmann, "Biography of a Polar City: Population Flows and Urban Identity in Norilsk," *Polar Geography* 40, no. 4 (2017): 306–323.

18. Robert Ferris, "Putin's Other Problem: Russia's Brain Drain," *CNBC*, December 17, 2014, http://www.cnbc.com/2014/12/17/putins-other-problem-russias-brain-drain.html.

19. Alexander Chyernich and Lolita Grusdeva, "Russia Looking to Reverse Brain Drain of Young Scientists," *Time*, November 18, 2011, http://content.time.com/time/world/article/0,8599,2099861,00.html.

20. *Sotsial'nyi atlas rossiiskikh regionov* (Moscow: Nezavisimyi institut sotsial'noi politiki, 2017), http://www.socpol.ru/atlas/overviews/social_sphere/kris.shtml.

21. John Witte and Michael Bourdeaux, *Proselytism and Orthodoxy in Russia: The New War for Souls* (Ossining, NY: Orbis Books, 1999).

22. Olga Filina, "Mapping Russia's Religious Landscape," *Russia & India Report*, September 1, 2012, https://www.rbth.com/articles/2012/08/30/mapping_russias_religious_landscape_17819.html.

23. See *Atlas religii i natsional'snostei Rossii*, 2012, http://sreda.org/arena/maps.

24. Whereas Jews numbered 537,000 in 1989, the 2010 census registered only 156,000 of them.

25. *Obshchestvennoe mnenie – 2013*, 168.

26. "Rossiiane o SMI," Levada Center, February 28, 2014, http://www.levada.ru/2014/02/28/rossiyane-o-smi/.

27. *Obshchestvennoe mnenie – 2013*, 170.

28. See the Levada survey question, "According to you, what will be the state policy toward television in the near future?," "Rossiiane o SMI," http://www.levada.ru/2014/02/28/rossiyane-o-smi.

29. "Russian Orthodox Church Seeks to Heal Centuries-Old Schism," *Orthodox Christian Laity*, December 25, 2013, http://ocl.org/russian-orthodox-church-seeks-to-heal-centuries-old-schism/.

30. Koozma J. Tarasoff, "More Doukhobors Moving from Georgia to Russia," April 1, 1999, http://doukhoborology.tripod.com/gdoukh.html.

31. Oleg Kavykin, *"Rodnovery": Samoidentifikatsiia neo-iazychnikov v sovremennoi Rossii* (Moscow: Institut Afriki RAN, 2007). See also Kaarina Aitamurto, "Reviving the Native Faith: Nationalism in Contemporary Slavic Paganism Rodnoverie," *Forum für osteuropäische Ideen- und Zeitgeschichte* 1, no. 2 (2011): 167–184.

32. Victor Shnirel'man, "Arkaim: arkheologiia, ezotericheskii turizm i natsional'naia ideia," *Antropologicheskii forum*, no. 114 (2014): 134–167.

33. *Obshchestvennoe mnenie – 2013*, 52.

34. *Obshchestvennoe mnenie – 2014*, 36.

35. "News conference of Vladimir Putin," *Johnson's Russia List*, December 19, 2013, http://russialist.org/transcript-continued-news-conference-of-vladimir-putin/.

CHAPTER 4. THE POLITICAL SYSTEM: A QUEST FOR CONSENSUS

1. Alexei Yurchak, *Everything Was Forever, Until It Was No More: The Last Soviet Generation* (Princeton, NJ: Princeton University Press, 2005).

2. Ilya Yablokov, *Fortress Russia: Conspiracy Theories in the Post-Soviet World* (New York: Polity Press, 2018).

3. Françoise Daucé, *La Russie postsoviétique* (Paris: La Découverte, 2008), 25–29.

4. See Dmitry Gorenburg, "Regional Separatism in Russia: Ethnic Mobilization or Power Grab?" *Europe-Asia Studies* 51, no. 2 (1999): 245–274; Gorenburg, *Minority Ethnic Mobilization*; Elise Giuliano, *Constructing Grievance: Ethnic Nationalism in Russia's Republics* (Ithaca, NY: Cornell University Press, 2011).

5. Jean Radvanyi, *La Russie face à ses régions: Problèmes politiques et sociaux* (Paris: La Documentation française, December 1994).

6. Nina Tumarkin, *The Living and the Dead: The Rise and Fall of the Cult of World War II in Russia* (New York: Perseus Books, 1994).

7. "Yeltsin o natsional'noi idee," *Nezavisimaia gazeta*, July 13, 1996.

8. More in Laruelle, *In the Name of the Nation*, 122–124.

9. Richat Sabitov, *Le fédéralisme russe contemporain et la République du Tatarstan* (Paris: Fondation Varenne, 2013). See also Gulnaz Sharafutdinova, "Paradiplomacy in the Russian Regions: Tatarstan's Search for Statehood," *Europe-Asia Studies* 55, no. 4 (2003): 613–629.

10. Anatol Lieven, *Chechnya: Tombstone of Russian Power* (New Haven, CT: Yale University Press, 1999).

11. Lev D. Gudkov, "Ethnic Phobias in the Structure of National Identification," *Russian Social Science Review* 39, no. 1 (1998): 89–103.

12. Mikhail Gorshkov, ed., *Mass Consciousness of the Russians during the Period of Social Transformations: Realities versus Myths* (Moscow: Russian Independent Institute of Social and Nationalities Problems, 1996), cited in Fiona Hill, "In Search of Great Russia: Elites, Ideas, Power, the State, and the Pre-Revolutionary Past in the New Russia, 1991–1996" (PhD diss., Harvard University, 1998).

13. See more in Hill, "In Search of Great Russia."

14. "Gosudarstvennaia programma 'Patrioticheskoe vospitanie grazhdan Rossiiskoi Federatsii na 2001–2005 gg.,'" Gosudarstvennaia sistema pravovoi informatsii, http://pravo.gov.ru/ipsdata/?doc_itself=&collection=1&backlink=1&nd=201006229&page=1&rdk=0#I0.

15. Alexander Agadjanian, "Religious Pluralism and National Identity in *Russia*," *International Journal on Multicultural Societies* 2, no. 2 (2000): 97–124.

16. On the role of the Federation Council, see Nikolai Petrov and Darrell Slider, "Putin and the Regions," in *Putin's Russia: Past Imperfect, Future Uncertain,* 2nd ed., ed. Dale Herspring (Lanham, MD: Rowman & Littlefield, 2005), 75–98; Anne Gazier, "La mise au pas des régions russes? La réforme institutionnelle de Vladimir Poutine," *Le Courrier des pays de l'Est*, no. 1015 (2001): 4–14; Jean-Robert Raviot, "Les rapports centre-région en Russie: Rééquilibrage et continuité," *Le Courrier des pays de l'Est*, no. 1033 (2003): 4–15; Thomas

F. Remington, "Majorities without Mandates: The Russian Federation Council since 2000," *Europe-Asia Studies* 55, no. 5 (2003): 667–691.

17. Beat Kernen, "Putin and the Parliamentary Election in Russia: The Confluence (Slijanie) of Russian Political Culture and Leadership," *East European Quarterly* 38, no. 1 (2004): 85–107.

18. "Vladimir Putin's Big Government and the 'Politburo 2.0,'" Minchenko Consulting, http://minchenko.ru/netcat_files/File/Big Government and the Politburo 2_0.pdf; see also Ievgenii Minchenko, "Sistemnye riski komandy Putina," *Nezavisimaia gazeta*, December 2, 2014, http://www.ng.ru/ng_politics/2014-12-02/9_risks.html.

19. "Ikh dom—Rossiia," in "Korporatsiia Rossiia: Putin s druz'iami podelili stranu," *Novoe vremia*, October 31, 2011, https://newtimes.ru/articles/detail/45648/.

20. Vladimir Pribylovskii, *Kooperativ Ozero i drugie proekty Putina* (Moscow: Algoritm, 2012).

21. On the situation of the children and spouses of the Russian political elite, see Aleksandr Limanov, "Vsio luchshee–detiam," *Novoe vremia*, no. 21 (206), June 18, 2011, http://newtimes.ru/stati/others/a5a575e9ae2376c2d343aa7057ab45ec-vse-lychshee-%E2%80%94-detyam.html.

22. See Karen Dawisha, "Vladislav Surkov, 1964–," in *Russia's People of Empire: Life Stories from Eurasia, 1500 to the Present*, ed. Stephen Norris and Willard Sunderland (Bloomington: Indiana University Press, 2012), 339–349; and Richard Sakwa, "Surkov: Dark Prince of the Kremlin," *Open Democracy*, April 7, 2011, https://www.opendemocracy.net/od-russia/richard-sakwa/surkov-dark-prince-of-kremlin.

23. "Gosudarstvennaia programma 'Patrioticheskoe vospitanie grazhdan RF na 2006-2010 gody,'" Gosudarstvennaia sistema pravovoi informatsii, http://pravo.gov.ru/proxy/ips/?docbody=&nd=102098946&intelsearch=1233+03.11.1994.

24. See Stephen White, "Soviet Nostalgia and Russian Politics," *Journal of Eurasian Studies* 1, no. 1 (2010): 1–9; and Charles Sullivan, "Motherland: Soviet Nostalgia in Post-Soviet Russia" (PhD diss., George Washington University, 2014).

25. The Second World War is one of the major historical contexts of these patriotic television series, but so are the years of the Soviet "Golden Age," the Brezhnev decades. The Tsarist past is exalted by series that stage the great Russian novels of the nineteenth century or major figureheads such as Admiral Alexander Kolchak.

26. Lev Gudkov, "Pamiat' o voine i massovaia identichnost' rossiian," *Neprikosnovennyi zapas*, no. 40–41 (2005), http://magazines.russ.ru/nz/2005/2/gu5.html.

27. "President Restores Name 'Stalingrad' to Moscow War Memorial," *RFE/RL Newsline*, July 23, 2004, www.hri.org/cgi-bin/brief?/news/balkans/rferl/2004/04-07-23.rferl.html#11.

28. "Stalin Monument to Be Erected by V-Day," *RFE/RL Newsline*, April 1, 2005, www.hri.org/cgi-bin/brief?/news/balkans/rferl/2005/05-05-10.rferl.html#15.

29. Kathy Rousselet, "Butovo: La création d'un lieu de pèlerinage sur une terre de massacres," *Politix* 20, no. 77 (2007).

30. Richard Sakwa, "Putin's Leadership: Character and Consequences," *Europe-Asia Studies* 60, no. 6 (2008): 879–897.

31. Marlene Laruelle, "Inside and around the Kremlin's Black Box: The New Nationalist Think Tanks in Russia," *Stockholm Papers* (October 2009), http://isdp.eu/content/uploads/images/stories/isdp-main-pdf/2009_laruelle_inside-and-around-the-kremlins-black-box.pdf.

32. See, for instance, Igor Yurgens, ed., *Obretenie budushchego: Strategiia 2012* (Moscow: INSOR, 2011), http://www.insor-russia.ru/files/Finding_of_the_Future percent20.FULL_.pdf.

33. "Elektoral'nyi reiting politicheskikh partii," VTsIOM, https://wciom.ru/news/ratings/elektoralnyj_rejting_politicheskix_partij/.

34. "Osnovy religioznykh kul'tur i svetskoi etiki stali obyazatel'nym predmetom dlia chetveroklassnikov," *News.ru.com*, September 1, 2012, www.newsru.com/religy/01sep2012/osnovrelig.html.

35. See Samuel Greene, *Moscow in Movement: Power and Opposition in Putin's Russia* (Stanford, CA: Stanford University Press, 2014); and Graeme Robertson, "The Election Protests of 2011–2012 in Broader Perspective," *Problems of Post-Communism* 60, no. 2 (2013): 11–23.

36. Eva Bertrand, "Pouvoir, catastrophe et représentation: Mise(s) en scène politique(s) des incendies de l'été 2010 en Russie occidentale" (PhD diss., Sciences Po, Paris, 2016).

37. Alfred B. Evans, "Protests and Civil Society in Russia: The Struggle for the Khimki Forest," *Communist and Post-Communist Studies* 45, no. 3–4 (2012): 233–242.

38. See Pål Kolstø, "Marriage of Convenience? Collaboration between Nationalists and Liberals in the Russian Opposition 2011–12," *Russian Review* 75, no. 4 (2016): 645–663.

39. Marlene Laruelle, "Alexei Navalny and Challenges in Reconciling 'Nationalism' and 'Liberalism,'" *Post-Soviet Affairs* 30, no. 4 (2014): 276–297.

40. See Maria Lipman, "How Putin Silences Dissent," *Foreign Affairs*, April 18, 2016, https://www.foreignaffairs.com/articles/russia-fsu/2016-04-18/how-putin-silences-dissent.

41. Alexandra Kulikova, "What Is Really Going on with Russia's New Internet Laws?" *Open Democracy*, October 29, 2014, https://www.opendemocracy.net/od-russia/alexandra-kulikova/what-is-really-going-on-with-russia's-new-internet-laws.

42. Aleksandr Sukharenko, "Kart blansh. Vserossiiskii gorodovoi," *Nezavisimaia gazeta*, April 7, 2016, http://www.ng.ru/politics/2016-04-07/3_kartblansh.html.

43. The reform represented a challenge to the Ministry of Defense, which saw itself excluded from internal security and now managing only the defense of Russia against external enemies; it also weakened the FSB, the citadel of Putin's power. Alexander Bortnikov, director of the FSB, who also heads the National Anti-Terrorism Committee, had to cede some of his power to the National Guard. In addition, two flagship institutions of the 2000s, the Federal Migration Service (led by Konstantin Romodanovsky) and Viktor Ivanov's Federal Drug Control Service, lost their status as independent agencies and became branches of the Ministry of the Interior. See Pavel Baev, "Newly Formed National Guard Cannot Dispel Putin's Multiple Insecurities," *Eurasia Daily Monitor* 13, no. 70 (2016), https://jamestown.org/program/newly-formed-national-guard-cannot-dispel-putins-multiple-insecurities/; Anna Baidakova, "Gennadii Gudkov: 'Natsional'nuiu gvardiiu gotoviat k podavleniiu sotsialnogo protesta," *Novaia gazeta*, April 6, 2016, https://www.novayagazeta.ru/articles/2016/04/06/68105-gennadiy-gudkov-171-natsionalnuyu-gvardiyu-gotovyat-k-podavleniyu-sotsialnogo-protesta-187.

44. Gulnaz Sharafutdinova, "The Pussy Riot Affair and Putin's Demarche from Sovereign Democracy to Sovereign Morality," *Nationalities Papers: Journal of Nationalism & Ethnicity* 42, no. 4 (2014): 615–621.

45. On Russia's policy in the cultural realm, see the special issue of *Kontrapuntk/Counterpoint*, no. 4 (2016), http://www.counter-point.org/.

46. Julie Ray and Neli Esipova, "Russian Approval of Putin Soars to Highest Level in Years," *Gallup*, July 18, 2014, http://www.gallup.com/poll/173597/russian-approval-putin-soars-highest-level-years.aspx.

47. See, for instance, Alexandre Motyl, "Putin's Russia as a Fascist Political System," *Communist & Post-Communist Studies* 49, no. 1 (2016): 25–36.

48. Michel Eltchaninoff, *Dans la tête de Vladimir Poutine* (Paris: Actes Sud, 2015), 134.

49. See, for instance, Anton Barbashin and Hannah Thoburn, "Putin's Brain: Alexander Dugin and the Philosophy behind Putin's Invasion of Crimea," *Foreign Affairs*, March 31, 2014, http://www.foreignaffairs.com/articles/141080/anton-barbashin-and-hannah-thoburn/putins-brain.

50. More in Yablokov, *Fortress Russia.*

51. Peter Pomerantsev, *Nothing Is True and Everything Is Possible: The Surreal Heart of the New Russia* (New York: PublicAffairs, 2014).

52. On Putin's glamour, see Valerie Sperling, *Sex, Politics, and Putin: Political Legitimacy in Russia* (New York: Oxford University Press, 2014).

53. Laruelle, "Inside and around the Kremlin's Black Box."

54. See more in Marlene Laruelle, "The Izborsky Club, or the New Conservative Avant-Garde in Russia," *Russian Review* 75, no. 4 (2016): 622–644.

55. Marlene Laruelle, *The 'Russian World': Russia's Soft Power and Geopolitical Imagination* (Washington, DC: Center on Global Interests, May 2015).

56. See more in Marlene Laruelle, "The Three Colors of Novorossiya, or the Russian Nationalist Mythmaking of the Ukrainian Crisis," *Post-Soviet Affairs* 32, no. 1 (2015): 55–74.

57. Henry Hale and Marlene Laruelle, "Civilizational Discourse in Russia" (forthcoming).

58. More in Marlene Laruelle, "Russia as an Anti-Liberal European Civilization," in *The New Russian Nationalism: Between Imperial and Ethnic*, ed. Pål Kolstø and Helge Blakkisrud (Edinburgh: Edinburgh University Press, 2016), 275–297.

59. Timothy Frye, "Are Sanctions Pushing Russians to 'Rally Around the Flag'? Not Exactly," *Washington Post's Monkey Cage*, June 15, 2017, https://www.washingtonpost.com/news/monkey-cage/wp/2017/06/15/are-sanctions-pushing-russians-to-rally-around-the-flag-not-exactly/?utm_term=.58f1d630ceab.

CHAPTER 5. THE ECONOMY: IS THERE A RUSSIAN DISEASE?

1. Vladimir Putin, "Mineral Natural Resources in the Strategy for Development of the Russian Economy," trans. Harley Balzer, in "Vladimir Putin's Academic Writings and Russian Natural Resource Policy," *Problems of Post-Communism* 53, no. 1 (2006): 48–54.

2. These debates can be followed by consulting the economy section of the editions since 2013 of the annual *Insights of the French-Russian Observatory* (Paris), http://obsfr.ru/fr/le-rapport-annuel.html.

3. Shinichiro Tabata, "Observations on Russian Exposure to the Dutch Disease," *Eurasian Geography & Economics* 53, no. 2 (2012): 231–243.

4. Among the first authors to diagnose that "disease," one may cite Julien Vercueil, *Transition et ouverture de l'économie russe: Pour une économie institutionnelle du changement* (Paris: L'Harmattan, 2000); Marshall I. Goldman, "The 'Russian Disease,'" *International Economy* 19, no. 3 (Summer 2005): 27–31; and Clifford G. Gaddy and Barry W. Ickes, "Resource Rents and the Russian Economy," *Eurasian Geography & Economics* 46, no. 8 (2005): 559–583.

5. *Rossiia v tsifrakh – 2017* (Moscow: Rosstat, 2017).

6. 29.2 percent in 2017, according to RBK. See Ekaterina Kopalkina, "Biudzhetnye iskopaemye. Neft' i gaz uvelichili svoi ves v nalogovykh postupleniiakh," *RBK*, March 6, 2018, https://www.rbc.ru/newspaper/2018/03/06/5a9818279a7947614fe7c2a3

7. Tsarist Russia made some considerable state-guaranteed loans at the beginning of the twentieth century. Their non-reimbursement by the Soviet regime was a cause of conflict until

an agreement was found in 1997. See Eric Toussaint, "Centenary of the Russian Revolution and the Repudiation of Debt," CADTM.org, October 23, 2017, http://www.cadtm.org/Centenary-of-the-Russian#nb2-13.

8. "The first thing we want to do now is re-establish a normal country, with a normal economy and a normal life. Not a super life, but a normal human way of life. Our tragic past has convinced us that one of the highest treasures that any human community can have is a normal way of life." Speech by Boris Yeltsin to the Canadian Parliament, June 19, 1992, http://www.lipad.ca/full/1992/06/19/13/.

9. These began in 1994 and ended with the Duma's ratification of Russia's admission in July 2012. On this topic, see Richard Connolly and Philip Hanson, "Russia's Accession to the World Trade Organization: Commitments, Processes, and Prospects," *Eurasian Geography & Economics* no. 53 (2012): 479–501.

10. Thomas Piketty, "La Russie poutinienne se caractérise par une dérive kleptocratique sans limites," *Le Monde*, April 7, 2018, http://www.lemonde.fr/idees/article/2018/04/07/piketty-la-russie-poutinienne-se-caracterise-par-une-derive-kleptocratique-sans-limites_5282016_3232.html.

11. Vladimir Putin, "Rossiia na rubezhe tysiacheletii," *Nezavisimaia gazeta*, December 31, 1999, http://www.ng.ru/politics/1999-12-30/4_millenium.html.

12. Putin, "Rossiia na rubezhe tysiacheletii."

13. Gertrude Schroeder, "Dimensions of Russia's Industrial Transformation, 1992 to 1998: An Overview," *Post-Soviet Geography & Economics* 39, no. 5 (1998): 243–270.

14. Goskomstat, *Trud i zaniatnost'* (Moscow: Goskomstat, 2017).

15. The crude oil price was around US$25 a barrel between 1986 and 2003 with a low point of $10 in 1999. It surpassed $100 between 2008 and 2013 and stabilized around $50 and $60 in 2017.

16. Aleksandr Naumov, "Perspektivy razvitiia rossiiskogo avtoproma," *Mirovoe i natsional'noe khoziaistvo*, no. 2 (2010): 51–59.

17. Aleksey Sinitskiy, "Lobovaia ataka rossiiskoi aviatsii," *Finansovye izvestiia*, May 8, 1999.

18. See "Amerikanskii sled na 'Permskikh motorakh," *War and Peace*, March 16, 2012, http://www.warandpeace.ru/ru/reports/view/67755/; and Aleksey Kondrashev, "Permskie motory: uroki istorii," *Nezavisimaia gazeta*, December 29, 2000.

19. J-P. Casamayou, "Sukhoï investit en Sibérie pour son Superjet-100," *Air & Cosmos*, May 1, 2007.

20. Andrei Bortsov, "Russko-kitaiskii samolet sotrudnichestva vzletaet vse vyshe," *Politicheskaia Rossiia*, June 27, 2016, http://politrussia.com/world/o-russko-kitayskom-dalnemagistral nom-602/.

21. Masaaki Kuboniwa, "Diagnosing the 'Russian Disease': Growth and Structure of the Russian Economy," *Comparative Economic Studies* 54, no. 1 (2012): 121–148; Julien Vercueil, "Russie: la 'stratégie 2020' en question," *Revue d'études comparatives Est-Ouest* 44, no. 1 (2013): 169–194.

22. See, for example, Jacques Sapir, "Stratégie industrielle russe," *RussEurope*, May 30, 2015, http://russeurope.hypotheses.org/3879; "La Russie sort de la crise," *RussEurope*, March 21, 2015, http://russeurope.hypotheses.org/3650.

23. Serguey Tsukhlo, "Importozameshchenie: mify i realnost'," in *Ezhegodnyi doklad Franko-rossiiskogo tsentra Observatorii Rossiia-2016*, ed. Arnaud Dubien (Paris: Le Cherche-Midi, 2016), 92–103.

24. Wladimir Andreff, *Économie de la transition. La transformation des économies planifiées en économies de marché* (Paris: Bréal, 2007).

25. Myriam Désert and Gilles Favarel-Garrigues, "Les capitalistes russes," *Problèmes politiques et sociaux*, no. 789 (August 1997).

26. This factory became American owned in 1998 through share purchases, causing a highly publicized scandal. An amicable solution was ultimately found with the factory's purchase in 2002 by a Russian oligarch.

27. "M. Poutine propose aux 'oligarques' russes une forme d'amnistie," *Le Monde*, July 30, 2000.

28. Richard Sakwa, *The Quality of Freedom: Khodorkovsky, Putin, and the Yukos Affair* (Oxford: Oxford University Press, 2009).

29. The first to be pushed out of Russia were Boris Berezovsky, owner of ORT Television, and Vladimir Gusinsky, owner of NTV (the only private television channel, which was highly critical of the government during the first Chechen war) and of the radio station Ekho Moskvy.

30. "Polozhitel'naia ekologicheskaia ekspertiza proekta 'Sakhalin-2' otmenena," *RIA Novosti*, September 19, 2006, https://ria.ru/company/20060919/54059888.html; "Britaniia ozabochena resheniem po 'Sakhalinu-2,'" BBC Russia, September 20, 2006, http://news.bbc.co.uk/hi/russian/russia/newsid_5363000/5363114.stm.

31. Terry Macalister, "BP Ups Stakes by Accusing Putin of Failing to Stop Hijack by Oligarchs," *Guardian*, June 13, 2008, https://www.theguardian.com/business/2008/jun/13/bp.russia; Carola Hoyos, Ed Crooks, and Catherine Belton, "Strained Relations Thaw Over TNK-BP," *Financial Times*, September 5, 2008, http://www.ft.com/cms/s/23a1bda6-7ae1-11dd-adbe-000077b07658.html.

32. Gaddy and Ickes, "Resource Rents and the Russian Economy"; Clifford Gaddy and Barry Ickes, "Russia's Declining Oil Production: Managing Price Risk and Rent Addiction," *Eurasian Geography & Economics* 50, no. 1 (2009): 1–13.

33. Mikhail Kasyanov, *Bez Putina. Politicheskie dialogi s Evgeniem Kiselevym* (Moscow: Novaia gazeta, 2009).

34. Tabata, "Observations on Russian Exposure."

35. See "Abramovich, Roman," *Lenta.ru*, https://lenta.ru/lib/14161457/.

36. "EU Sanctions against Russia over Ukraine Crisis," European Union Newsroom, March 16, 2017, https://europa.eu/newsroom/highlights/special-coverage/eu-sanctions-against-russia-over-ukraine-crisis_en.

37. Viktoriia Nikitina, "Dorogi RF v 38 raz dorozhe i v 2 raza 'nezhnee' kanadskikh," *Argumenty i fakty*, June 8, 2011, http://www.aif.ru/money/25863.

38. Matthew Sagers, "Russia's Energy Policy: A Divergent View," *Eurasian Geography & Economics* 47, no. 3 (2006): 314–320; Matthew Sagers, "The Regional Dimension of Russian Oil Production: Is a Sustained Recovery in Prospect?" *Eurasian Geography & Economics* 47, no. 5 (2006): 505–545.

39. William Tompson, "Back to the Future? Thoughts on the Political Economy of Expanding State Ownership in Russia," *Les cahiers Russie*, no. 6 (2008).

40. Sergey Guriev, "New Wave of Russian Privatization," *Note of the French-Russian Observatory*, no. 2 (January 2013), http://obsfr.ru/uploads/media/130115_Policy_Paper_2_Gouriev_EN.pdf.

41. "Ukaz Prezidenta RF ot 7 maia 2012 g. N 596 'O dolgosrochnoi gosudarstvennoi ekonomicheskoi politike,'" http://base.garant.ru/70170954/.

42. "Stenogramma vystupleniia Vladimira Putina pered federal'nym sobraniem," *Rossiiskaia gazeta*, March 1, 2018. https://rg.ru/2018/03/01/stenogramma-vystupleniia-vladimira -putina-pered-federalnym-sobraniem.html.

43. Ildar Ablaev, "Innovation Clusters in the Russian Economy: Economic Essence, Concepts, Approaches," *Procedia Economics & Finance* 24 (2015): 3–12, http://www.sciencedirect .com/science/article/pii/S221256711500605X.

44. See Ekaterina Gloriozova and Aude Merlin, eds, "Sotchi-2014: La Russie à l'épreuve de ses Jeux, les Jeux à l'épreuve du Caucase," special issue of *Connexe, les espaces post-communistes en question(s)* (December 2016).

45. "Global Corruption Barometer 2016: Europe and Central Asia," Transparency International, http://www.transparency.org/files/content/feature/GCB_ECA_Regional_Results.xlsx and https://files.transparency.org/content/download/2039/13168/file/2016_GCB_ECA_ EN.pdf.

46. Lennart Dal'gren, *Vopreki absurdu, ili kaki ia pokorial Rossiiu, a ona – menia: Vospominaniia byvshego general'nogo direktora IKEA v Rossii* (Moscow: Al'pina Biznes Buks, 2010).

47. In Moscow, a police officer shielded by his leaders killed four clients in a supermarket; in Kuchevskaya, a mafia group that has for years terrorized this small town with the complicity of the local authorities massacred twelve members of a family that was resisting its hold. See Aleksandr Khinshtein [appointed adviser to the director of the National Guard in 2016], "Tsapnut' Tsapka," *Moskovskii komsomolets*, December 6, 2010, http://www.mk.ru/ incident/2010/12/06/549780-tsapnut-tsapka.html. See also Jean Radvanyi, *Retour d'une autre Russie: Une plongée dans le pays de Poutine* (Lormont: Le Bord de l'eau, 2013).

48. See, for instance, the documentary film by Andrei Nekrasov on the topic, *Magnitsky Act–Behind the Scenes* (2016) and, about it, Mark Landler, "Film about Russian Lawyer's Death Creates an Uproar," *New York Times*, June 9, 2016, https://www.nytimes.com/2016/06/10/ world/europe/sergei-magnitsky-russia-vladimir-putin.html.

49. Boris Nemtsov and Vladimir Milov, *Putin. Itogi. 10 let* (Moscow: Solidarsnost', 2010); Vladimir Milov, Boris Nemtsov, Vladimir Ryzhkov, and Ol'ga Shorina, *Putin. Korruptsiia* (Moscow: Solidarnost', 2011).

50. On Navalny's case, see, for example, "Naval'nyi, Aleksei," *Lenta.ru*, https://lenta.ru/ lib/14159595/; "Navalnyi, Aleksei Anatol'evich," Wikipedia, https://ru.wikipedia.org/wiki/ Навальный,_Алексей_Анатольевич.

51. "Doing Business 2017: Russian Federation," World Bank, http://www.doingbusiness .org/~/media/wbg/doingbusiness/documents/profiles/country/rus.pdf.

52. See Isabelle Mandraud, "A Moscou, le Comité d'enquête, bras judiciaire de Poutine," *Le Monde*, February 25, 2015, http://www.lemonde.fr/international/article/2015/02/05/ a-moscou-le-bras-arme-de-poutine_4570142_3210.html.

53. "Chinovnikam zapretili imet' scheta za rubezhom," *Interfax*, April 24, 2013, http:// www.interfax.ru/russia/303553.

54. "Infliatsiia na potrebitel'skom rynke: Ianvar' 2015 god," Central Bank of Russia, http://www.cbr.ru/statistics/infl/Infl_01012015.pdf; https://tradingeconomics.com/russia/ inflation-cpi.

55. "International Reserves of the Russian Federation," Central Bank of the Russian Federation, http://www.cbr.ru/eng/hd_base/?Prtid=mrrf_m.

56. *Sotsial'no-ekonomicheskoe polozhenie Rossii: 2016 god* (Moscow: Rosstat, 2016), 15.

57. *Sotsial'no-ekonomicheskoe polozhenie Rossii: 2016 god*, 67–68.

58. *Sotsial'no-ekonomicheskoe polozhenie Rossii: Ianvar' 2017 goda* (Moscow: Rosstat, 2017), 208–209.

59. Dmitrii Kozlov, "Minpromtorg zanialsia arkticheskoi inzheneriei," *Kommersant,* January 25, 2017, http://www.kommersant.ru/doc/3200888?utm_source=kommersant&utm_medium=business&utm_campaign=four; Iurii Ban'ko, "Importozameshchenie dlia arkticheskogo shel'fa: gonki ne nada, no i ne rasteriat' by uzhe dostignutogo," *Arktik–TV,* June 2, 2016, http://xn———7sbhwjb3brd.xn—p1ai/news/analitika/importozameshenie-dlya-arkticheskogo-shelfa-gonki-ne-nado-no-i-ne-rasteryat-by-uzhe-dostignutogo; "Shel'fovye proekty," Rosneft, https://www.rosneft.ru/business/Upstream/offshore/.

60. "Gross Domestic Product Based on Purchasing-Power-Parity (PPP) Valuation of Country GDP (Current International Dollar)" and "Gross Domestic Product Based on Purchasing-Power-Parity (PPP) Per Capita GDP (Current International Dollar)," World Economic Outlook Database, IMF, October 2016.

61. Goldman, "The 'Russian Disease.'"

62. Vercueil, *Transition et ouverture.*

63. "Zerkalo zastoia: Shto nuzhno znat' o novom reitinge RBK 500," *RBK,* September 21, 2017, http://www.rbc.ru/newspaper/2017/09/22/59c061fd9a7947581a01ed0c.

CHAPTER 6. BETWEEN EUROPE AND ASIA: THE DOUBLE-HEADED EAGLE

1. We are not counting the brief intervention of Russian paratroopers at Pristina airport in Kosovo in June 1999.

2. See the comment on Sputnik News, "Paranoia Over 'Imminent Russian Invasion of Poland' Gives Analysts a Good Laugh," *Sputnik,* July 28, 2016, https://sputniknews.com/politics/20160728/1043716396/analysts-commentary-polish-russian-threat.html.

3. Mary Elise Sarotte, "A Broken Promise? What the West Really Told Moscow about NATO Expansion," *Foreign Affairs,* September/October 2014, https://www.foreignaffairs.com/articles/russia-fsu/2014-08-11/broken-promise.

4. Zbigniew Brzezinski, *The Grand Chessboard: American Primacy and Its Geostrategic Imperatives* (New York: Basic Books, 1998).

5. Maria Repnikova and Harley Balzer, "Chinese Migration to Russia: Missed Opportunities," *WWICS Eurasian Migration Paper,* no. 3 (2010), https://www.wilsoncenter.org/sites/default/files/No3_ChineseMigtoRussia.pdf.

6. Yuri Slezkine, "The USSR as a Communal Apartment, or How a Socialist State Promoted Ethnic Particularism," *Slavic Review* 53, no. 2 (July 1994): 414–452.

7. Gerald Toal, *Near Abroad: Putin, the West and the Contest over Ukraine and the Caucasus* (Oxford: Oxford University Press, 2017).

8. Petr Vail', "Itogi sammita SNG v Kishineve," Radio Svoboda, October 8, 2002, http://www.svoboda.org/a/24193749.html.

9. See the site "GUAM Organization for Democracy and Economic Development," http://guam-organization.org/.

10. Franck Tétart, *Géopolitique de Kaliningrad* (Paris: Presses de l'université Paris-Sorbonne, 2007).

11. Isabelle Facon, *La nouvelle stratégie de sécurité nationale de la Fédération de Russie* (Paris: Fondation pour la recherche stratégique, February 10, 2016), https://www.frstrategie.org/pub lications/notes/la-nouvelle-strategie-de-securite-nationale-de-la-federation-de-russie-2016-05.

12. On this complex question, see Stephen Blank, ed., *Russia and the Current State of Arms Control* (Carlisle, PA: Strategic Studies Institute, 2012); from the Russian perspective, Aleksei Arbatov, Vladimir Dvorkin, and Sergei Oznobishchev, eds., *Rossiia i dilemmy iadernogo razoruzheniia*, 2nd ed. (Moscow: IMEMO, Russian Academy of Sciences, 2012).

13. See Jacob W. Kipp, "Russia's Future Arms Control Agenda and Posture," in Blank, *Russia and the Current State of Arms Control*, 1–62.

14. "Voennaia doktrina Rossiiskoi Federatsii," approved by presidential edict February 5, 2010, http://kremlin.ru/supplement/461; "Voennaia doktrina Rossiiskoi Federatsii," approved by presidential edict December 26, 2014, http://kremlin.ru/events/president/news/47334.

15. The list of sixty Russian officials under sanction (visa prohibition) continues the tradition of the Jackson-Vanik amendment, which tied trade with the Soviet Union to the right of Soviet Jews to emigrate.

16. See Eric Ehrmann, "Washington, WikiLeaks and Russian Soft Power," Russian International Affairs Council, August 23, 2013, http://russiancouncil.ru/en/blogs/eric -ehrmann/?id_4=628.

17. Richard Sokolsky, "Not Quiet on NATO's Eastern Front," Carnegie Endowment for International Peace, June 29, 2016, http://carnegieendowment.org/2016/06/29/not-quiet -on-nato-s-eastern-front-pub-63984.

18. "Russia Suspends Joint Consultations on Treaty on Conventional Armed Forces in Europe," *ITAR-TASS*, March 10, 2015, http://tass.com/russia/781973; "NATO Strategic Communications Center Unveiled in Riga," Latvian Public Broadcasting, August 20, 2015, http:// www.lsm.lv/en/article/societ/society/nato-strategic-communications-center-unveiled-in-riga. a142243/; "NATO Opens Training Center in Georgia," Radio Free Europe / Radio Liberty, August 27, 2015, http://www.rferl.org/a/georgia-nato-training-center/27212128.html.

19. Yeltsin met with Belorussian president Stanislaw Shushkevich and Ukrainian president Leonid Kravchuk near Minsk on December 8, 1991. The other leaders, who had not been invited, insisted that a second summit be organized at Alma-Ata on December 18. Apart from the three already mentioned, representatives also came from Moldova, Armenia, and Azerbaijan, as well as the five Central Asian states. No one came from Georgia because its president, Zviad Gamsakhurdia, was overthrown on the very same day. Georgia only joined the CIS in October 1993 under the presidency of Eduard Shevardnadze.

20. Zbigniew Brzezinski and Paige Sullivan, eds., *Russia and the Commonwealth of Independent States: Documents, Data, and Analysis* (Armonk, NY: M. E. Sharpe, 1997), 41.

21. Yann Breault, Pierre Jolicœur, and Jacques Lévesque, *La Russie et son ex-empire: Reconfiguration géopolitique de l'ancien espace soviétique* (Paris: Presses de Sciences Po, 2003).

22. Begun in 1992, negotiations were concluded in 1997 with the leasing of this strategic base for 20 years; Kiev reserved for itself the use of one of the base's bays.

23. This was one of the interpretations spread in *Izvestiia* on December 9, 1991, under the title "Three Slavic Leaders Have Decided the Union's Destiny." The interpretation is easily seen to be misleading.

24. "US Army Trainers Land in Georgia," BBC, May 19, 2002, http://news.bbc.co.uk/2/ hi/europe/1996833.stm.

25. Katya Kalandadze and Mitchell A. Orenstein, "Electoral Protests and Democratization beyond the Color Revolutions," *Comparative Political Studies* 42 (2009): 1403–1425; Joshua Tucker, "Enough! Electoral Fraud, Collective Action Problems, and Post-Communist Colored Revolutions," *Perspectives on Politics* 5 (3): 537–553; Lucan Way, "The Real Causes of the Color Revolutions," *Journal of Democracy* 19, 3 (2008): 55–69.

26. Vladimir Putin, "Vystuplenie i diskussiia na Miunkhenskoi konferentsii po voprosam politiki bezopasnosti" (speech delivered at the Munich Security Conference, Munich, February 10, 2007), http://kremlin.ru/events/president/transcripts/24034.

27. Steven Erlanger and Steven Lee Myers, "NATO Allies Oppose Bush on Georgia and Ukraine," *New York Times*, April 3, 2008, http://www.nytimes.com/2008/04/03/world/europe/03nato.html; Paul Gallis, "The NATO Summit at Bucharest, 2008," Congressional Research Service, May 5, 2008, https://www.fas.org/sgp/crs/row/RS22847.pdf; Steven Erlanger, "Georgia and Ukraine Split NATO Members," *New York Times*, October 30, 2008, http://www.nytimes.com/2008/11/30/world/europe/30iht-nato.4.18268641.html; Judy Dempsey, "U.S. Pushing to Bring Ukraine and Georgia into NATO," *New York Times*, November 3, 2008, http://www.nytimes.com/2008/02/13/world/europe/13iht-nato.4.10021504.html.

28. See the EU's Tagliavini Report: "Report: Volume I, Independent International Fact-Finding Mission on the Conflict in Georgia," September 2009, http://news.bbc.co.uk/2/shared/bsp/hi/pdfs/30_09_09_iiffmgc_report.pdf.

29. See Pascal Marchand, *Géopolitique de la Russie* (Paris: Presses Universitaires de France, 2014).

30. See, for example, Putin's explicit articulation of this position and these resentments in his "Crimean Speech": Vladimir Putin, "Obrashchenie Prezidenta Rossiiskoi Federatsii," March 18, 2014, http://kremlin.ru/events/president/news/20603.

31. Cooley, *Scripts of Sovereignty.*

32. Piotr Dutkiewicz and Richard Sakwa, eds., *Eurasian Union: The View from Within* (London: Routledge, 2015).

33. See Schenk, "Open Borders, Closed Minds"; and Marlene Laruelle, "Russia as a Xenophobic Empire: Multiethnicity, the Nation and the Empire in Russia's 'Political Thought,'" in *Russia: State Power Is Back* (Milan: Reset Dialogue on Civilizations, 2016).

34. Timothy Colton and Samuel Sharap, *Everyone Loses: The Ukraine Crisis and the Ruinous Contest for Post-Soviet Eurasia* (London: Routledge, 2017).

35. See Françoise Daucé, *L'État, l'armée et le citoyen en Russie post-soviétique* (Paris: L'Harmattan, 2001).

36. See Dmitry Gorenburg, "Russian Military Reform" (blog), https://russiamil.wordpress.com/author/gorenbur/.

37. Dmitry Gorenburg, "Russia's Military Modernization Plans: 2018–2027," *PONARS Eurasia Policy Memo*, no. 495, November 2017, http://www.ponarseurasia.org/memo/russias-military-modernization-plans-2018-2027.

38. Jakov Hedenskog and Robert L. Larsson, *Russian Leverage on the CIS and the Baltic States* (Stockholm: FOI, Swedish Defence Research Agency, 2007).

39. "'Inter RAO' ne vyderzhalo armianskikh dram," *Kommersant*, June 29, 2015, http://www.itogi.ru/archive/2000/16/110943.html.

40. Susanne Nies, "Nabucco et South Stream: Des gazoducs trop politisés?" Institut Français des relations internationales, January 4, 2008, https://www.ifri.org/fr/publications/editoriaux/edito-energie/nabucco-south-stream-gazoducs-politises.

41. Putin eventually proposed completely ending the export of oil via the Baltic republics' ports by 2018. See Liudmila Podobedova, and Natal'ia Derbysheva, "V Pribaltiku ni truboi," *RBK*, September 12, 2016, http://www.rbc.ru/newspaper/2016/09/13/57d6c5779a79 47b83d50f2d3.

42. See the website "Nord Stream 2," https://www.nord-stream2.com/.

43. Aleksei Topalov, "Obnulit' ukrainskii tranzit," *Gazeta.ru*, January 23, 2015, https://www.gazeta.ru/business/2015/01/22/6383865.shtml.

44. Maria-Raquel Freire and Roger E. Kanet, eds., *Key Players and Regional Dynamics in Eurasia: The Return of the "Great Game"* (New York: Palgrave, 2010).

45. See more in Marlene Laruelle and Sebastien Peyrouse, *The "Chinese Question" in Central Asia: Domestic Order, Social Changes and the Chinese Factor* (London and New York: Oxford University Press and Hurst, 2012).

46. Peter Ferdinand, "Westward Ho: The China Dream and 'One Belt, One Road': Chinese Foreign Policy under Xi Jinping," *International Affairs* 92, no. 4 (2016): 941–957. See also Marlene Laruelle, ed., *China's Belt and Road Initiative (BRI) and Its Impact in Central Asia* (Washington, DC: George Washington University's Central Asia Program, 2017), http://centralasiaprogram.org/wp-content/uploads/2017/12/OBOR_Book_.pdf.

47. "Russia: Trade Statistics," UN Comtrade via GlobalEdge, Michigan State University, https://globaledge.msu.edu/countries/russia/tradestats.

48. The initials of the states (Brazil, Russia, India, China, South Africa) that make up this set; a Goldman Sachs analyst gave it this moniker in 2001.

49. Marcin Kaczmarski, *Russia-China Relations in the Post-Crisis International Order* (London: Routledge, 2015).

50. Ferdinand, "Westward Ho."

51. Kira Latukhina, "S gazom!," *Rossiiskaia gazeta*, May 22, 2014, https://rg.ru/2014/05/21/gaz-site.html.

52. Elena Domcheva, "Rossiia naladit innovatsionnoe sotrudnichestvo s Kitaiem," *Rossiiskaia gazeta*, July 9, 2016, https://rg.ru/2016/07/09/rossiia-naladit-innovacionnoe-sotrud nichestvo-s-kitaem.html.

53. "Backing Ukraine's Territorial Integrity, UN Assembly Declares Crimea Referendum Invalid," *UN News Centre*, March 27, 2014, http://www.un.org/apps/news/story.asp?NewsI D=47443&Cr=ukraine&Cr1=#.UzgPNqLRUdw; Voting Record of "Item 33(b) A/68/L.39 Draft Resolution Territorial Integrity of Ukraine, Resolution 68/262," https://papersmart.un meetings.org/media2/2498292/voting-record.pdf; "UN Security Council Action on Crimea Referendum Blocked," *UN News Centre*, March 15, 2014, http://www.un.org/apps/news/story.asp?NewsID=47362#.WMLR00eltVo.

54. Henry Plater-Zyberk and Andrew Monaghan, *Strategic Implications of the Evolving Shanghai Cooperation Organization* (Carlisle, PA: Strategic Studies Institute and U.S. Army War College Press, 2014).

55. With India and Pakistan, the SCO now has eight member states, four observers (Afghanistan, Belarus, Iran, and Mongolia), and six dialogue partners (Armenia, Azerbaijan, Cambodia, Nepal, Sri Lanka, and Turkey).

56. See Dmitry Gorenburg, "The Southern Kuril Islands Dispute," *PONARS Eurasia Policy Memo*, no. 226 (September 2012), https://www2.gwu.edu/~ieresgwu/assets/docs/ponars/pepm_226_Gorenburg_Sept2012.pdf.

57. "Rossiia i Iaponiia dogovorilis' o sovmestnom ispol'zovanii Kuril'skikh ostrovov," *Nastoiashchee vremia*, December 15, 2016, http://www.currenttime.tv/a/28178217.html.

58. See Julien Vercueil, *Les pays émergents: Brésil-Russie-Inde-Chine* (Paris: Bréal, 2012).
59. Recall that Russia, invited to the G8 in 1997, was excluded from it in 2014. It is remarkable that when the Australian prime minister (a member of the G7) wanted to exclude Russia from the G20 summit in Brisbane in November 2014, he was confronted by a general outcry from "emerging nations" that forced him to backpedal.
60. Brice Pedroletti, "La Chine façonne son nouvel ordre mondial," *Le Monde*, January 9, 2015, http://www.lemonde.fr/asie-pacifique/article/2015/09/01/la-chine-faconne-son-nouvel-ordre-mondial_4742315_3216.html.
61. Paul Stronski and Richard Sokolsky, *The Return of Global Russia: An Analytical Framework* (Washington, DC: Carnegie Endowment for International Peace, 2017), http://carnegieendowment.org/2017/12/14/return-of-global-russia-analytical-framework-pub-75003.
62. "Zaiavlenie MID Rossii," Ministry of Foreign Affairs of the Russian Federation, June 6, 2017, http://www.mid.ru/ru/press_service/spokesman/official_statement/-/asset_publisher/t2GCdmD8RNIr/content/id/2717182.

CHAPTER 7. RUSSIA IN THE WORLD: BESIEGED FORTRESS OR NEW CRUSADER?

1. "Vladimir Putin's Interview with the BBC (David Frost)," BBC, March 13, 2000, www.gazeta.ru/2001/02/28/putin_i_bbc.shtml.
2. The phrase has occasionally been uttered by Putin, for the first time in February 2000, then in 2005; it is also to be found in the memoirs of General Alexander Lebed.
3. Vladimir Putin, "Russia's Place in a Changing World" (English translation), *Moskovskie novosti*, February 27, 2012, http://worldmeets.us/Moskovskiye.Novosti000001.shtml#axzz4SVaGrHcN.
4. Kristopher Natoli, "Weaponizing Nationality: An Analysis of Russia's Passport Policy in Georgia," *Boston University International Law Journal* 28 (2010): 389–417, http://www.bu.edu/law/journals-archive/international/documents/natoli_weaponizingnationality.pdf.
5. Anna Brezhneva and Daria Ukhova, "Russian as a Humanitarian Aid Donor," Oxfam Discussion Paper, July 2013, https://www.oxfam.org/sites/www.oxfam.org/files/dp-russia-humanitarian-donor-150713-en.pdf.
6. See Patrick Moreau and Stéphane Courtois, eds., *En Europe, l'éternel retour des communistes 1989–2014* (Paris: Vendémiaire, 2014).
7. Quoted by Sinikukka Saari in "Russia's Post-Orange Revolution Strategies to Increase Its Influence in the Former Soviet Republics: Public Diplomacy *po russki*," *Europe-Asia Studies* 66, no. 1 (2014): 50.
8. Simon Shuster, "Inside Putin's On-Air Machine," *Time*, March 5, 2015, http://time.com/rt-putin/.
9. Shuster, "Inside Putin's On-Air Machine."
10. Available at http://www.sho.com/the-putin-interviews.
11. The Russian Orthodox Church Outside of Russia (ROCOR) is the name given to the Russian Orthodox Church of the emigration, which left the fold of the Moscow Patriarchate during the Soviet era in protest of the church's submission to an atheist power and the religious repression of the Soviet state.

12. Adam Federman, "How US Evangelicals Fueled the Rise of Russia's 'Pro-Family' Right," *The Nation*, January 7, 2014, https://www.thenation.com/article/how-us-evangelicals-fueled-rise-russias-pro-family-right/.

13. Miranda Blue, "Globalizing Homophobia, pt. 1: How The American Right Came to Embrace Russia's Anti-Gay Crackdown," *Right Wing Watch*, October 3, 2013, www.rightwingwatch.org/content/globalizing-homophobia-part-1-how-american-right-came-embrace-russia-s-anti-gay-crackdown#sthash.Bu2BQQ5q.dpuf; Miranda Blue, "Globalizing Homophobia, pt. 2: Today the Whole World Is Looking at Russia," www.rightwingwatch.org/content/globalizing-homophobia-part-2-today-whole-world-looking-russia#sthash.wdyrKObx.dpuf.

14. Peter Stone, David Smith, Ben Jacobs, Alec Luhn, and Rupert Neate, "Donald Trump and Russia: A Web That Grows More Tangled All the Time," *Guardian*, July 30, 2016, https://www.theguardian.com/us-news/2016/jul/30/donald-trump-paul-manafort-ukraine-russia-putin-ties.

15. "Meeting of the Valdai International Discussion Club," *Kremlin.ru*, September 19, 2013, http://en.kremlin.ru/events/president/news/19243.

16. "Marine Le Pen fait l'éloge de Vladimir Poutine 'le patriote,'" *Le Figaro*, May 18, 2014, www.lefigaro.fr/politique/le-scan/citations/2014/05/18/25002-20140518ARTFIG00118-marine-le-pen-fait-l-eloge-de-vladimir-poutine-le-patriote.php.

17. Anton Shekhovtsov, "Pro-Russian Extremists Observe the Illegitimate Crimean 'Referendum,'" Anton Shekhovtsov (blog), March 17, 2014, http://anton-shekhovtsov.blogspot.com/2014/03/pro-russian-extremists-observe.html.

18. More in Anton Shekhovtsov, *Russia and the Western Far Right: Tango Noir* (London: Routledge, 2017), and Marlene Laruelle, ed., *Eurasianism and the European Far Right: Reshaping the Europe-Russia Relationship* (Lanham, MD: Lexington, 2015).

19. *The Foreign Policy Concept of the Russian Federation*, July 12, 2008. See Luke March, "Is Nationalism Rising in Russian Foreign Policy? The Case of Georgia," *Demokratizatsiya: Journal of Post-Soviet Democratization* 19, no. 3 (2011): 187–207.

20. "Putin: nevozmozhno bez otvrashcheniia smotret' na kadry ubiistva Kaddafi," *RIA Novosti*, October 26, 2011, https://ria.ru/arab_ly/20111026/471693000.html.

21. Andrei Soldatov and Irina Borogan, *The Red Web: The Struggle between Russia's Digital Dictators and the New Online Revolutionaries* (New York: PublicAffairs, 2015).

22. Fyodor Lukyanov, "Why Russia's Soft Power Is Too Soft," *Russia in Global Affairs*, February 1, 2013, http://eng.globalaffairs.ru/redcol/Why-Russias-Soft-Power-Is-Too-Soft-15845.

23. "Hollande: Russia Is a Partner, Not a Threat," Radio Free Europe / Radio Liberty, July 8, 2016, http://www.rferl.org/content/hollande-russia-is-a-partner-not-a-threat/27847690.html.

CONCLUSION

1. Mathieu Boulegue, "The Russia-NATO Relationship between a Rock and a Hard Place: How the 'Defensive Inferiority Syndrome' Is Increasing the Potential for Error," *Journal of Slavic Military Studies* 30 (2017): 361–380.

2. Ol'ga Kuvshinova and Aleksandra Prokopenko, "Eshche 20 let stagnatsii prognoziruet Minekonomrazvitiia," *Vedomosti*, October 20, 2016, http://www.vedomosti.ru/economics/articles/2016/10/20/661689-20-let-stagnatsii.

Bibliography

Ablaev, Ildar. "Innovation Clusters in the Russian Economy: Economic Essence, Concepts, Approaches." *Procedia Economics and Finance* 24 (2015): 3–12.

Agadjanian, Alexander. "Religious Pluralism and National Identity in *Russia*." *International Journal on Multicultural Societies* 2, no. 2 (2000): 97–124.

Aitamurto, Kaarina. "Reviving the Native Faith: Nationalism in Contemporary Slavic Paganism Rodnoverie." *Forum für osteuropäische Ideen- und Zeitgeschichte* 1, no. 2 (2011): 167–184.

Andreff, Wladimir. *Économie de la transition: La transformation des économies planifiées en économies de marché.* Paris: Bréal, 2007.

Arbatov, Aleksei, Vladimir Dvorkin, and Sergei Oznobishchev, eds. *Rossiia i dilemmy iadernogo razoruzheniia,* 2nd ed. Moscow: IMEMO, Russian Academy of Sciences, 2012.

Arnold, Richard. "Visions of Hate: Explaining Neo-Nazi Violence in the Russian Federation." *Problems of Post-Communism* 57, no. 2 (2010): 37–59.

Avdeyeva, Olga A. "Policy Experiment in Russia: Cash-for-Babies and Fertility Change." *Social Politics: International Studies in Gender, State & Society* 18, no. 3 (2011): 361–386.

Balzer, Harley. "Vladimir Putin's Academic Writings and Russian Natural Resource Policy." *Problems of Post-Communism* 53, no. 1 (2006): 48–54.

Bantekas, Ilias. "Bilateral Delimitation of the Caspian Sea and the Exclusion of Third Parties." *International Journal of Marine & Coastal Law* 26, no. 1 (2011): 47–58.

Bertrand, Eva. "Pouvoir, catastrophe et représentation: Mise(s) en scène politique(s) des incendies de l'été 2010 en Russie occidentale." PhD diss., Sciences Po, 2016.

Blank, Stephen, ed. *Russia and the Current State of Arms Control.* Carlisle, PA: Strategic Studies Institute, 2012.

Boulegue, Mathieu. "The Russia-NATO Relationship between a Rock and a Hard Place: How the 'Defensive Inferiority Syndrome' Is Increasing the Potential for Error," *Journal of Slavic Military Studies* 30 (2017): 361–380.

Breault, Yann, Pierre Jolicœur, and Jacques Lévesque. *La Russie et son ex-empire: Reconfiguration géopolitique de l'ancien espace soviétique.* Paris: Presses de Sciences Po, 2003.

Brudny, Yitzhak M. *Reinventing Russia: Russian Nationalism and the Soviet State, 1953–1991.* Cambridge, MA: Harvard University Press, 2000.

Brzezinski, Zbigniew. *The Grand Chessboard: American Primacy and Its Geostrategic Imperatives.* New York: Basic Books, 1998.

Brzezinski, Zbigniew, and Paige Sullivan, eds. *Russia and the Commonwealth of Independent States: Documents, Data, and Analysis.* Armonk, NY: M. E. Sharpe, 1997.

Colton, Timothy, and Samuel Sharap, *Everyone Loses: The Ukraine Crisis and the Ruinous Contest for Post-Soviet Eurasia.* London: Routledge, 2017.

Connolly, Richard, and Philip Hanson. "Russia's Accession to the World Trade Organization: Commitments, Processes, and Prospects." *Eurasian Geography & Economics*, no. 53 (2012): 479–501.

Cooley, Alexander. *Scripts of Sovereignty: The Freezing of the Russia-Ukraine Crisis and Dilemmas of Governance in Eurasia.* Washington, DC: Center on Global Interests, January 2015.

Dal'gren, Lennart. *Vopreki absurdu, ili kaki ia pokorial Rossiiu, a ona – menia: Vospominaniia byvshego general'nogo direktora IKEA v Rossii.* Moscow: Al'pina Biznes Buks, 2010.

Daucé, Françoise. *La Russie postsoviétique.* Paris: La Découverte, 2008.

———. *L'État, l'armée et le citoyen en Russie post-soviétique.* Paris: L'Harmattan, 2001.

Dawisha, Karen. *Putin's Kleptocracy: Who Owns Russia?* New York: Simon & Schuster, 2015.

———. "Vladislav Surkov, 1964–." In *Russia's People of Empire: Life Stories from Eurasia, 1500 to the Present*, edited by Stephen Norris and Willard Sunderland, 339–349. Bloomington: Indiana University Press, 2012.

Désert, Myriam, and Gilles Favarel-Garrigues. "Les capitalistes russes." *Problèmes politiques et sociaux*, no. 789 (August 1997).

Dutkiewicz, Piotr, and Richard Sakwa, eds. *Eurasian Union: The View from Within.* London: Routledge, 2015.

Eberstadt, Nicholas. *Russia's Peacetime Demographic Crisis: Dimensions, Causes, Implications.* Seattle, WA: National Bureau of Asian Research, 2010.

Eltchaninoff, Michel. *Dans la tête de Vladimir Poutine.* Paris: Actes Sud, 2015.

Evans, Alfred B. "Protests and Civil Society in Russia: The Struggle for the Khimki Forest." *Communist & Post-Communist Studies* 45, no. 3–4 (2012): 233–242.

Fabry, Mikulas. "The Contemporary Practice of State Recognition: Kosovo, South Ossetia, Abkhazia, and Their Aftermath." *Nationalities Papers: Journal of Nationalism & Ethnicity* 40, no. 5 (2012): 661–676.

Ferdinand, Peter. "Westward Ho: The China Dream and 'One Belt, One Road': Chinese Foreign Policy under Xi Jinping." *International Affairs* 92, no. 4 (2016): 941–957.

Freire, Maria-Raquel, and Roger E. Kanet, eds. *Key Players and Regional Dynamics in Eurasia: The Return of the "Great Game."* New York: Palgrave, 2010.

Gaddy, Clifford G., and Barry W. Ickes. "Resource Rents and the Russian Economy." *Eurasian Geography & Economics* 46, no. 8 (2005): 559–583.

———. "Russia's Declining Oil Production: Managing Price Risk and Rent Addiction." *Eurasian Geography & Economics* 50, no. 1 (2009): 1–13.

Gazier, Anne. "La mise au pas des régions russes? La réforme institutionnelle de Vladimir Poutine." *Le Courrier des pays de l'Est*, no. 1015 (2001): 4–14.

Gerber, Theodore. "Beyond Putin? Nationalism and Xenophobia in Russian Public Opinion." *Washington Quarterly* 37, no. 3 (2014): 113–134.

Giuliano, Elise. *Constructing Grievance: Ethnic Nationalism in Russia's Republics.* Ithaca, NY: Cornell University Press, 2011.

Gloriozova, Ekaterina, and Aude Merlin, eds. "Sotchi-2014: La Russie à l'épreuve de ses Jeux, les Jeux à l'épreuve du Caucase." Special issue of *Connexe, les espaces post-communistes en question(s)* (December 2016).

Goldman, Marshall I. "The 'Russian Disease.'" *International Economy* 19, no. 3 (Summer 2005): 27–31.

Gorenburg, Dmitry. *Minority Ethnic Mobilization in the Russian Federation.* New York: Cambridge University Press, 2003.

———. "Regional Separatism in Russia: Ethnic Mobilization or Power Grab?" *Europe-Asia Studies* 51, no. 2 (1999): 245–274.

———. "Russia's Military Modernization Plans: 2018–2027," *PONARS Eurasia Policy Memo,* no. 495 (November 2017).

———. "The Southern Kuril Islands Dispute." *PONARS Eurasia Policy Memo,* no. 226 (September 2016).

Gorshkov, Mikhail, ed. *Mass Consciousness of the Russians during the Period of Social Transformations: Realities versus Myths.* Moscow: Russian Independent Institute of Social and Nationalities Problems, 1996.

Greene, Samuel. *Moscow in Movement: Power and Opposition in Putin's Russia.* Stanford, CA: Stanford University Press, 2014.

Gudkov, Lev D. "Ethnic Phobias in the Structure of National Identification." *Russian Social Science Review* 39, no. 1 (1998): 89–103.

———. "Pamiat' o voine i massovaia identichnost' rossiian." *Neprikosnovennyi zapas,* no. 40–41 (2005).

Guillot, Michel, Natalia Gavrilova, and Tetyana Pudrovska. "Understanding the 'Russian Mortality Paradox' in Central Asia: Evidence from Kyrgyzstan." *Demography* 48, no. 3 (August 2011): 1081–1104.

Guriev, Sergey. "New Wave of Russian Privatization." *Note of the French-Russian Observatory,* no. 2 (January 2013).

Hale, Henry, and Marlene Laruelle. "Civilizational Discourse in Russia." Forthcoming.

Hashimova, Umida. "What 2015 Is Promising for Labor Migrants from Central Asia." *Central Asia Policy Brief,* no. 23 (March 2015).

Hedenskog, Jakov, and Robert L. Larsson. *Russian Leverage on the CIS and the Baltic States.* Stockholm: FOI, Swedish Defence Research Agency, 2007.

Henriksen, Tore, and Geir Ulfstein. "Maritime Delimitation in the Arctic: The Barents Sea Treaty." *Ocean Development & International Law* 42, no. 1–2 (February 2011): 1–21.

Hill, Fiona. "In Search of Great Russia: Elites, Ideas, Power, the State, and the Pre-Revolutionary Past in the New Russia, 1991–1996." PhD diss., Harvard University, 1998.

Holland, Edward, and Eldar Eldarov. "'Going Away on Foot' Once Again: The Revival of Temporary Labour Migration from Russia's Dagestan." *Central Asian Survey* 31, no. 4 (2012): 379–393.

Jurczyszyn, Lukasz. "Russian Radical Nationalist Interpretation of the French Riots of November 2005." *Demokratizatsiya: Journal of Post-Soviet Democratization* 19, no. 3 (Summer 2011): 277–285.

Kaczmarski, Marcin. *Russia-China Relations in the Post-Crisis International Order.* London: Routledge, 2015.

Kaganskii, Vladimir. *Kul'turnyi landshaft i sovetskoe obytaemoe prostranstvo: sbornik statei.* Moscow: NLO, 2001.

Kalandadze, Katya, and Mitchell A. Orenstein. "Electoral Protests and Democratization beyond the Color Revolutions," *Comparative Political Studies* 42 (2009): 1403–1425.

Karpova, Galina G., and Maria A. Vorona. "Labour Migration in Russia: Issues and Policies." *International Social Work* 57, no. 5 (September 2014): 535–546.

Kastoryano, Riva, ed. *Les codes de la différence: Race, origine, religion. France, Allemagne, Etats-Unis.* Paris: Presses de Sciences Po, 2005.

Kasyanov, Mikhail. *Bez Putina. Politicheskie dialogi s Evgeniem Kiselevym.* Moscow: Novaia gazeta, 2009.

Kavykin, Oleg. *"Rodnovery": Samoidentifikatsiia neo-iazychnikov v sovremennoi Rossii.* Moscow: Institut Afriki RAN, 2007.

Kernen, Beat. "Putin and the Parliamentary Election in Russia: The Confluence (*Slijanie*) of Russian Political Culture and Leadership." *East European Quarterly* 38, no. 1 (Spring 2004): 85–107.

Khodorkovsky, Mikhail. *My Fellow Prisoners.* New York, Overlook Books, 2015.

Kipp, Jacob W. "Russia's Future Arms Control Agenda and Posture." In *Russia and the Current State of Arms Control,* edited by Stephen Blank, 1–62. Carlisle, PA: Strategic Studies Institute, 2012.

Kolosov, Vladimir, and Olga Vendina, eds. *Rossiisko-ukrainskoe pogranich'e. Dvadtsat' let razdelennogo edinstva.* Moscow: Novyi Khronograf, 2011.

Kolstø, Pål. "Marriage of Convenience? Collaboration between Nationalists and Liberals in the Russian Opposition, 2011–12." *Russian Review* 75, no. 4 (2016): 645–663.

———. "Russia's Nationalists Flirt with Democracy." *Journal of Democracy 25, no.* 3 (2014): 120–134.

Kuboniwa, Masaaki. "Diagnosing the 'Russian Disease': Growth and Structure of the Russian Economy." *Comparative Economic Studies* 54, no. 1 (2012): 121–148.

Laruelle, Marlene. "Alexei Navalny and Challenges in Reconciling 'Nationalism' and 'Liberalism.'" *Post-Soviet Affairs* 30, no. 4 (2014): 276–297.

———, ed. *China's Belt and Road Initiative (BRI) and Its Impact in Central Asia.* Washington DC: GW's Central Asia Program, 2017.

———, ed. *Eurasianism and the European Far Right: Reshaping the Europe-Russia Relationship.* Lanham, MD: Lexington, 2015.

———. "Inside and around the Kremlin's Black Box: The New Nationalist Think Tanks in Russia." *Stockholm Papers* (October 2009).

———. *In the Name of the Nation: Nationalism and Politics in Contemporary Russia.* New York: Palgrave MacMillan, 2009.

———. "The Izborsky Club, or the New Conservative Avant-Garde in Russia." *Russian Review* 75, no. 4 (2016): 622–644.

———, ed. *Migration and Social Upheaval as the Face of Globalization in Central Asia.* London: Brill, 2013.

———. "Russia as a 'Divided Nation,' from Compatriots to Crimea: A Contribution to the Discussion on Nationalism and Foreign Policy." *Problems of Post-Communism* 62, no. 2 (2015): 88–97.

———. "Russia as an Anti-Liberal European Civilization." In *The New Russian Nationalism: Between Imperial and Ethnic,* edited by Pål Kolstø and Helge Blakkisrud, 275–297. Edinburgh: Edinburgh University Press, 2016.

———. "Russia as a Xenophobic Empire: Multiethnicity, the Nation and the Empire in Russia's 'Political Thought.'" In *Russia: State Power Is Back.* Milan: Reset Dialogue on Civilizations, 2016.

———. *The 'Russian World': Russia's Soft Power and Geopolitical Imagination*. Washington, DC: Center on Global Interests, May 2015.

———. "The Three Colors of Novorossiya, or the Russian Nationalist Mythmaking of the Ukrainian Crisis." *Post-Soviet Affairs* 32, no. 1 (2015): 55–74.

Laruelle, Marlene, and Sophie Hohmann. "Biography of a Polar City: Population Flows and Urban Identity in Norilsk." *Polar Geography* 40, no. 4 (2017): 306–323.

Laruelle, Marlene, and Sebastien Peyrouse. *The "Chinese Question" in Central Asia: Domestic Order, Social Changes and the Chinese Factor*. London and New York: Oxford University Press and Hurst, 2012.

Laruelle, Marlene, and Natalia Yudina, "Islamophobia in Russia: Trends and Societal Context." In *Religious Violence in Russia*, edited by Olga Oliker and Jeffrey Mankoff. Washington DC: CSIS, 2018, 43–63.

Lieven, Anatol. *Chechnya: Tombstone of Russian Power*. New Haven, CT: Yale University Press, 1999.

Mälksoo, Lauri. "Which Continuity? The Tartu Peace Treaty of 2 February 1920, the Estonian-Russian Border Treaties of 2005, and the Legal Debate about Estonia's Status in International Law." *Archiv des Völkerrechts* 43, no. 4 (December 2005): 513–524.

March, Luke. "Is Nationalism Rising in Russian Foreign Policy? The Case of Georgia." *Demokratizatsiya: Journal of Post-Soviet Democratization* 19, no. 3 (2011): 187–207.

Marchand, Pascal. *Géopolitique de la Russie*. Paris: Presses Universitaires de France, 2014.

Mendras, Marie. "Russie: Le débat sur l'intérêt national." *Problèmes économiques et sociaux*, no. 694. Paris: La Documentation française, December 1992.

Milov, Vladimir, Boris Nemtsov, Vladimir Ryzhkov, and Ol'ga Shorina. *Putin: Korruptsiia*. Moscow: Solidarnost', 2011.

Mitrokhin, Nikolai. *"Russkaia partiia": dvizhenie russkikh natsionalistov v SSSR 1953–1985 gg.* Moscow: NLO, 2003.

Moreau, Patrick, and Stéphane Courtois, eds. *En Europe, l'éternel retour des communistes 1989–2014*. Paris: Vendémiaire, 2014.

Motyl, Alexander. "Putin's Russia as a Fascist Political System." *Communist & Post-Communist Studies* 49, no. 1 (2016): 25–36.

Natoli, Kristopher. "Weaponizing Nationality: An Analysis of Russia's Passport Policy in Georgia." *Boston University International Law Journal* 28 (2010): 389–417.

Naumov, Aleksandr. "Perspektivy razvitiia rossiiskogo avtoproma." *Mirovoe i natsional'noe khoziaistvo*, no. 2 (2010): 51–59.

Nemtsov, Boris, and Vladimir Milov. *Putin. Itogi. 10 let.* Moscow: Solidarsnost', 2010.

Obshchestvennoe mnenie – 2013. Moscow: Levada Center, 2014.

Obshchestvennoe mnenie – 2014. Moscow: Levada Center, 2015.

Petrov, Nikolai, and Darrell Slider. "Putin and the Regions." In *Putin's Russia: Past Imperfect, Future Uncertain*, 2nd ed., edited by Dale Herspring, 75–98. Lanham, MD: Rowman & Littlefield, 2005.

Peyrouse, Sébastien. "Former 'Colonists' on the Move? The Migration of Russian-Speaking Populations." In *Migration and Social Upheaval as the Face of Globalization in Central Asia*, edited by Marlene Laruelle, 215–238. London: Brill, 2013.

Pilkington, Hilary, Elena Omel'chenko, and Al'bina Garifzianova. *Russia's Skinheads: Exploring and Rethinking Subcultural Lives*. London: Routledge, 2010.

Plater-Zyberk, Henry, and Andrew Monaghan. *Strategic Implications of the Evolving Shanghai Cooperation Organization*. Carlisle, PA: Strategic Studies Institute and U.S. Army War College Press 2014.

Pomerantsev, Peter. *Nothing Is True and Everything Is Possible: The Surreal Heart of the New Russia.* New York: PublicAffairs, 2014.

Pribylovskii, Vladimir. *Kooperativ Ozero i drugie proekty Putina.* Moscow: Algoritm, 2012.

Radvanyi, Jean. *La Russie face à ses régions: Problèmes politiques et sociaux.* Paris: La Documentation française, December 1994.

———. "Quelques réponses à une question non posée: l'islam et le recensement de la population de Russie en 2002." In *Islam et politique en ex-URSS,* edited by Marlene Laruelle and Sébastien Peyrouse, 159–169. Paris: L'Harmattan, 2005.

———. *Retour d'une autre Russie: Une plongée dans le pays de Poutine.* Lormont: Le Bord de l'eau, 2013.

Raviot, Jean-Robert. "Les rapports centre-région en Russie: Rééquilibrage et continuité." *Le Courrier des pays de l'Est,* no. 1033 (2003): 4–15.

Reeves, Madeleine. "Clean Fake: Authenticating Documents and Persons in Migrant Moscow." *American Ethnologist* 40, no. 3 (2013): 508–524.

Remington, Thomas F. "Majorities without Mandates: The Russian Federation Council since 2000." *Europe-Asia Studies* 55, no. 5 (2003): 667–691.

Repnikova, Maria, and Harley Balzer. "Chinese Migration to Russia: Missed Opportunities." *WWICS Eurasian Migration Paper,* no. 3 (2010).

Robertson, Graeme. "The Election Protests of 2011–2012 in Broader Perspective." *Problems of Post-Communism* 60, no. 2 (2013): 11–23.

Rossiia v tsifrakh – 2014. Moscow: Rosstat, 2014.

Rossiia v tsifrakh – 2016. Moscow: Rosstat, 2016.

Rossiiskii statisticheskii ezhegodnik – 2015. Moscow: Rosstat, 2015.

Rousselet, Kathy. "Butovo: La création d'un lieu de pèlerinage sur une terre de massacres." *Politix* 20, no. 77 (2007).

Saari, Sinikukka. "Russia's Post-Orange Revolution Strategies to Increase Its Influence in the Former Soviet Republics: Public Diplomacy po russki." *Europe-Asia Studies* 66, no. 1 (2014) : 50–66.

Sabitov, Richat. *Le fédéralisme russe contemporain et la République du Tatarstan.* Paris: Fondation Varenne, 2013.

Sagers, Matthew J. "The Regional Dimension of Russian Oil Production: Is a Sustained Recovery in Prospect?" *Eurasian Geography & Economics* 47, no. 5 (2006): 505–545.

———. "Russia's Energy Policy: A Divergent View." *Eurasian Geography & Economics* 47, no. 3 (2006): 314–320.

Sakwa, Richard. "Putin's Leadership: Character and Consequences." *Europe-Asia Studies* 60, no. 6 (2008): 879–897.

———. *The Quality of Freedom: Khodorkovsky, Putin, and the Yukos Affair.* Oxford: Oxford University Press, 2009.

Schenk, Caress. "Controlling Immigration Manually: Lessons from Moscow (Russia)." *Europe-Asia Studies* 65, no. 7 (2013): 1444–1465.

———. "Open Borders, Closed Minds: Russia's Changing Migration Policies: Liberalization or Xenophobia?" *Demokratizatsiya: Journal of Post-Soviet Democratization* 18, no. 2 (April 2010): 101–121.

Schroeder, Gertrude. "Dimensions of Russia's Industrial Transformation, 1992 to 1998: An Overview." *Post-Soviet Geography & Economics* 39, no. 5 (1998): 243–270.

Serrano, Silvia. *Géorgie: Sortie d'empire.* Paris: CNRS Editions, 2007.

Sharafutdinova, Gulnaz. "Paradiplomacy in the Russian Regions: Tatarstan's Search for Statehood." *Europe-Asia Studies* 55, no. 4 (2003): 613–629.

————. "The Pussy Riot Affair and Putin's Demarche from Sovereign Democracy to Sovereign Morality." *Nationalities Papers: Journal of Nationalism & Ethnicity* 42, no. 4 (2014): 615–621.

Shekhovtsov, Anton. *Russia and the Western Far Right: Tango Noir.* London: Routledge, 2017.

Shevel, Oxana. "The Politics of Citizenship Policy in Post-Soviet Russia." *Post-Soviet Affairs* 28, no. 1 (2012): 111–147.

————. "Russian Nation-Building from Yeltsin to Medvedev: Ethnic, Civic, or Purposefully Ambiguous?" *Europe-Asia Studies* 63, no. 1 (2011): 179–202.

Shnirel'man, Victor. "Arkaim: arkheologiia, ezoterischeskii turizm i natsional'naia ideia," *Antropologicheskii forum*, no. 114 (2014): 134–167.

Slezkine, Yuri. "The USSR as a Communal Apartment, or How a Socialist State Promoted Ethnic Particularism." *Slavic Review* 53, no. 2 (July 1994): 414–452.

Soldatov, Andrei, and Irina Borogan. *The Red Web: The Struggle Between Russia's Digital Dictators and the New Online Revolutionaries.* New York: PublicAffairs, 2015.

Sperling, Valerie. *Sex, Politics, and Putin: Political Legitimacy in Russia.* New York: Oxford University Press, 2014.

Sotsial'no-ekonomicheskoe polozhenie Rossii: 2016 god. Moscow: Rosstat, 2016.

Sotsial'no-ekonomicheskoe polozhenie Rossii: Ianvar' 2017 goda. Moscow: Rosstat, 2017.

Stolberg, Eva-Maria. "The Siberian Frontier between 'White Mission' and 'Yellow Peril,' 1890s–1920s." *Nationalities Papers: Journal of Nationalism & Ethnicity* 32, no. 1 (March 2004): 165–181.

Stronski, Paul, and Richard Sokolsky. *The Return of Global Russia: An Analytical Framework.* Washington, DC: Carnegie Endowment for International Peace, 2017.

Sullivan, Charles. "Motherland: Soviet Nostalgia in Post-Soviet Russia." PhD diss., George Washington University, 2014.

Suny, Ronald Grigor, and Terry Martin, eds. *A State of Nations: Empire and Nation-Making in the Age of Lenin and Stalin.* New York: Oxford University Press, 2001.

Tabata, Shinichiro. "Observations on Russian Exposure to the Dutch Disease." *Eurasian Geography & Economics* 53, no. 2 (2012): 231–243.

Tétart, Franck. *Géopolitique de Kaliningrad.* Paris: Presses de L'université Paris-Sorbonne, 2007.

Tetruashvily, Esther. "How Did We Become Illegal? Impacts of Post-Soviet Shifting Migration Politics on Labor Migration Law in Russia." *Region* 1, no. 1 (January 2012): 53–74.

Thorez, Julien. "*Khorosho, gde nas net*. L'émigration des 'Russophones' d'Asie centrale." *EchoGéo*, no. 9 (2009): 1–25.

Tinguy, Anne de. *La grande migration.* Paris: Plon, 2004.

Tishkov, Valerii. *Rossiiskii narod: Istoriia i smysl natsional'nogo samosoznaniia.* Moscow: Nauka, 2013.

Toal, Gerald. *Near Abroad: Putin, the West and the Contest over Ukraine and the Caucasus.* Oxford: Oxford University Press, 2017.

Tolz, Vera, and Sue-Ann Harding. "From 'Compatriots' to 'Aliens': The Changing Coverage of Migration on Russian Television." *Russian Review* 74, no. 3 (2015): 452–477.

Tompson, William. "Back to the Future? Thoughts on the Political Economy of Expanding State Ownership in Russia." *Les cahiers Russie*, no. 6 (2008).

Tsukhlo, Serguey. "Importozameshchenie: mify i real'nost'." In *Ezhegodnyi doklad Frankorossiiskogo tsentra Observatorii Rossiia-2016*, edited by Arnaud Dubien, 92–103. Paris: Le Cherche-Midi, 2016.

Tucker, Joshua. "Enough! Electoral Fraud, Collective Action Problems, and Post-Communist Colored Revolutions." *Perspectives on Politics* 5 (3): 537–753.

Tumarkin, Nina. *The Living and the Dead: The Rise and Fall of the Cult of World War II in Russia.* New York: Perseus Books, 1994.

Vercueil, Julien. *Les pays émergents: Brésil-Russie-Inde-Chine.* Paris: Bréal, 2012.

———. "Russie: La 'stratégie 2020' en question." *Revue d'études comparatives Est-Ouest* 44, no. 1 (2013): 169–194.

———. *Transition et ouverture de l'économie russe: Pour une économie institutionnelle du changement.* Paris: L'Harmattan, 2000.

Way, Lucan. "The Real Causes of the Color Revolutions." *Journal of Democracy* 19, 3 (2008): 55–69.

Welt, Cory. "The Thawing of a Frozen Conflict: The Internal Security Dilemma and the 2004 Prelude to the Russo-Georgian War." *Europe-Asia Studies* 62, no. 1 (2010): 63–97.

White, Stephen. "Soviet Nostalgia and Russian Politics." *Journal of Eurasian Studies* 1, no. 1 (2010): 1–9.

Wilson, Jeanne. *Strategic Partners: Russian-Chinese Relations in the Post-Soviet Era.* Armonk, NY: M. E. Sharpe, 2004.

Witte, John, and Michael Bourdeaux. *Proselytism and Orthodoxy in Russia: The New War for Souls.* Maryknoll, NY: Orbis Books, 1999.

Yablokov, Ilya. *Fortress Russia: Conspiracy Theories in the Post-Soviet World.* New York: Polity Press, 2018.

Yudina, Natalia, and Vera Al'perovich. *Starye problemy i novye soiuzy: Ksenofobiia i radikal'nyi natsionalizm i protivodeistvie im v 2016 godu v Rossii.* Moscow: SOVA-Center, 2017.

Yadrintsev, Nikolay. *Sibir' kak koloniia: sovremennoe polozhenie Sibiri, eia nuzhdy i potrebnosti, eia proshloe i budushchee.* St. Petersburg, 1882.

Yurchak, Alexei. *Everything Was Forever, Until It Was No More: The Last Soviet Generation.* Princeton, NJ: Princeton University Press, 2005.

Yurgens, Igor, ed. *Obretenie budushchego: Strategiia 2012.* Moscow: INSOR, 2011.

Zaionchkovskaya, Zhanna, ed. *Migranty v Moskve.* Moscow: Tri kvadrata, 2009.

Index